W9-AQE-510

PRINCIPLES OF THANATOLOGY

Principles of Thanatology

Edited by
AUSTIN H. KUTSCHER,
ARTHUR C. CARR,
and LILLIAN G. KUTSCHER

A Foundation of Thanatology Text

COLUMBIA UNIVERSITY PRESS NEW YORK 1987

Library of Congress Cataloging-in-Publication Data

Principles of Thanatology.

(Columbia University Press/Foundation of Thanatology series)
"A Foundation of Thanatology Text."
Includes bibliographies and index.
1. Thanatology. I. Kutscher, Austin H. II. Carr, Arthur C. III. Kutscher, Lillian G. IV. Foundation of Thanatology. V. Series
HQ1073.P75 1987 306.9 86-24210
ISBN 0-231-04494-1

Columbia University Press
New York Guildford, Surrey

Printed in the United States of America

Book designed by J.S. Roberts

To Lillian

Who brought academic excellence of the highest order to all of the work of the Foundation of Thanatology, who so significantly moved mountains, and who brought life and love to everyone she touched.

Contents

Acknowledgment

The editors wish to acknowledge the support and encouragement of the Foundation of Thanatology in the preparation of this volume. All royalties from the sale of this book are assigned to the Foundation of Thanatology, a tax exempt, not-for-profit, public scientific and educational foundation.

Thanatology, a new subspecialty of medicine, is involved in scientific and humanistic inquiries and the application of the knowledge derived therefrom to the subjects of the psychological aspects of dying; reactions to loss, death, and grief; and recovery from bereavement.

The Foundation of Thanatology is dedicated to advancing the cause of enlightened health care for the terminally ill patient and the family. The Foundation's orientation is a positive one based on the philosophy of fostering a more mature acceptance and understanding of death and the problems of grief and the more effective and humane management and treatment of the dying patient and bereaved family members.

Introduction

The original impetus for attempting to state in succinct form the "Principles of Thanatology" was the result of two specific exchanges between one of the editors (ACC) and colleagues at the College of Physicians and Surgeons, Columbia University. His affiliation with the Foundation of Thanatology led within a period of two weeks to having beliefs attributed to him that he did not know himself to have or that he did not know he was supposed to have.

The first exchange involved a confrontation that actually occurred on the street, when a physician who was then working on the heart surgery unit challenged the belief that patients always either know or should know (i.e., be told) that they are terminally ill, a belief he attributed to "all you thanatologists." He was reacting to data that indicated that denial often is an adaptive defense and that patients who use denial may do better and actually live longer after a heart attack than those who do not.

The second exchange was also as fortuitous and occurred in just as unlikely a location. At this chance encounter, a colleague attributed to thanatologists a belief in euthanasia, apparently having the misconception that the concepts were identical. Here, at least, it was possible to stress to the colleague that an interest in thanatology in no way carried any specific belief concerning the complicated issue of euthanasia. ACC stressed that he, at least, had no conviction about euthanasia as to what it might mean in terms of its application or limits.

These two encounters were not easily forgotten, not only because there seemed to be something aggressive about what was presented in each, but also because they represented serious misconceptions about the efforts of those of us then attempting to promote a greater interest in and dedication to the psychological management of death and dying and of loss and grief.

Within the next few weeks, ACC found himself struggling to formulate for himself what he felt were the basic assumptions and beliefs underlying the thanatological movement which were shared by his co-workers. The tentative statements arrived at were later rounded out, honed, and polished with the help of AHK and LGK, and finally reached publication in 1980.

With no practical experience in handling the issues that precipitated the endeavor, ACC had originally become involved in thanatology through the direct efforts of AHK (to whom he was introduced by Dr. Bernard Schoenberg) who was soon thereafter to become President of the newly organized Foundation of Thanatology.

As is so often the case, the Foundation owes its meaning to the impelling force of its origin. It came into being a few weeks after AHK's young wife's death from cancer. AHK found from his own quests that there was scant consolidated literature covering both emotional and practical problems to serve as an aid to griefstricken persons in their recovery from bereavement—although many articles on bereavement were *scattered* in the psychological, medical, and social science literature. The scope of the work of the Foundation emerged from months of conscious and unconscious efforts, bringing together the counsel of as many authorities in their respective fields as possible.

Inaugurated now almost 20 years ago and based at Columbia-Presbyterian Medical Center, The Foundation of Thanatology is a public tax-exempt educational and scientific organization. Directly affiliated with the activities of the Foundation are professionals in the allied health sciences—including psychiatry, more than 13 other specialties of medicine, psychology, nursing, social work, dentistry, law, religion and theology, social sciences, funeral service, communications, volunteer service, geriatrics, history, philosophy, and so forth—who give care and counsel to the dying patient and to the family. The Foundation of Thanatology is served by a distinguished multidisciplinary Professional Advisory Board.

The third editor of this volume, Lillian G. Kutscher (LGK), to whose memory this volume is dedicated, died on April 7, 1986. She had married AHK in 1966 after having herself been a widow for some six years following the death of her husband, also from cancer. She devoted the entirety of her academic life from the time of the origin of the Foundation until her death to sculpting by far the largest individual and composite collection/library of recent knowledge in this field, the 79 volumes which she edited, constituting the publication efforts of the Foundation until the time of her death.

The plan for the present volume was to submit each principle to an outstanding authority in the field for development and explication. The task has been approached somewhat differently by each author—some have stayed close to the specific principle while others have expanded the scope of their individual assignment. As different as are the points of departure, however, the material that follows offers sound consideration of the issues involved in the complicated problems surrounding death, dying, and bereavement. For both the professional and the layperson, the volume should have interest and relevance.

AHK
ACC
LGK

PRINCIPLES OF THANATOLOGY

Prologue: Principles of Thanatology

ARTHUR C. CARR

Preamble: Simply by being human, we are confronted with experiences related to death and dying. Consequently, a healthy view of life recognizes the finite nature of our lives and affirms death as an inevitable part of the living process.

Principle 1: A Healthy Outlook on Life Necessarily Comprehends Death

Preamble: Although forces in our culture seem to lead on the one hand to repression and denial, and on the other to exploitation and sensationalism, death and dying should ideally be accepted as inevitable aspects of reality that need not be imbued with anxiety and fear.

Principle 2: Death and Dying Are Not and Should Not Be Taboo Topics

Preamble: Since death and dying have traditionally been taboo topics in our culture, the logical means of combating the influences of repression, denial, exploitation, and sensationalism is through education. Education at all levels is indicated, beginning in kindergarten and continuing through courses for the mature adult and the aged. Training should be related, where appropriate, to all aspects and ramifications of death and dying, including loss and grief, care of the terminally ill, and recovery from bereavement—that is, to the discipline of Thanatology.

Principle 3: Education in Thanatology Is Necessary

Preamble: While the medical profession is usually most intimately involved with care of the dying patient, a continuous program of education in Thanatology requires a multidisciplinary approach that unites nursing, social work, philosophy, psychology, psychiatry, and religion, as well as other professional and lay groups. The development of adequate programs in the sensitive areas of Thanatology requires services, training, and research workers.

Principle 4: Education in Thanatology Requires a Multidisciplinary Approach

Preamble: Dying patients should neither be abandoned nor exploited. They are entitled to the same respectful care as those patients who are expected to fully recover. They should be given, where this is appropriate, information about their illness and treatment, and know that they have the right to refuse treatment. Confidentiality should always be respected. Care should be responsive and considerate and should always be given by qualified personnel.

Principle 5: Dying Patients Have Human Rights That Should Be Respected

Preamble: While the circumstances surrounding dying vary greatly, the care of dying patients should give emphasis to their psychosocial as well as to their physical needs. In usual circumstances, patients should be entitled to a relatively pain-free death, and with the maximum maintenance of control of self and self-esteem—in short, since death with dignity often seems hardly achievable, the goal to be sought should be death with as few indignities as possible.

Principle 6: An Ultimate Ideal in the Care of Dying Patients Should Be That of Death Without Indignity

Preamble: Earlier formulations in Thanatology may have created the impression that terminally ill patients always know or always should be told they are dying. While patients differ greatly in their ability, need, or desire to acknowledge imminent death, the concept of "death without indignity" subsumes the right of the patients to express, or not to express, their fears, hopes, gratitudes, and dissatisfactions about their fate. Therefore, absence of shared communication about dying should maximally reflect the patient's choice or circumstances, rather than the anxieties or impatience of caregivers and relatives.

Principle 7: Death Without Indignity Is Most Likely to Occur in an Atmosphere of Open Communication

Preamble: The capacity of one person to form an affiliation with another carries with it the potential for grief and mourning when that affiliation or relationship is broken. These reactions can be observed even in the very young child. Thus, there is nothing unusual or abnormal about grief and mourning among relatives after the death of a loved person.

Principle 8: Grief Is a Normal Response to the Death of a Loved One

Preamble: Bereaved persons should not be exploited; nor should they have to experience undue loss to their own self-esteem. These goals are most likely to be achieved when the bereaved have had information concerning the illness and treatment of the patient, when the patient has experienced death without indignity, and when communication surrounding the patient's dying has been marked by clarity, candor, and compassion.

Principle 9: Bereaved Persons Have Rights That Should Be Respected

Preamble: Bereaved persons bring special physical and psychological needs to the health-care professional; these needs should not be ignored. Among the effects of bereavement are disruptions of normal bodily and sensory reactions, loss of appetite, tearfulness, insomnia, feelings of numbness, fatigue, irritability, and diminished sexual interest—all these occur and support the contention that a grieving person is in a physically vulnerable state that may include a susceptibility to other illnesses.

Principle 10: Although a Normal Response, Bereavement Has Physiological and Psychological Manifestations That Qualify It Symptomatically as a Temporary Illness

Preamble: The course of bereavement is usually predictable and is characterized, in time, by a returning of the person to a state of productivity and well-being, even if not totally unaffected by the nature and the extent of the loss. When, in addition to expected depression, the reaction includes undue loss of self-esteem, feelings of self-condemnation, suicidal thoughts, or grief that is inappropriate to the occasion, special professional assistance may be necessary.

Principle 11: Especially Severe Reactions to Bereavement May Require Special Professional Care

Preamble: The overwhelming context of Thanatology resides primarily in approaching what should be the ideal routine doctor-patient-family care relationships, such care forming the indispensable base upon which the core of care specific to Thanatology can and will easily be extended.

Principle 12: The Essence of Good Thanatologic Care Is Good Patient Care

Summary Preamble: Thanatology encompasses the broad areas of death and dying, loss and grief, and the accompanying issues and problems. It stresses the need for comprehending dying as part of a healthy outlook on living. It emphasizes the need for education and communication in these sensitive areas. It stresses the rights and needs of dying patients and their families to competent, considerate care responsive to their particular physical and psychosocial needs. It recognizes the necessity for new and better approaches to the care of the dying and the bereaved. It encourages inquiry into how attitudes and approaches to loss, grief, death, and dying can lead to fuller, happier living.

Summary Principle: Thanatology Is Both an Art and a Science. As an Art, It Emphasizes Humanistic Approaches to Death, Dying, and Bereavement. As a Science, It Stresses the Need for Education, Inquiry, Systematic Investigation, and Research in Approaching These Once Taboo Topics.

Preamble: Simply by being human, we are confronted with experiences related to death and dying. Consequently, a healthy view of life recognizes the finite nature of our lives and affirms death as an inevitable part of the living process.

Principle 1: A Healthy Outlook on Life Necessarily Comprehends Death

1

A Healthy Outlook on Life Necessarily Comprehends Death

VANDERLYN R. PINE

> Since death is a fate that comes to everyone, nobody can ever say why it comes precisely to a person or why it comes just when it does. As the values of culture increasingly unfold and are sublimated to immeasurable heights, such ordinary death marks an end where only a beginning seems to make sense.
>
> Max Weber (1958:335)

A persistent endeavor throughout recorded human history has been the attempt to make life understandable by relating the meaning of death to the meaning of life. In this pursuit, the philosophical and theological outlooks on life and death have been an integral part of the cultural heritage of all societies. To a great extent, it is also the reason societies develop rituals to help cope with the passage from life to death.

The idea of "progress" for any society carries with it the hope of attaining perfection in its culture. The effects of changes that have been made in an attempt to attain this goal, however, have not solved the problems surrounding human dissatisfaction, death denial, fear, and death itself (Becker 1973). The threat of war remains (Lifton 1967), the destruction of humankind is a reality, social unrest exists (Freud 1962), and numerous other forms of discontent prevail (Brown 1959). In addition to these "age-old" problems, it seems safe to say that we are caught in a paradoxical trap: ever-increasing advances toward the extension of life versus ever-increasing developments threatening the extinction of life. How we cope with these complex issues reflects the extent to which we develop and maintain a healthy outlook on life.

It is instructive to explore the way people comprehend death and how that "way" fits into an overall view of life. Our purpose here, therefore, is to examine the ways a healthy outlook on life both depends upon and enables our comprehension of death.

Clarifying a Healthy Outlook on Life

There are many ways to define a healthy outlook on life. The difficulty of this task resides in both the psychological outlook of the beholder and in the philosophical context of the society in which one lives (Choron 1964). It is essential to determine what constitutes a healthy outlook on life and its meaning in terms of our current social values.

First, in order to have a healthy outlook a person needs a developed, individualized social identity. Social identity refers to a person's individual selfhood as an interacting human being, one capable of establishing and maintaining relationships with others. This is true even though the society in which we live has elements of alienation and anonymity. One's social identity also consists of those reflective elements of self, the nurturance of which depends upon other people and the input and feedback they provide. This means that a person's social identity is intricately connected with significant others and social interactions with them.

Second, in order to have a healthy outlook it is necessary to have the ability and willingness to be accepting of self, others, and the world. As suggested above, one of the primary elements in a healthy outlook is acceptance of one's self. Although this may appear to be a tautology, there are many elements of self that one may not perceive as being perfect. It is important in maintaining a healthy outlook on life to develop a rational basis of judgment and a reasonable acceptance of "who" one is. This does not suggest that change is not possible, for it is. Furthermore, acceptance of one's self does not mean blind acceptance of all one's traits, but it does suggest a conscious evaluation of one's personality and cognitive skills.

It also is essential to develop the ability to accept others as they are. Again, this does not mean blind acceptance of undesirable traits, immoral characteristics, or socially unacceptable behaviors. It requires one not to take a hopeless view of others, and it is important to strive for a realistic assessment of others' selfhood.

The final aspect of accepting is of the world in which one lives. Acceptance of the world around us includes the outright rejection of unacceptable attitudes and behaviors. It is necessary for one to perceive the world, the self, and others, and to make a conscious judgment to accept the facts as they are, regardless of one's decision about how to behave in light of those facts. Hence, the ability to accept is a prerequisite for perceiving, recognizing, and acknowledging reality in an honest and morally acceptable framework.

Of course, this means that one who rejects elements of one's own environment and seeks to change them must be able to do so with a grasp of the actual facts of the situation in order to qualify for accepting the world, self, and others. Likewise, someone who does not feel compelled or motivated to change or alter those elements but who is able to recognize the limitations and drawbacks of reality also could possess the necessary accepting components for a healthy outlook.

Third, in order to have a healthy outlook one must maintain

meaningful relationships. Meaningful relationships may be defined as interpersonal relationships that have substantive emotional and reciprocal social dimensions. A major component in evaluating the meaningfulness of a relationship involves the intangible concept of value. In this sense, some relationships have a higher quality than others and have a more important place in our lives than other relationships. Therefore, less meaningful relationships can be lost without a major impact on our lives, while the loss of the most meaningful relationships can produce great trauma.

Fourth, there is the need to have a sense of affection for one's self and for others. Thus, in addition to acceptance of self, others, and the world, affection also is needed. This means that beyond the perception and recognition of one's own attributes, it is important for each of us to give and to receive as much affection as possible. One view of this characteristic is the sense in which affection supersedes any connotation of egotistical affection. Instead, it involves a realistic sense of self in which one is seen positively.

Fifth, in order to have a healthy outlook an individual needs a clear perception of one's place in home, work, and leisure. A "sense of place" provides a setting and opportunities for developing enduring community friendships and meaningful relationships. In regard to one's place in these different surroundings, it is important to recognize that it is from our concept of "place" that we derive our sense of companionship and develop the feeling of connectedness with others. In addition, place can promote our sense of "belonging."

Sixth, in order to have a healthy outlook one must feel an absence of loneliness. Having interpersonal relationships may reduce loneliness, but death or the threat of death has the ultimate power to destroy relationships and produce loneliness. Death is the most complete separator, a phenomenon thought to distinguish people as individuals, but also one that ends life with a futility and desperation that often requires reinforcement and support from others (Freud 1963; Brown 1959).

Seventh, in order to maintain a healthy outlook toward life one must have an *awareness* of the social supports in one's life. Those elements of social behavior that connect us to other people provide a sense of community in which we can lean on others at the interpersonal level for sustenance in our everyday activities. For many, this involves those cultural components of life that are embodied in ceremony and ritual. It is important in maintaining a healthy outlook that these supports be available during times of stress. Unfortunately, for many highly mobile people, the recognition and awareness of a sense of social support is not available in everyday life. This *lack* of social supports may intensify or even worsen a stressful situation. Loss of family or friends through death serves as a stressor that tests both the availability and adequacy of one's social supports.

In a fast-changing society a key concern centers around the concept of tradition and the ways "traditional" activities have meaning for people. There are several definitions of tradition, but for our purposes tradition means social customs, beliefs, and values that are passed down from one generation to another by word of mouth or by practice and everyday usage. Not incidentally, there is increasing evidence that many people are seeking and enjoying a rediscovery of tradition.

This definition of tradition inherently includes a sense of community. People often express having a feeling of being "from" some place, which refers to having experienced the interdependent social bonds of a "community." These social bonds are a complex mix of dependence, independence, and reliability. In such a setting, there often evolves a sense of community understanding, and hopefully a clearly defined use of the traditions of the community. The point is that feelings of tradition, community, and social support are important to a healthy outlook and equally important in the event of illness, loss, and death.

In order to have a healthy outlook on life, it is critical to be able to distinguish between the past, the present, and the future. This may appear to be self-explanatory, but it is essential in developing a sense of perspective in regard to one's being.

Although the past is bounded by specific dates and occurrences, it can in some sense be seen as involving an infinite passage of time. The past is infinite not only because it passes backward beyond recognizable measures of time, but also because time allows for the past to be reconstructed so that each past experience possesses an unlimited number of variations on a theme. This allows for different interpretations of the reality, meaning, and significance of past experiences, including the loss of someone who has died.

Grappling with temporality in the present is restricted by finite bounds and the constant awareness that "this too shall pass." This often is problematic, however, because death or dying interrupts the commonly understood meaning of life.

Finally, a view of temporality must involve a cognizance of the future and its meaning. Herman Feifel (1977:5) states "In a society that emphasizes achievement and the future, the prospect of no future at all and loss of identity is an abomination." The future is both finite and infinite. The finite future is what we can know, experience, and measure in hours, days, weeks, or a number of other socially meaningful units. Nevertheless, future time, at the abstract level, contains no measurable boundaries. Regardless of how we measure the future, it can be viewed as an indefinite postponement of death (Weisman 1972). This belief can be interpreted as a form of denial of death and self-deception.

Clarifying the Comprehension of Death

To comprehend death, one must be aware of its psychological, cultural, and social implications. Let us examine brief excerpts from some of the critical thinkers who have addressed this issue. From the psychological perspective we have the ideas of Sigmund Freud and Erich Lindemann.

In "Mourning and Melancholia," Freud (1917:153) refers to grief as a "painful" state of mind and locates it in terms of the "economics of the mind." By bringing in the concept of economics, Freud is able to identify grief as part of a psychological exchange process, with tasks and activities being carried out as "labour" in exchange for a kind of psychic "freedom" from the dead person.

In this vein, Freud (1917:156–161) refers to "the work of grief" as the need for the bereaved individual to become free from the attachments to the dead person, from the inhibitions of becoming a separate being, and from conflicts and ambivalence over the lost love relationship. Therefore, we comprehend "the work of mourning" as a temporal process occurring over time. From this viewpoint a dimension of psychoanalytical comprehension of death has grown.

In "The Symptomatology and Management of Acute Grief," Lindemann (1944) explains that acute grief is an observable syndrome with psychological and somatic symptoms and that with *comprehension,* understanding, and clinical intervention, unresolved grief is manageable. This concept has fostered the "generally accepted" understanding that death gives rise to a grief experience that can be assuaged by appropriate ongoing conventional or therapeutic relationships—that is, through social contact.

These concepts eventually must link individuals to their particular culture. This raises the matter of rites and rituals used to help people cope with their emotional and intellectual perspectives.

From the cultural perspective, we have the ideas of the anthropologists Bronislaw Malinowski and Raymond Firth. In *Magic, Science, and Religion,* Malinowski (1948:53) emphasizes that mourning behavior serves to demonstrate the emotions of the bereaved and the loss experienced by the whole group. The rituals of death reinforce as well as reflect the natural feelings of the survivors. Therefore, they help foster and enhance the way people comprehend death.

In most societies, it is during the funeral ceremony that death reactions reflect our social outlook on life and death. Funeral rites provide bereaved people with a defined social role to help them pass through a period of adjustment following the death. The rites set boundaries on the period of mourning, assist the bereaved by providing the opportunity for the public expression of grief, and help in commemorating an individual's death.

In *Elements of Social Organization,* Firth (1964:63) observes that there are societal elements that help resolve many ambivalent feelings about death. Firth states that the funeral provides three elements to the living. The first element is the resolution of uncertainties in the behavior of the immediate kin. The funeral provides relatives with an opportunity to display their grief publicly and establishes a period of time for mourning. As such, it is a ritual of closure that also links our understanding of death at the psychological and societal level.

The second element is the fulfillment of social consequence. This means that the ceremony helps to reinforce the appropriate attitudes of the members of society to each other. Although it focuses on the dead person, the funeral points out the value of the services of the living. Once again, societal and individual comprehensions of death are reflected in everyday ritualistic practices.

The third element is the economic aspect. Firth explains that every funeral involves the expenditure of money, goods, and services. In this sense, the exchange process is important to the bereaved on a tangible social and economic level. Bereaved people may feel the need to make restitution to the deceased by purchasing such nonabstract items as funeral feasts, funeral merchandise, religious services, and so forth.

Analytically, this last point is connected to Freud's reference to the concept of psychic economics and the exchange process in relation to grief and mourning. From Freud's perspective, the bereaved feel they must "compensate" in some way for the death. He was referring to a psychological rather than a socioeconomic exchange process, but clearly they are related. In exploring the three elements of the funeral ceremony, Firth illustrates that the different ways in which one views life in general or the life of someone in particular are inextricably linked with one's understanding of life and comprehension of death.

Inherent in the framework of a psychocultural analysis of the practical meaning of death is the sociological view, which encompasses the dynamic, interactive elements through which a person evaluates "just what" a particular death really means. Durkheim (1915) and Weber (1947) shed divergent light on this concern from the sociological perspective.

In *The Elementary Forms of Religious Life,* Durkheim (1915:435) points out that funeral rites are ceremonies that designate a state of "uneasiness or sadness." From this perspective, death produces personal anxieties, which are addressed by the funeral, a ceremony that is indicative of a society's overall comprehension of death. In this sense, then, funeral rites mirror a society's interpretation of life and death. Thus, according to Durkheim, mourning behavior does not demonstrate a spontaneous release of emotions. He posits that bereaved people are social actors who feel obliged to "play out" their emotions through behaviors that are sanctioned by society (1915:443). From the social perspective, therefore, comprehending death requires knowledge of the social "context" of the social behaviors in a particular culture.

In *The Theory of Social and Economic Organization,* Weber (1947) explains that to understand human behavior it is necessary to comprehend the subjective meaning individuals give to their actions. Moreover, human action must possess and supply inherent meaning to an individual; otherwise the actions truly cannot be understood. Weber (1947:93–94) explains that "*human mortality,* indeed the organic cycle generally from the helplessness of infancy to that of old age, is naturally of the greatest sociological importance through the various ways in which human action has been oriented to these facts." Nevertheless, it is not only the mere existence of such facts and a person's psychological makeup that form the basis for comprehension but also the sociocultural meaning that is contained within the actions. As Weber (1947:102) states, "these concepts of collective entities . . . have a meaning in the minds of individual persons, partly as something actually existing, partly as something with normative authority." Death with its attendant attributes clearly fits into the above discussion, for it not only has an actual presence, but it also manifests a full set of norms and values. Thereby, death provides us with both intrinsic and extrinsic levels of understanding.

In order for any person to have an understanding of death that allows its true comprehension, there must be a fusion of the various dimensions just described. This means, of course, that one must possess a developed psychological comprehension of death as a real force in human existence. This would militate against the full use of denial at the personal, interpersonal, and institutional levels.

In addition, one must possess a clear understanding of the cultural elements inherent in death. The exact meaning of death and the carrying out of death-related behavior occur only in a particular cultural context. This enables individuals to practice the various customs of a given culture *and* to benefit from doing so. There is a very important distinction here between the need to have some means of containing the impact of death and the actual practices that do just that.

Before the full meaning of death can be comprehended the psychological and cultural meanings must come to have a coherent everyday meaning to the "real live" person. This extends death and all its trappings to the sociological realm, for it is this interactive significance that provides the full measure of our understanding. Thus, a person must be able not only to recognize death and its reality, but also to locate death as a reality in life. Moreover, death must possess a social significance to have any psychocultural importance.

Reasoning and Understanding Death

Comprehending death is a complex multidimensional process, and most people have to face it frequently and often painfully. We are constantly exposed to death through media reports and personal experience. All such awarenesses are part of this complex psychosocial process. Furthermore, most of us use believable organizing frameworks, hypothetical models, or plausible explanatory theories to help cope with and understand death and bereavement.

There are three ways that the reasoning process can be used to help understand death. First, there is the deductive reasoning model, which occurs when one possesses a general concept or understanding of death and then particularizes it for a given person's death. For example, employing the reasoning that everyone must die someday may help us understand that the death of a specific person is a natural consequence of life. Second, there is the inductive reasoning model that is used by inferring something from a specific person's death and then generalizing that everyone must die. For example, "knowing" that a particular person has died eventually may lead to understanding that death will happen to all of us. Third, there is the retroductive reasoning model that is utilized by looking at a death and then seeking logical reasons for its occurrence. For example, knowing that a loved person has died may force us to "look back" in an attempt to understand the plausible reasons for the death's occurrence.

To consider the reasoning process and our understanding of death is neither philosophical nor esoteric, although the actual process is both. Quite simply, it is important because death is brought into our consciousness through a combination of the three reasoning styles. Some ideas about death may emerge from our belief in widespread, culturally accepted theories about God or the universe, and then we deduce ideas about specific deaths (deduction). From a specific individual's death we gain understanding that all of us will die someday (induction). We gain additional understanding through the process of trying to "figure out and explain to ourselves" a death, and this act of putting a death into our own common-sense perspective may help us come to grips with death (retroduction). The real-life process of comprehending death actually involves a complex mixture of all three reasoning models.

The basic premises we make about the nature of humankind also influence and help us form our theories of death. For example, acceptance of the premise that death is inevitable generally facilitates a more realistic attitude toward one's own death. A belief in immortality may lead to a different perception of death. Recently, many of our premises and hypotheses concerning death have become inappropriate and obsolete. The high technology, prolongevity, and artificial life that we see and hear almost every day through the media or firsthand experience have rendered our past views of death outdated. Today, many people feel that death is appropriate only at a certain time in life and only for certain people. For instance, some may feel that death is "appropriate" for a ninety year old whereas the death of a teenager is viewed by many as inappropriate.

Coping with Today's World

In a stable, unchanging society, one's philosophical outlook and one's state of mind are important in determining how one handles everyday events. In a complex, rapidly changing society, there are additional important reasons for having a healthy outlook on life. This is true regardless of what aspect or dimension of life we face, but it is of even greater consequence when we consider the events of dying and death.

Let us turn to some of today's complex concerns as they relate to dying, death, and life processes. One potentially powerful change involves the daily advances in our technological abilities and desires. Not surprisingly, many of the answers we seek regarding complicated life-and-death matters involve technological issues. Accompanying such advancing technology is the temptation to use it to resolve moral dilemmas and social questions.

Such attempts can be defined only as wishful thinking. For example, computers can process information more rapidly than a human, but they cannot solve paradoxical or "morally insoluble" questions unless they are reduced to programmable dilemmas. The situation historically parallels the nineteenth century when philosophers and social observers were confronted with questions about production and consumption (Marx 1956), capitalism and industrialization (Durkheim 1933), and economic models (Weber 1947). Today, the focus increasingly centers on social, psychological, and moral dilemmas and the limited abilities of our most technologically sophisticated machines to resolve them.

The high technology available today intersects with the issue of health care. Because of sophisticated computer-based equipment and technologically advanced laser beam, light ray, and X-ray technology, many health services are possible today that were unimaginable a few years ago. For recipients of advanced health care, the present circumstances appear enviable. Nevertheless, health care services have the dilemma of the enormous expense of sophisticated technology versus the ability of recipients to pay for it. This raises the serious moral question, "Who has the right to receive treatment?" While this question is not a new one, it is more salient today because highly technical medical treatments are costly not only to obtain but also to provide, and raise the issue about who shall die and who shall live (Fuchs 1974).

Contributing to the problem is the matter of health care organization. Specifically, in technological societies, formal institutions, such as hospitals, have come to replace informal institutions, such as families. When America was basically nontechnological, people took care of their sick, their elderly, and their dying at home. Obviously, this provided a quite different setting and atmosphere from what is provided today in an institution. With the growth of institutionalization and the change from an industrial to a technological society, today's health care system has evolved to be different from prior systems.

Today, American health care is also different in regard to attitudes and values. Such societal attitudes exercise a powerful influence on the overall collective outlook on life and death. Therefore, the question "What is death" is not just a rhetorical one but rather is a real issue in the field of medicine and everyday life. As Veatch (1976:21) notes,

> now that technology permits us to treat the body organ by organ, cell by cell, we are forced to develop a more precise understanding of what it means to call a person dead. There is a complex interaction between the technical aspects of deciding a person is dead. . . . and the more fundamental philosophical considerations which underlie the judgment that a person in a particular condition should be called dead.

Although there are many values that govern the general field of health care, there are four major ones that influence today's health care system (Pine 1977:135–136).

First, we value human life and consider it to have special meaning. In general, we believe that there are certain basic human qualities that inhere a special value just to being "human." This view differs from cultures in which such sanctity is reserved for the nobility, the rich, and other select groups of people.

Second, we value the humanitarian belief that we should prevent suffering at almost all costs. This belief is different from certain former views about suffering. For instance, in some religions, those who suffered were thought to be blessed, in a sense, because through suffering one became a "better" person. Present-day American attitudes tend to consider humane treatment to be a right of individuals. This is especially so for the sick and the dying.

Third, we value utilitarianism—that is, to provide the greatest good for the greatest number. The counterpoint, of course, involves the allocation of resources. In health care there is often a problem in providing medical services for the greatest number, without regard to their affordability. Put bluntly, those chosen to receive extraordinary life-sustaining measures may be selected not by need but by their ability to pay for the measures. In other words, as a character on the *St. Elsewhere* television program aptly points out, "what we have in this country is an abundance of highly developed and advanced medical technology with a horse and buggy delivery system."

Fourth, complicating these values is the existence of widespread patterns of social differentiation. Naturally this raises the issue of social inequality; nevertheless, the present use refers to another type of differentiation. Health care social differentiation occurs when some people are seen as being "appropriately" dying (the ninety-year-old) and other people are seen as being "inappropriately" dying (the teenager). At the practical level, the care given is different in each case. Clearly, such a norm violates certain values, and the violation is instructive about our overall comprehension of death.

Another illustration of "appropriateness" and differentiation is the common occurrence of there being one nurse on duty to care for two patients on the same floor (Sudnow 1967). What happens when both patients call for assistance simultaneously? To which patient should the nurse go? Generally, the nurse makes such a decision instantly. When asked how the decision was made, nurses often explain that it had to do with "appropriateness," and that a patient who is "inappropriately" dying receives the attention first. It appears that nurses react almost instinctively and give their services where there may be a better chance for life to continue. Such differentiation has serious consequences not only for patients, but also in terms of helping to comprehend our overall societal view of death.

In addition to these four points, health care increasingly depends upon our view of dying and death. Interest in the subject of dying and death has increased drastically over the past twenty years, a period during which more writings have been published about dying and death than in all previously recorded history. This suggests that there is an important difference in terms of focus and interest today, and it has a direct bearing on how health care is being and will be provided.

This issue has an impact on the expanding gerontological population of our society. The elderly are living longer, and when they become ill they increasingly will use the latest highly sophisticated equipment. A dilemma is inherent: many are not able to afford these new services. How we solve this and other associated dilemmas depends upon moral judgments, available resources, and considerations that are philosophical, theological, social, and economic in nature. As mentioned earlier, the technology that enables us to save and extend lives cannot be expected to solve the question of whose lives will be saved or extended.

The technological advances raise another issue because our attention is drawn not just to the matter of the length of life and life as we believe it to be "proper and appropriate" but also to the matter of prolongevity. The scientific developments that have enabled us to prolong the living process beyond what was once considered normal and acceptable have led to the emergence of the notion of prolongevity.

The problems associated with prolongevity involve fitting a new or revised view of aging into what we comprehend about dying and death. In this case, our common-sense understanding of what extended life brings is clouded by our legacy from the past, and we tend to cling to the idea that long life is desirable only up to a certain point. That point is neither clearly defined nor universally accepted. Nonetheless, our traditional understanding of death fosters the notion that death is quite "appropriate" at an advanced age. Paradoxically, at the same time we continue to try to extend life even longer.

Facing Life and Death Dilemmas

Social and political responses to changing moral values emerge only over a long period of time. Therefore, part of our present difficulty is the inherent lag between the availability of technology and its benefits and the application of that technology in a socially and morally responsible manner. Carr (1973:5) points out that "present technological advances make possible increasing prolongation of life to an extent where the question may sometimes be whether one is humanely prolonging life or inhumanely prolonging dying."

Another aspect of coping with today's world involves the multifaceted dilemmas surrounding life and death. There are numerous indicators of the difficulties that we face in modern society, but let us consider five life/death dilemmas.

The widespread controversy surrounding the case of Karen Ann Quinlan is a classic example of a society with outdated moral standards, which have rendered us unable to deal with the matter of life versus death. Many viewed the life of Ms. Quinlan as having ended long before her actual death, because, in our society's view, social interaction is held to be the most significant factor in determining the existence of life. Since she had no awareness of her surroundings, she could not maintain, establish, or perpetuate relationships with other people. Thus, according to Western society's paradigm, Karen Ann Quinlan could be viewed as dead.

The question raised in her court cases was whether or not it would be permissible to disconnect her from life support systems, thereby supposedly allowing her to "die in peace." As Veatch (1976:117) notes, however, "dying in 'peace' has become difficult to achieve in this day of biological revolution." The first court decision ruled that this was a matter that should be decided among doctor, patient, and family. The second trial ended in the decision that failure to disconnect Ms. Quinlan from the life support machines was an invasion of her privacy. It is noteworthy that nothing was said directly in that decision about her right to live or die.

Confounding the paradox is the fact that after being disconnected from life support systems, Ms. Quinlan's body sustained life. Consequently, she came to be viewed as socially dead but physiologically alive. To condense the dilemma, consider these simple questions: When and by what means is it appropriate to disconnect someone from life support mechanisms? If an individual is disconnected and continues to live, what options remain?

What appears to be even more paradoxical and ironic is that we are spending time, energy, and large amounts of money in the development of more sophisticated technology. Increasingly, people become attached to life-sustaining mechanisms, and then they or their families fight in our court system to be disconnected from them. This occurs when the individuals or their families no longer feel life is worth living under such "mechanized" circumstances. A person can be disconnected from a life support machine and continue to live, if only in the physiological sense. This situation gives rise to questions about the usefulness of our technology when matched against nature.

There are other life and death questions that have been created by our technological advances. There is the apparently straightforward question of whether or not people should be allowed to die if that is their wish. For example, there was a case of a young man who was badly injured when a leaking propane gas line exploded, killing his father and resulting in second- and third-degree burns over 68 percent of the young man's body; his eyes, ears, and most of his face were burned away. After many months of skin grafts, his hands had been amputated, he was susceptible to infections, and he had to be bathed daily in a special tank. Although he accepted treatment, he said he wanted to die. Eventually he refused further treatment and insisted on going home, a transfer that would mean certain death. This gives rise to complex questions.

Under such circumstances, does a person have the right to refuse treatment?

What are the responsibilities of the medical profession?

Are the "necessary" treatments involved a contributing factor to this person's unwillingness to live?

Another example of how technology can create new dilemmas in the life/death spectrum involves technological advances and the law. France's Napoleonic Code has 2281 articles, but none of them anticipated the case of a young widow who sued to get her late husband's semen from a sperm bank. Before he was married, the man agreed to undergo chemotherapy for testicular cancer. Knowing that the treatment might make him sterile, he made a deposit of his semen with France's Center for the Study and Conservation of Sperm (CECOS).

Two years after they had met, the couple married, just two days before he died. The woman still wanted to bear her husband's child and asked for his sperm deposit. CECOS refused and pointed out that no law indicated who should inherit the sperm. Although the French court eventually ruled against the woman, the case contains many critical issues that fall into that grey area where technology has outstripped the law.

Still another area of the life/death dilemmas involves business responsibilities in the health care arena. For example, a couple's infant son was born prematurely and was diagnosed as having apnea. Apnea is the interruption or cessation of breathing that has been linked to sudden infant death syndrome (SIDS). After discussing their son's condition and the potential threat of SIDS, the couple decided to lease an apnea monitor, which records sleep data for infants and has an alarm system to warn of irregularities in an infant's breathing.

When the child was eight months old, he stopped breathing while asleep and died. The parents had not heard the monitor's alarm, even though their son was connected to it. Furthermore, the parents had tried to obtain a new alarm for the monitor because it would go off sporadically. The parts did not arrive at the dealer's until the day after the infant died.

The couple was not consoled by the fact that their son's death was the only one reported out of over 7000 monitors in use. They were so distraught that they brought a $2 million product liability lawsuit against the three companies responsible for the monitor. The case, filed in Federal court, charged that the manufacturer, leasing company, and parts supplier were negligent because the monitor apparently malfunctioned.

In this case, at least one question arises. If an event, i.e., death, would occur without a certain technological device, does the failure of the device amount to negligence if the predictable event does occur? An event that at one time would have been explained as "an act of God" now precipitates lawsuits to determine who should be held financially responsible for its occurrence.

Our technological advances have created seemingly insoluble dilemmas that, once decided upon, will be the precedents for the future and help establish new and emerging understandings about life and death. To illustrate this point further, consider the case of Elsa Rios, who learned that she and her husband, Mario, could not conceive another child by natural means. They very much wanted to have more children, so they went to the Melbourne Australia Medical Center to seek the help of a well-known test-tube baby team there and were accepted into the program.

Using the in vitro method, doctors fertilized an ovum from Mrs. Rios' womb in the laboratory with sperm from an anonymous donor. One of the developed embryos was implanted in her womb but the pregnancy failed after 10 days. Extra embryos produced at the time were frozen for later implantation, a technique pioneered by the Melbourne team. Mrs. Rios never returned, however, because this Argentina-born woman and her Chilean-American husband were killed in a plane crash.

In an unmarked steel chamber at a Melbourne medical center, a pair of glass vials bearing the initials ER stood in a container of liquid nitrogen. Inside the vials were two frozen human embryos no bigger than the period at the end of this sentence. The embryos were kept at −328° F. An Australian state legislature ultimately stated that "the two frozen embryos will go anonymously to prospective parents."

Many life/death questions are involved. For example, is it "right" for doctors to "create" life in a laboratory?

When does human life begin?

Must the embryos be implanted in another woman and carried to term, if possible?

No matter what our personal answers may be to these questions, they cannot help but reflect our outlook on life and death.

As we learn about these and similar dilemmas, our established, conventional wisdom does not provide adequate comprehension to enable us to answer the attendant questions. In particular, we do not have the ability even to know the "right questions." This should be neither surprising nor especially disturbing. The real issue is how all modern societies will come to locate life and death reality as part of our sociomoral system; it will require revised norms and values. Such controls generally evolve slowly, over time, even though the need for them is great right now.

The main danger occurs when precedents are set too rapidly and are based on outmoded values. In the past, the normative structure of society generally involved folkways and mores with informal social sanctions and regulations and laws with formal sanctions. The problem has now become extremely difficult because of the new sociomoral dilemmas that confound the norms. The situation is made more complex when attempts are made to maintain stability in the face of existing norms that are inappropriate and counterproductive.

Today we face such problems in the area of life and death concerns. While it is not a guarantee for solving these dilemmas, a full comprehension of death may enable us to grapple with the issues involved.

Comprehending Death on an Everyday Basis

Comprehension is the act of recognizing and processing the nature, meaning, and significance of a concept. The dynamics of attaining personal and interpersonal meanings of death and bereavement are intricate, complicated, and often emotionally and physically draining. As we pass through life events, we use past experiences, abstract organizing models, individual emotional reactions, and a vast repertoire of personal responses as a foundation from which our psychosocial reactions evolve. The significance of each previous event then becomes a component in future situations in which we must "comprehend" similar events. All these aspects are woven into and are necessary for the comprehension of death.

Comprehension of death requires an understanding of the powerful emotions involved. From this perspective, rather than simply acknowledging the *need* to cry, it is also crucial to address the complex cognitive elements of the awareness of death. Bereaved people often need assistance in attaining a understanding of *why* they are crying and in determining the psychosocial and personal meanings of their emotions. In other words, while an initial emotive step may be crying, the next step is understanding the significance of the crying. Furthermore, "just crying" may not be sufficient for the expression of one's emotions, and an additional release of feelings may be warranted.

Comprehension of death involves an intellectual understanding. That is, death must be meaningful in one's visual mind as a phenomenon of life. Unfortunately, there may be problems when an individual believes that one's own theory about death is the only answer. Such a belief weakens one's ability to adjust to death. Moreover, there is no specific way to comprehend death to the exclusion of other options or alternatives. Finally, the uniqueness and specific needs of each individual must be taken into consideration in order to deal with death in a healthy fashion. Hence, each person's reactions to a particular death may differ considerably from all others to the same death.

Our society's technological/scientific paradigm is typified by the desire to "know and understand." The only way to *know* death is to die, but accepting death may help us to know, understand, and appreciate life. Furthermore, acceptance of the inevitability of death is important and enables us to live more meaningfully after experiencing the loss of a key person in our lives. In this manner, a coherent comprehension of death can assist in the successful passage through the crises of life.

The outlook one has on life profoundly influences one's comprehension of death and vice versa. From any of the perspectives examined in this chapter, regardless of how one defines a so-called healthy outlook on life, in order for it to be truly complete, it must both include and contribute to a comprehension of death.

References

Becker, E. 1973. *The Denial of Death*. New York: The Free Press.

Brown, N. O. 1959. *Life Against Death*. New York: Vintage Books.

Carr, A. C. 1973. "A Commentary on Tolstoi's The Death of Ivan Illych." In *The Death of Ivan Illych.* New York: Health Sciences Publishing Corp., p. 5.
Choron, J. 1964. *Modern Man and Mortality.* New York: The Macmillan Company.
Durkheim, E. 1915. *The Elementary Forms of the Religious Life.* New York: The Free Press.
Durkheim, E. 1933. *The Division of Labor in Society.* New York: The Free Press.
Feifel, H., ed. 1977. *New Meanings of Death.* New York: McGraw-Hill Book Company.
Feifel, H., ed. 1959. *The Meaning of Death.* New York: McGraw-Hill.
Firth, R. 1964. *Elements of Social Organization.* Boston: Beacon Press.
Freud, S. 1917. "Mourning and Melancholia." In *Collected Papers,* 1959. New York: Basic Books, pp. 152–170.
Freud, S. 1962. *Civilization and Its Discontents,* Trans. and ed. James Strachey. New York: W. W. Norton, Inc.
Freud, S. 1963. *Beyond the Pleasure Principle.* New York: Bantam Books.
Fuchs, V. R. 1974. *Who Shall Live.* New York: Basic Books, Inc.
Fulton, R. 1965. *Death and Identity.* New York: John Wiley and Sons, Inc.
Gerth, H. H. and C. W. Mills. 1958. *From Max Weber: Essays in Sociology.* New York: Oxford University Press.
Lifton, R. 1967. *Death in Life.* New York: Random House, Inc.
Lindemann, E. 1944. "The Symptomatology and Management of Acute Grief." *American Journal of Psychiatry* 101: 141–148.
Malinowski, B. 1948. *Magic, Science, and Religion.* Garden City, N.Y.: Doubleday.
Marx, K. 1956. *Selected Writings in Sociology & Social Philosophy.* New York: McGraw-Hill Book Company.
Pine, V. R. 1977. "Health Care Delivery and Social Change." In Gerchick, E., D. Huttunen, A. H. Kutscher, and D. J. Cherico, eds., *The Role of the Community Hospital in the Care of the Dying Patient and the Bereaved,* New York: MSS Information Corporation, pp. 134–144.
Sudnow, D. 1967. *Passing On: The Social Organization of Dying.* New Jersey: Prentice-Hall, Inc.
Veatch, R. M. 1976. *Death, Dying, and the Biological Revolution.*New Haven: Yale University Press.
Weber, M. 1958. "Religious Rejections of the World and Their Directions." In H. H. Gerth and C. W. Mills, eds. and trans. *From Max Weber: Essays in Sociology.* New York: Oxford University Press, p. 335.
Weber, M. 1947. *The Theory of Social and Economic Organization.* New York: The Free Press.
Weber, M. 1958. *The Protestant Ethic and The Spirit of Capitalism.* New York: Charles Scribner's Sons.
Weisman, A. D. 1972. *On Dying and Denying: A Psychiatric Study of Terminality.* New York: Behavioral Publications, Inc.

Preamble: Although forces in our culture seem to lead on the one hand to repression and denial, and on the other to exploitation and sensationalism, death and dying should ideally be accepted as inevitable aspects of reality that need not be imbued with anxiety and fear.

Principle 2: Death and Dying Are Not and Should Not Be Taboo Topics

2

Death and Dying Are Not and Should Not Be Taboo Topics

THERESE A. RANDO

The operative word in the title, one which foreshadows much of the discussion to come, is "taboo." The following are several of the definitions offered for taboo by Webster's New Universal Unabridged Dictionary (1983): "among primitive tribes, a sacred prohibition put upon certain people, things, or acts which makes them untouchable, unmentionable. . . . the highly developed system or practice of such prohibitions." The reader will note four dimensions of the word as it relates to death and dying, as well as to a significant amount of American culture's responses to these topics. First, it has the element of sacredness. In this regard, death is accorded the attribute of being hallowed or sacrosanct. Following naturally from this feature are additional distinctions of a taboo, such as the qualities of being "untouchable" and "unmentionable." These reveal death's ineffability. That is, it is too overwhelming to be adequately expressed or described in words, an attribute that Shneidman (1973) has cited as the main reason why death has become taboo. Second, reference is made to the fact that taboos are usually found among primitive peoples. This suggests that the necessity of designating a subject or behavior as taboo stems from a fear so powerful that rational thought and refined behavior cannot be expected to cope with it. Rather, prohibitions must be established to protect the society. This gives one a clue as to the posture that has been assumed toward death in this country. That such a primitive mechanism as the rendering of death and dying as taboo subjects should occur in a country that prides itself on its logic and civilized behaviors shows the power of the emotions generated by contemplation of these topics. Third, taboos are based on a "highly developed system and practice." This suggests that there is concerted effort at the banning or forbidding. Consequently, regarding the issue of death and dying as taboo, there will exist a methodical process for excluding and ostracizing interaction with these events and with thoughts and feelings regarding them. Fourth, a "prohibition" is a refusal to permit a thing to be done. Someone who violates a prohibition usually is punished, so when the taboo around death and dying is breached, one can expect that social responses will be disapproving, and perhaps penalizing, designed to reduce the possibility of recurrence. These third and fourth dimensions both act to prevent the contact required to confront death and dying and to realize the inappropriateness of their being designated as taboo. In this way, the taboo is perpetuated.

What should become clear is that the consequences of maintaining death and dying as taboo topics are distinctly malignant. They rob individuals and society of the therapeutic benefits that accrue when human mortality is recognized as a basic limitation with which one must contend in all areas of existence. The strong nature of social taboos reduces the opportunities for open confrontation with and examination of man's finite nature, undermining its efficacy as the factor creating meaning, purpose, and drive by its delimitation of life. Failure to maintain awareness of the realities of the human condition, of death and of dying, constitutes a denial of the inexorable fate of each individual. And such denial, along with the self-deceit it embodies, compromises that very existence the individual attempts to save by denying that it will ever be lost.

In general, this article explores the various personal and social elements contributing to the need to deny death and dying and to assign them some degree of taboo status. (I do not subscribe to the notion that death and dying are completely taboo in American society, but I do believe that they retain a significant degree of taboo status.) The article then examines the consequences of such assignments and concludes by offering a realistic and healthy perspective from which to view and then capitalize upon the uniquely positive effects of death and dying on life.

Meanings of Death and Dying

For any two individuals the words "death" and "dying" may have vastly different idiosyncratic connotations. While several fairly general denotations of the words exist, these are significantly enhanced by the personal meanings and fears one accords to death and dying. Any one, or a combination, of these can prompt the response(s) that indicate an individual's emotional reaction to death and dying. To understand a given response or the reason for it, one must first comprehend what has generated it by appreciating exactly what death and dying represent to that individual.

GENERAL DENOTATIONS

Death is "all the time" and is lodged in our bowels. It is not just fortuity, mischance, or an exclusivity of the old and moribund. We are all observer-participants with respect to death. (Feifel 1977b: 352)

From the intimate and integral position that it occupies in the human consciousness, death confronts us with the threat of termination of all that is known, felt, valued, and loved. While death may carry numerous idiosyncratic meanings to each individual, it also presents several interrelated general denotations; death limits futurity and it represents nonbeing as we know it.

Death's signifying the ending of futurity presents us with an incomprehensible conception. We are future-oriented creatures, a capacity that distinguishes us from other animals. It makes death an ultimate threat, since it colors the anticipation that guides the majority of our actions and dampens the expectation that serves as a principal mediator of goal-directed and purposeful behavior (Feifel 1968). The place of the future is critical in determining how we respond.

> The underemphasis on the place of the future in psychological thinking is surprising because, in many moments, man responds much more to what is coming than to what has been. Indeed, what a person seeks to become may, at times, well decide what he attends to in his past. The past is an image that changes with our image of ourselves. It has been said that we may *learn* looking backward—we *live* looking forward. A person's thinking and behavior may be influenced more than we recognize by his views, hopes, and fears concerning the nature and meaning of death. (Feifel 1959: 116).

Consequently, the absence of an infinite future into which to project the self confronts us with a limit that, by implication, has a profound impact on our current experiences. Death is ever present. It compels our attention, since it threatens our being in the very future that steers our present behavior (Feifel 1971).

Death, representing nonbeing as we know it, engenders significant anxiety. This fear of extinction is regarded as the basic fear of death (Kastenbaum and Aisenberg 1972). The psychoanalysts have long written about the impossibility of conceiving of our own death in our unconscious. They assert that our narcissism perpetuates a myth in the unconscious that we are immortal despite conscious attitudes to the contrary (Freud 1915). A number of thanatologists have taken issue with this contention (for example, Kalish 1981 and Kastenbaum and Aisenberg 1972). Nevertheless, it is clear that we cannot fully imagine entering a state of nonbeing in which we do not become spectators to the event and therefore are not truly dead to ourselves. Most of the time when we contemplate what we think are our own deaths we are actually deluding ourselves. For death-of-ourselves means total disintegration and dissolution of the personal world. By definition it cannot include our presence as external observers of our own death scenes. Death-of-ourselves also involves the disintegration of our entire world, for the entire scene vanishes with our death. In contrast, the death of another involves the elimination of an object within our world, not of ourselves or of our world. It is for this reason that clear confrontation with anticipation of our own personal death evokes such deep, extraordinary, and unspeakable anxiety: it entails the disappearance of the world itself and means an encounter with nothingness, the confrontation of a void (Koestenbaum 1971). We tend to protect ourselves from the realization of this by conceptualizing instead the death of another when we try to think of our own death. In this manner we hide from ourselves the true and demolishing nature of our own anxiety about the tragedy of our own death.

Related to these issues of nonbeing and lack of futurity is the issue of death as an end of the opportunity to achieve (Kastenbaum 1977). Death erases us as experiencing and producing beings. In this regard death is the greatest of calamities, for it not only robs us of a vehicle for definition of self (that is, through achievement and productivity) but also erases us as experiencing beings. It ceases our inner experiences of thinking and feeling. Additionally, for those of us who need to think our way through problems, death is the ultimate enigma, since we cannot understand, unravel, or logically comprehend it. Therefore, many of our typical coping mechanisms are rendered useless.

PERSONAL MEANINGS AND FEARS

Besides its embodiment of the aforementioned general denotations, death can have many personal meanings and significances to a given individual. Like the general denotations of death and dying, each of these can generate diverse idiosyncratic fears. Reasons why specific meanings or fears of death are salient for a particular individual stem from the influence of such variables as the psychosocial characteristics of the individual and the level of and temporal distance from the threat of death.

In a classic study, Bromberg and Schilder (1933) wrote that death may be seen as a means of vengeance to force others to give more affection than they would otherwise be willing to give, as an escape from an unbearable situation to a new life lacking the difficulties of the present, as a final narcissistic perfection granting lasting and unchallenged importance, or as a means of punishment and atonement. Feifel (1959, 1968) has articulated the multidimensional meanings that death holds for people. He has said that for many death can represent a teacher of transcendental truths incomprehensible during life; the "gentle night," a friend who brings an end to pain through peaceful sleep; an adventure, a great new oncoming experience; a "great destroyer," which should be fought to the bitter end; or it can reflect surcease from pain and tribulation, reunion with one's family, loss of control, punishment, or loneliness. Kastenbaum (1977) noted four broad perspectives from which death may be viewed: as the great leveler, a powerful relentless force that brings death to the high and mighty as well as the lowliest of mortals; as the great validator, a view emphasizing the ways that death can confirm and support the status or distinction of an individual, especially through funeral practices; as something that unites or separates—in either case radically altering relationships with others; as the ultimate solution (as in homicide or suicide) or as the ultimate problem, through its ending of the opportunity to achieve and experience.

There are, in addition, a number of distinct death fears. These, too, vary among individuals. The wise clinician knows that a major way in which an individual can be aided in managing his generalized anxiety about death or dying is by being assisted in breaking down the anxiety into its component parts. The person is helped to delineate his specific fears and concerns, and then each one is addressed and solved separately. It is always easier to cope with explicit, well-defined fears than to grapple with more global, undifferentiated, and thus more terrifying anxiety .

A number of writers have delineated a host of specific fears related to dying, death, the results or consequences of death, and the death of others. The following is a synthesis of fears culled from the writings of Brantner (1971), Gordon (1970), Kastenbaum and

Aisenberg (1972), Neale (1973), Pattison (1977), Rando (1984), and Simpson (1979).

Fears of Dying. Leaving unfinished, with things undone and secrets poorly concealed; dying alone; facing the unknown; loneliness; impairment and loss of functions, roles, objects, body parts, and people; loss of control; loss of consciousness; altered body-image; shame; dependency; loss of integrity; becoming a burden; indignity; disability; suffering and pain; loss of identity; sorrow; and regression.

Fears of Death. Losing time; irreversibility; facing the unknown; loss of self and cessation of thought; loss of pleasure; loss of mastery; incompleteness and failure; separation; loss of identity; loss of control; extinction, "ceasing to be," or annihilation; mutilation; decomposition; and premature burial.

Fears of the Results or Consequences of Death. Fate of the body; judgment; punishment or rejection from God; facing the unknown; fate of loved ones left behind; what will happen to one's property, plans, and projects; and loss of control.

Fears of the Dying or Death of Others. Separation from and loss of others and the relationships with them; repetition of an unpleasantly experienced dying of another; vicarious suffering and disintegration; retaliation by the deceased; being haunted by spirits of the dead; abandonment; and vulnerability.

Although most people are afraid of and anxious about their deaths, the same concerns will not be equally significant to each person. Every individual will have his own unique combination of specific fears about death and dying. These fears are not fixed or invariant. They will change in meaning and intensity as the individual's life experience changes. Those factors most directly pertinent to formation of an attitude toward death at a given point in time include the individual's: personality; sex; age; coping styles and abilities; religion or philosophy of life; social, cultural, and ethnic background; previous experiences with loss and death; maturity;

intelligence; mental health; lifestyle; psychosocial support; perceived fulfillment in life; perceived timeliness of death; specific fears about dying and death; previous experiences with and personal expectations about illness and death; and personal meanings of specific illnesses (Rando 1984).

Not only do the individual's conceptions of and attitudes toward death vary over time, but responses to it vacillate as well within the same individual (Feifel 1971; 1977a). These can fluctuate from strong avoidance toward anxious hope and uneasy resignation to calm acceptance. In addition, Feifel has also demonstrated the *simultaneous* coexistence of contradictory attitudes toward death within a person. There appear to be coinciding acceptance-rejection orientations toward death, with acknowledgment and manageable fear dictating verbal or conscious considerations, and denial and dread ruling the "gut level" reactions. Frequently there is delicate maintenance of a subtle equilibrium between realistic acceptance of death and its concomitant rejection. This concurrence of contradictory attitudes toward death seems to allow a terminally ill patient to maintain communal associations and yet to organize his resources to contend with oncoming death. Consequently, any assessment of reaction to personal death must recognize the differing levels of awareness on which the individual simultaneously operates.

Attitudes Toward Death That Influence Life

Regardless of the particular meaning that death has for a given individual, it is incontrovertible that the fact of one's mortality and whatever one construes death to mean will influence that individual's life in the most profound ways. The human being is the only animal that can conceive of its own existence, and hence its nonexistence. This knowledge influences the experience and course of life. Much of "how-I-live" is determined by one's response to "I-will-die." As Feifel has noted, "We are mistaken to consider death as a purely biologic event. The attitudes concerning it, and its meaning for the individual, can serve as an important organizing principle in determining how he conducts himself in life." (Feifel, 1959: 128).

The existentialists have long proclaimed that the posture one assumes toward death influences the quality of one's life. Psychotherapists and philosophers note that the way an individual orients himself in life, such as world-view, defenses, attitudes, psychopathology and so forth, reflects his responses to the threat of death and to its symbolic representations.

The individual's response to death is not relegated solely to those events that are clearly death-related. Responses to events associated with death (such as sleep, illness, coldness, and darkness) or to experiences that are viewed as aspects of death (such as separation, loss, experience of the unknown, loss of control, and saying goodbye) may all arouse the same threat of death and may be responded to in much the same manner as more traditional death stimuli. Further, it is not the death of ourselves in the physical sense that is the sole threat to us. *Symbolic death* brings with it an equal threat. A symbolic death is the collapse of a particular world toward which energies and goals are directed. Examples include the collapse of someone's business, the loss of a job, the personal slight by someone whose attention we prize and esteem, rejection from someone who is important to us, and so forth (Koestenbaum 1971).

The issue of death, its meaning to us, and also our emotional responses to it play a major role in directing and influencing our lives. Research suggests that the threat of death is instrumental in fostering the sense of self, personality patterns, and psychological defenses of the individual. From infancy, our responses to death—as experienced through such symbolic equivalents as separation and absence—initiate our modes of adaptation to death, as well as to life. How children experience, think about, and attempt to cope with these situations not only will shape their adult conceptions of death, but also will be incorporated with their personality and experience, and influence subsequent character, feelings, thoughts, and behaviors in their lives (Kastenbaum 1968; Kastenbaum and Aisenberg 1972; Rochlin 1965).

That at some future we shall not be renders an infinite amount of ramifications and reactions in the present. The knowledge of the human condition of death and limitation, and the implications derived therefrom, are stimuli we are all subjected to; and we react in response (Rando 1981). The threat of the negation of the self and all that is valued, which is most often prompted by thoughts of death, demands this response. Human beings are future-oriented animals. To conceive that at some time there will be no future arouses anxiety. This anxiety initiates subsequent responses, which influence the quality, experience, and course of human life as we know it (Rando 1981). From infancy, the individual is constantly in relationship to death. The "death" may be a physical (tangible) one; or a symbolic (psychosocial) one; a permanent or reversible fact; an issue to be confronted presently or in a future time. The relationship may be acknowledged or denied. As in communication, however—where there is no such thing as "not communicating" (since not to communicate is to communicate that one is not communicating)—so there is no such thing as not having a relationship to death, barring extreme organicity on one's part.

Our reactions to recognition of our relationship to death may be subtle or blatant. They may range from complete denial to complete and existential acceptance of death. They will pervade our entire experience and existence, having an impact in our psychological, social, physical, and spiritual realms. Death is the ultimate threat in the presence of which we constantly exist. As a result, the coping mechanisms employed to deal with the threat of death are integrated with other behaviors in the individual's repertoire, and will serve as significant influencing variables for other aspects of life. For example, Ms. A is someone who cannot accept the fact of her own mortality; she will avoid the topic of death at all costs, missing wakes and funerals, and postponing the necessity of making wills or scheduling yearly physical exams. She will mimimize separations and losses. Mr. B will attempt to master the threat of death through the use of counterphobic mechanisms. He will be the "daredevil," the one who disregards the physician's orders or who constantly teases and tempts death in a grandiose effort to assert to himself that he has control over it and will be master of his own fate.

Ms. C will adhere to the religion that promises her an eternal life that death cannot vanquish. Her life has meaning only as a portal to the more important afterlife and she acts accordingly. Mr. D will recognize that the threat of death is constantly present and that his life must be geared to maximizing the opportunity for creating meaning at every moment. He will live so as to ensure the mimimum amount of unfinished business when death interrupts. Whatever the lifestyle, it reflects information about individuals' responses to their ultimate death.

AMERICAN SOCIAL INFLUENCES ON THOUGHTS OF DEATH AND DYING

Just as individuals vary in their ability to tolerate the thought of their own deaths, so, too, are societies distinguishable in response to death. Such a response is a function of how death fits into the society's teleological view of life. There appear to be three general patterns of response: death-accepting, death-defying, and death-denying. All societies fall somewhere on the continuum that spans these three perspectives. The United States today is often cited as an example of a more or less death-denying culture. It is described as having a widespread refusal to confront death, with a declining number of rituals for recognizing it, and with the replacement of contrivances for coping with it. There is a general attitude that death is antithetical to living and not a natural part of human existence.

An analysis of the development of Western attitudes toward death from the middle ages to the present illustrates the changing relationship between the individual and his thoughts and feelings about death, as influenced by changes in society (Aries 1974). These attitudes have progressed from an era of "Tamed Death," in which death was accommodated as an everyday occurrence. It was not feared, but perceived as the common destiny for all, with rituals developed to deal with it. Social changes eventuated and there were shifts to attitudes about death that focused on "One's Own Death." During this time the individual specifically prepared for and accepted his own death. Further social developments led to the era of

"Thy Death," wherein the attitudes of acceptance of death declined further, death was romanticized, and there was increased emphasis on memorialization of the dead and an emotional and obsessive preoccupation with death that was increasingly perceived as alien.

Finally, the present era, which began in the mid-nineteenth century, has been termed "Forbidden Death." Death is perceived as shameful and prohibited—distasteful. Lying about the true state of the dying person's condition is commonplace. It often involves the dying being taken to institutions and left there to die, largely unaided by the living who attempt to put death as far as possible from them. Ritual or emotion of bereavement is notably suppressed.

In the United States there have been in recent years a series of social, technological, and medical changes that have dramatically complicated the dying and grieving process. These transitions have made dying and grieving increasingly difficult to undergo; and as a result, thoughts, attitudes, and feelings toward death and dying have also been affected. Such changes have not only influenced the dominant Western perspectives on a macrolevel, but have, as is normally the case, infiltrated and shaped the social, cultural, religious/philosophical, and ethnic beliefs, mores, norms, standards, and restrictions that nurture a particular individual's response to death and dying.

It is important to appreciate the changes manifested in the post-industrial United States because they tend to distance death further from the normal life experience and, through making it more foreign, they tend to reinforce the notion of death and dying as topics that are somewhat taboo. These changes increase the likelihood that anxiety and fear will be the predominant emotional reactions to such topics, as indeed they are to all topics that are denied and prevented by societal prohibitions from being examined and understood. Many of them also rob us of traditional sources of support for coping with death and the feelings it generates. Among these changes are industrialization and urbanization; exclusion of the aged and dying; advances in medical technology; social reorganization, social mobility, and the movement toward the nuclear family; advances in technology and increasingly rapid social changes, with an increasing impersonality of social life resulting from dominance by technology; secularization from religion; the possibility of mass death and ecological disaster; deritualization; American expectations of success, control, individuality, and the rights to life, liberty, and the pursuit of happiness; the impact of the mass media.

While these changes have made death more removed from the individual in American society, they have simultaneously also made him more vulnerable to it because of his decreased experience and familiarity with it. Combined with the diminishing power of traditional resources for coping with death, this results in the increased power of death as a threat to the individual. Previously, these traditional resources had provided matrices for developing coping strategies to deal with the dilemma of death. These included, for example, family, religion, ritual, community, and personal immortality through continuation in social and biological modes within a world expected to continue after the individual's death. Now such resources and assurances are missing. Their absence supports the maintenance of taboo-like qualities of death and dying in our society, leaving us with little but denial, magical thinking, or overcompensation as options for coping with the handling of the anxiety generated by thoughts of death.

AMERICAN RESPONSES TO DEATH AND DYING

In contemporary American society one most often witnesses variations on three distinct responses to death and dying. They constitute types of defensive overcompensation and denial that are frequently manifested as alternatives to the realistic acceptance of death and dying as inevitable aspects of reality that ought not necessarily be overly imbued with anxiety and fear. These three postures are repression/denial, sensationalism/exploitation, and romanticization of death. All serve to remove death and dying from their natural places in human existence.

The processes of repression and denial are psychological coping mechanisms designed to exclude from awareness a particular threat or its significance. In repression the individual forces anxious or unacceptable thoughts, feelings, or impulses into the unconscious. The failure of repression to function adequately necessitates the emergence of auxiliary mechanisms aimed at barring the threat from consciouness: suppression, denial, and rationalization (Rando 1984). For our purposes here, we need examine only denial.

Denial is a form of avoidance that temporarily negates or pushes into the unconscious painful and intolerable thoughts and stimuli. With regard to the contemplation of death and dying, there are adaptive amounts of both repression and denial. Some amounts of each are necessary to continue to exist in the face of human mortality. Continued, unremitting contemplation about death would be paralyzing to action in life. Consequently, there are times when it is therapeutic to put thoughts about our demise out of conscious awareness. For example, an optimum amount of denial has been found to have particularly useful consequences for terminally ill patients (Feifel 1971; Lazarus 1981; Schoenberg and Senescu 1970; Weisman and Worden 1975).

Nevertheless, excessive repression or denial is unwarranted; it interferes with healthy functioning. After reviewing the studies on the effects of denial and denial-like processes, Lazarus (1981) concluded that denial "can be both adaptationally sound *and* capable of eliciting a heavy price" (p. 53). For example, the persistent social denial of the human condition of mortality with the distancing of death from life, as evidenced in such social practices as the segregation of the aged and the attempts to shield children from death and dying, results in diminished respect for the significance of death, as well as for life. It tends to eventuate in a lack of appreciation for life, its meaning, its values, and its brevity. On an individual level, ongoing denial of death perpetuates a myth of personal invulnerability that can be viciously assaulted when one experiences the death of a beloved other. In some cases, it interferes with appropriate anticipatory grief during a terminal illness. In other cases, one's ability to accept the reality and permanence of the loss may be compromised and can interfere with successful address of the initial task of mourning after the death, that is, to accept the reality of the loss (Worden 1982). In situations where a specific oncoming death or death in general has been denied, survivors are often quite unprepared. When this is coupled with the lack of formal or informal e repression and denial, the sensationalism and exploitation and dying serves only to remove it from its natural place in e and to stimulate unhealthy responses in its wake.

third response to death and dying is the romanticization of ler to make it more manageable, death is glorified, with an hasis put on what some perceive as its positive aspects—its serenity, and capacity to draw people together. While death eed hold these attributes for some, problems arise when s to it and expectations for it are generated based on the on of death in these glowingly romantic and affectionate 'his of course ignores the reality that death takes unwilling separates loved ones, involves the loss of everything and e, and generates profound grief. Unfortunately, many care-spouse a romantic view of death. They believe that if the hings are done, a lovely, calm, and accepted death can be in which all business will be finished and the exit will be acefully after well-articulated goodbyes (Rando 1984). They of ardor and zeal, seeking passionately to bring the "beauti-th to their patients. Although armed with good intentions re than passing knowledge about death and dying, these rs are poorly equipped for what they inevitably must con-or death, in far too many cases, is not romantic. It is not . It is not beautiful. In fact, often death stinks—literally and vely! It is clammy, too. It can sound bad, and it often is ugly. hneidman (1971, 1973) noted that death attitudes are ciously sentimental" and asserted that it is the "curse to end s," arguing that it is about as loving as kidnapping or rape. the romanticization of death as particularly severe, since it norized suicide and presented the fallacy of it as an ally and enemy. Other related examples can be found wherein our has romanticized and sensationalized certain types of homi-d other violent acts. In these situations death is not recog-all of its true realism. It may then be robbed of its ability to eople to act to avoid premature death, as they would for if they recognized the true horror of suicide and its reper-s. Just as it is inappropriate to take a view of life that negates o is it equally inappropriate to take a view of death that

education about death, decreasing rituals for mourning, and inappropriate social and personal expectations for grievers stemming from a denial of the impact of death and its consequences, survivors are forced to confront death and loss in a most vulnerable fashion. Because of an unrealistic image of death by survivors or those who would assist them, survivors are left without the resources necessary to cope with death. One who has not dealt with death in the abstract will find it even more difficult to contend with it in the concrete terms involved in the permanent separation from a significant other.

Related to this, Stephenson (1985), echoing Feifel's (1977a) earlier observations about the coexistence of contradictory attitudes toward death and dying, recently made some interesting distinctions pertinent to repression and denial. He asserted that Americans do appear to accept the notion of abstract death—that is, death distant from and extrinsic to them and close loved ones. He contended, however, that they tend to avoid, and have significant confusion about and difficulty dealing with, their own personal mortality. Stephenson felt that the reality of existential death is more often denied and avoided, not only because of the personal issues it arouses, but because basically death is antithetical to America's values and cannot easily be incorporated into the internal imagery of American society.

Disproportionate repression and denial frequently result in death-denying behaviors. In a pompous attempt to assert control and mastery over mortality, individuals often assume roles and behaviors that suggest their need to dispute their vulnerability or, at the very least, flaunt their defiance of it. The stunts of motorcyclist Evel Knievel in the 1970s are prime examples of this. Immoderate repression and denial led to what Gorer (1965) termed "the pornography of death." He noted a replacement of the repression and prudery previously evidenced around the natural processes of birth and copulation by that surrounding the processes of death and physical decomposition. Gorer observed that the emotions typically concomitant with death (that is, those of grief) are given little or no attention. This is similar to the overlooking of the emotion of love within a pornographic focus on sex. Gorer saw this as occurring because of reliance on fantasies to titillate our curiosity since the real events are shrouded in mystery and have become viewed as "disgusting. . . . morbid and unhealthy, to be discouraged in all and punished in the young" (Gorer 1965:196).

Notwithstanding the assertion that death and dying frequently are relegated to taboo-like status in our culture, some writers have perceptively and correctly noted recent changes that illustrate that it is not *entirely* true that the subject of death and dying is completely taboo in America (Kalish 1981; Parsons and Lidz 1967; Stephenson 1985). What is apparent is that while there are denials and exclusions of death in some instances—for example, in shielding children from death, using euphemisms for death-related words, and in dispatching the dying to institutions—in other instances there is open acceptance of death and dying. Newspapers do print obituaries, artificial heart patients are candidates for media attention, death education courses are offered, grief is discussed on television talk shows, people are more attuned to health promotion, and so forth. Because this is the case, perhaps Gorer's conception must be updated. While current American behaviors and attitudes do not warrant an "X-rating," they are sufficient to suggest some degree of taboo-like quality and avoidance. Hence, they could properly be upgraded to a rating of "PG-13,"—not to be witnesssed by children under 13, but one which has made room for some socially redeeming values and messages for adults.

At the polar opposite of repression and denial, but as unhealthy as responses to death and dying, are sensationalism and exploitation. Sensationalism refers to that which is intended to arouse intense interest, to shock and thrill. Exploitation means to make unethical use of someone or something for one's own profit. Both these behaviors have been increasingly relied upon by the mass media. While there has been a decline in the average individual's personal contact with death and dying, due to sociological changes and advances in medicine and technology, there has been an increase in exposure to violence and death through television, movies, and the print media. Commencing with the television coverage of the war in Vietnam, ravages, which many may have previously avoided confronting, are now witnessed in the family living room.

Not infrequently, a type of "death overl
enced as viewers are bombarded with st
result in the mass extinction of human li
astation. Acts of murder, war, violenc
crime, natural disasters, and so forth
tionalized in the name of the public's rig
for the media and its sponsors are obvi
aggressive aspects of human personalit
profit of others, frequently stimulating i
aggression or violence. Fears and insecu
heightened either purposely for entertain
of normal reactions to an increasingly vi
timization is not uncommon. Psychologic
tionalism and exploitation can be quite de
behaviors increase denial of death and d
frequently result in an increase of annihil
ings of personal vulnerability. These can
several reactions: one can become overlo
one can overcompensate by becoming ag
becoming detached from others and from a
one can depersonalize, desensitize, and/or
order to minimize the impact; or one can c
and heighten defenses by repressing and de
of death and dying.

The irony is that while death is bro
are inundated by increased media exposu
having a personal impact and affecting our
been pushed further away. This can breed c
or can serve to make death seem almost u
with fictionalized productions reinforcing
death as a reality, with characters "killed"
and then reappearing in another, this leads
lence may not have permanent effects. Such
provides us with false illusions of being ab
watching others die while remaining unsc
serves only to reinforce the denial of death or
anesthetized or indifferent to aspects of it. Si

attributes positive qualities to it that fail to recognize its grim reality as well.

Anxiety and Fear of Death

In order to arrive at an appropriate perspective on death and dying, it is important to examine the concepts of anxiety and fear and to see how they interrelate in the individual. These emotions constitute the bases for development of taboos and are necessary to maintain them.

It is imperative to differentiate between anxiety and fear. Both present threats to different psychological levels of the personality, but anxiety is a diffuse, undifferentiated emotional response to a threat, while fear is a differentiated emotional response to a specific, localized danger. Fear derives from anxiety, which is the basic, underlying reaction. Anxiety is the generic term; fear is the expression of the same capacity in its specific form (May 1977).

Initially, one must distinguish between normal and neurotic anxiety. Anxiety is the apprehension cued by a threat to some value that the individual holds essential to his existence as a personality (May 1977). The threat may be to physical life (which makes some amount of anxiety quite normal when considering ultimate death), to psychological existence, or to a value identified with one's existence. Normal anxiety is defined as follows:

> First, it is proportionate to the stress. *You and I have to bear the anxiety of ultimately dying* and whatever other anxieties there are; the contingencies of life do not let us escape the necessity of anxiety . . . Second, it does not require repression; rather it increases awareness. Its purpose, as a matter of fact, is to increase our consciousness. Third, it does not result in symptom formation. Fourth, it can result in creative productiveness. (May 1982:18, italics mine)

In contrast, anxiety is neurotic when it is disproportionate to the threat, requires repression, results in symptoms, and renders creative capacities ineffective by the shrinking of the individual's consciousness (May 1982). Therefore, anxiety about one's death can be normal or it can become neurotic in nature.

Freud perceived anxiety about death as a secondary derivative stemming from more primary anxieties centering around separation and castration. His position was that it is impossible for the individual to conceive of his own nonbeing; thus, fear of death is neurotic and necessarily covers up more "legitimate" conflicts. In contrast, Feifel (1971) asserted that while death fears can be secondary phenomena, as suggested by the Freudians, the data increasingly suggest that the reverse may be more valid. He noted how apprehensiveness over body annihilation and concerns about death assume dissembling guises, such as depressed mood, fears of loss, insomnia, psychosomatic symptoms, and various psychological disturbances—all of which have been linked to anxieties concerning death.

May (1977) noted that normal anxiety includes our vulnerability to nature, sickness and fatigue, and to eventual death. He felt that it is often difficult to distinguish the normal from the neurotic elements in anxiety connected with death, since in most persons the two kinds are intermingled. May observed that in American culture neurotic anxiety about death is prevalent because the normal recognition of death as an objective reality is so widely repressed. In our culture one is supposed to ignore the fact of ultimate death, as though living can be enhanced if one can remain oblivious to it. In contrast, however, the exact opposite occurs: the experience of living tends to become vacuous and to lose its zest and savor if the fact of death is ignored.

UNHEALTHY RESPONSES TO THOUGHTS OF DEATH AND DYING

There are high psychological prices that one must pay to avoid perceiving death and dying in their rightful places as inevitable aspects of reality. First, it must be recognized that any defense that persistently enables one to escape the perception of a fundamental or external reality is psychologically exorbitant (Wahl 1959). In most cases it exacts more to deny than to deal with death. Wahl noted that the defenses we employ against the fear of death would be seen as ludicrous if they were used to this degree for something else. He called attention to the fact that "any heavy reliance upon magical thinking and delusion formation, even when collectively shared, raises problems of emotional sickness and health, both for the individual and society" (Wahl 1959: 19).

Impressive evidence documents that death anxiety can precipitate psychological disorder in which impaired imagery of death and the continuity of life is a unitary theme around which mental illness can be described and in some degree understood (Lifton 1975). This corroborates assertions that anxieties, obsessions, and other neurotic symptom formations are genetically related to the fear of death or its symbolic equivalents, with the symptons serving as symbolic substitutive attempts to bind death anxiety (Wahl 1959). In addition there is evidence that fear of death is the most dramatic factor in senile psychosis (Gillespie 1963) and is one of the causes of schizophrenic denial of reality (Feifel 1968; Searles 1961). Others have also persuasively argued that the effort to escape facing death can lead to mental illness (for example, Becker 1973; May 1977; Murphy 1959; Rochlin 1965).

The theme of Becker's (1973) *The Denial of Death* is that it is precisely the recognition of one's mortality that leaves man with no choice but to deny the fact of his death. That man is a god and separate from the other animals by the consciouness of his symbolic self, and yet is also one with them by his fundamental expendability in nature, is the dualism with which man must live. This recognition brings a terror of death that would drive man insane if he fully apprehended it. For some this can stimulate creativity. For most of humanity, according to Becker, the only recourse left is to deny mortality and practice self-deceit via character and behaviors, driving oneself into blind obliviousness with social games, psychological tricks, and personal preoccupations so far removed from the reality of one's human situation as to be forms of madness. "Agreed madness, shared madness, disguised and dignified madness, but madness all the same" (p. 27).

This response of denial of death may ultimately prevent the actions needed to eliminate "deathogenic factors," those human-created factors within the global community that cause premature, horrible, and torturous death (Leviton and Wendt 1983). Leviton and Wendt hypothesize that by removing the denial factor, the "horrific death-fear of death denial of death-inaction" chain will be broken and individuals will act in the best interests of the society and those to come. As examples of such "breakthroughs" they cite the massive demonstrations in this country and abroad against the proliferation of nuclear weaponry and the arms buildup. For far too many individuals, however, denial prevents those actions that are important to undertake in order to address the critical issues that are destructive to personal and global well-being.

Another way in which reactions to death are manifested is in violent behavior. Feifel (1977a) and Kübler-Ross (1969) both noted that violence may be an indicator of difficulty in facing death with acceptance and dignity. Attacking and destroying others can often be construed as attempts to exert control, to conquer and master death, to experience a type of ascendancy over the inevitable against which one is helpless. In this way violence can be perceived as an active response to unmastered dread of death.

There are other negative sequelae of excessive fear of death; among them despair, self-destructiveness (often evidenced in alcohol and drug abuse, self-sabotage behavior, accident-proneness, and so forth), and increased anxiety (leading to denial, psychiatric symptom formation, immobilization, disillusionment, and the need for counterphobic and other behaviors to assert control). The question is posed, "Why be rational, civilized, and delay gratification if there may be no world tomorrow?"

THE DELETERIOUS EFFECTS OF FEAR OF DEATH AND DEATH ANXIETY ON CAREGIVERS AND THEIR PATIENTS

Caregivers are not immune to the fear of death and death anxiety. Indeed, death anxiety has propelled some professionals into working with the dying and the bereaved. For others, anxiety is stimulated by these populations and they find themselves unable to respond in a concerned and caring manner. Death anxiety is what Harper (1977) said must be worked through if caregivers are ever to relate compassionately to the dying patient, in full acceptance of the impending death, and in ways that will be translated into constructive and appropriate activities to meet the needs of the dying patient and family. If the death anxiety that is engendered in working with these populations is not successfully overcome, the caregiver is susceptible to burnout (Maslach and Jackson 1979; Shubin 1978; Vachon 1978; Worden 1982).

The tendency to use professional knowledge as a buffer against encounters with dying and the anxiety it evokes is often manifested in the use of distancing techniques such as jargon, spending limited time with the patient, professional distance, overlooking psychosocial aspects, avoiding being present, premature decathexis, and increased attempts at control. Caregivers in the field of thanatology are required to address their own death fears and anxieties. These do not all have to be completely resolved, but they must have at least been examined, with the caregivers being consciously aware of them and of the necessity to continue working on them. They must discover and identify those stressors that generate the greatest effect, as well as those fears and anxieties that have the most impact, and develop appropriate responses to them.

In cases where fear of death, death anxiety, or burnout are prevalent, unrealistic expectations often arise. These steal from the dying the emotion, warmth, and outgoingness of their caregivers. Caregivers must close themselves off in order to cope with the high anxiety. Numerous unhealthy responses to this anxiety have been documented. For example, nurses have been reported to respond less readily to the needs of those near death than to other patients in their care (Bowers et al. 1964). Sociological trends contribute to the development of a role for the caregiver as "surrogate griever" (Fulton 1979). Because of the faltering of traditional kinship networks, disengagement of family members from the dying, and absence of family because of social mobility or the segregation of the dying, professional caregivers often find themselves participating in the emotional and social care of their patients. This results in caregivers taking emotional risks and forming bonds that will eventually demand a grief response when terminated by death. This close involvement obviously predisposes the caregiver to the heightened death anxiety that can develop in any of us who are touched personally, as well as professionally, by death. Such anxiety is not unusual secondary to any experiences that make us feel vulnerable and mortal. Consequently, the caregiver is well-advised to follow appropriate regimens to manage the stress generated by the professional experience (Rando 1984).

Positive Effects of Death on Life

Despite the problems that can arise when feelings about death and dying are overly negative and when the defenses established to defend against them interfere with healthy functioning, the idea of death creates life's unique meaning and provides the elements most contributory to the positive experiences of life.

Forster's (1962) aphorism summarizes the beneficial and positive aspects of the impact of the notion of death on man's life: "Death destroys a man but the *idea* of death saves him." The knowledge of our finiteness serves as a galvanizing and positive force pulling us toward creativity and accomplishment. The awareness of death sharpens and intensifies the awareness of life. Our lives would be inconceivable without the tacit assumption that they must end. Reproduction, emotion, competition, and ambition would be pointless if there were never any death (Verwoerdt 1966). It is precisely because we are finite that the quality of life is all the more poignant and meaningful. Were we immortal, there would be no reason for aspiring, hoping, striving, and attempting to make meaning out of life. Existence would continue ad infinitum and the quality and value of the experiences of life would pale in intensity in an endless supply of tomorrows with limitless opportunities (Rando 1984). Our goals and our purposes, from the most trivial to the most consummate, are enhanced by the knowledge that our time is limited. This disallows time for casualness, thoughtlessness, selfishness, and resentment, and it stimulates the development of self that is accomplished only in relationships with other persons (Brantner 1971).

In this regard, awareness of death makes it easier to define our values, our priorities, our life goals. It gives a poignancy to the present that demands the creation of meaning. It calls upon us to live life in such fashion as to minimize the unfinished business remaining should it suddenly be taken away. Our uncertain futurity focuses us and provides the tension necessary to stimulate and catalyze us. Psychologists are clear on the fact that an absence of tension and anxiety leads to boredom and apathy, with a lack of that stimulation necessary to prod us to achieve and produce. Indeed, if we did not fear death, we would not exert at much effort trying to avoid it or to leave our mark in the world. The normal anxiety inherent in the realization that our activity and creativity will eventually be cut off can be a motivation, like death itself, for more responsible, zestful, and purposeful use of the time available in which we do live (May 1977).

Confronting death can have a positive developmental value in that it can foster a positive philosophy of life (Maddi 1975). If properly understood, small confrontations with death can have positive value. Such encounters with death occur, for example, whenever something ends that you did not want to end, whenever you are overwhelmed by the insufficiency of time and energy to do all that you sincerely wish to do, whenever events are monotonous, and whenever conventional values are contradicted by events. These events are legitimate reminders of death because they directly threaten psychological death. They demonstrate the real fact of our limited control over events and the naïveté of conventional values. These confrontations lead to conclusions about life and are the stuff of philosophies of life. Those who can emerge from life with personal resources of self-confidence and a predilection for symbolizing, imagining, and judging (the cognitive capabilities that create meaning), with the experience of at least small encounters with death, will be able to use these resources to recognize the true significance of the dire realities of life and react by constructing a positive philosophy of life.

Such a philosophy alerts us to the importance of using every moment to the fullest, lending meaning and direction to future activities, propelling us to creative endeavor. The philosophy emphasizes (1) the acceptance that one has only partial control over events and that conventional values are inapplicable, (2) the importance of creating one's own meaning in the form of values and preferences, (3) the necessity of identifying and pursuing those matters of special importance, and (4) the view that life, properly led, is challenging and strenuous (Maddi 1975).

Other authors have supported the notion of death leading to creativity (Becker 1973); May 1977) and stimulating a sense of connection to others that can be provided by genuinely communal relationships (Killilea 1980–81; May 1977). To face death is a beginning of mastery over the terror of life, helping us not to be alienated by our nature and destiny. If death can be accepted as a necessity, and not denigrated to the level of accident, our energies will be freed for constructive aspects of living. We will remain in basic contact with who we are, with a potential for creativity and a decreased need to project fear of death outside of ourselves in violent and destructive ways (Feifel 1971). In this way pleasure is actually a product of death, not an escape from it (Fowles 1964).

"THE VITALITY OF DEATH"

Perhaps the greatest reason why death and dying should not be taboo is that when this occurs, ones loses the benefits of what the awareness of death and finitude can bring. No other author has explicated this more clearly and dramatically than Koestenbaum (1971), author of "The Vitality of Death." This seminal work will be drawn upon heavily here to explicate and elucidate the salutary consequences of death.

Unless real and symbolic death are both confronted, the individual cannot live a healthy life or achieve genuine happiness and authentic success. Koestenbaum gives the illustration of a secretary to an important executive. She has a good and well-compensated position, with status, good working conditions, and an excellent relationship with her boss. Her boss is a strong personality and she is relatively submissive and weak. In spite of the advantages of her position, however, she is beginning to feel that she is getting on in years and should think about marriage and children. Her excessive dependence on her job makes it impossible for her to see any man as a serious prospect, so she feels she should (1) quit her present job and select one with more emotional freedom that she can leave without elaborate preparation, or (2) abandon work altogether for a while to acquire the necessary emotional independence from her present employer to make eventual marriage possible. Yet the secretary is heavily dependent emotionally on the strong personality of the executive who becomes angry, cold, and indifferent to her when she intimates that she may leave her job. She dreads this response and finds it impossible to quit.

Koestenbaum noted that the secretary is plagued by self-deception. She dreads leaving her job and as result procrastinates making and executing a decision, accepting stupid excuses as rational. She strives to avoid thinking about the matter altogether. This self-deception is made possible only by the secretary's tacit acceptance of the promise of immortality. It is as if she interprets the executive as saying, in effect, "Stay with me and I will give you eternal life." Koestenbaum notes that it is because she has not learned to respond maturely to the general problem of death in her life that she is unable to manage this symbolic form of death in the potential rejection by her boss. It will only be by the correct appraisal and full acceptance of death that she will be freed from the painful, anxiety-filled, and guilt-ridden predicament in which she finds herself, as she is confused about the nature of her own death.

According to Koestenbaum, the secretary must recognize that the threat of death—real and symbolic—is inevitable and inescapable. With this she will quickly recognize that the symbolic promise of immortality, in the form of her employer's emotional acceptance of her, is a fraud. Once she completes this difficult task, accepting the certainty of her own real death, she will no longer be intimidated by symbolic death. With this recognition she realizes full well that her employer's eventual rejection is inescapable, just as is her own death, and that she is being foolish to hope secretly that life is different from what it really is—that is, with no death. Once she focuses her attention on death she will recognize that time is running out and that she has but one life to lead, and that if she relinquishes this she will have lost all there is. It will soon become apparent to her that her boss is not worth all that, and that his symbolic promise of immortality can be fulfilled no more reliably than immortality in relation to real death. If she keeps the fact of her inevitable death clearly in mind, she will develop the courage and decisiveness needed to quit her job and to engage forthwith in the task of building a family for herself. The realization of her death will place immediate and tremendous presssure upon her to make the problem of meaning of life one of primary importance to her. She will realize she has no time to waste, that she must face the facts and come to a decision.

Koestenbaum talked about the perspective that one must take:

> Authentic success and happiness in human existence demand uncompromising realism; we must understand and acknowledge the facts of life. Paradoxically, the most vitalizing fact of life is the utter inevitability of death! Man must constantly keep before his eyes the reality, the nature, and the inevitability of that fact. He must make every effort to understand exactly what his own death means to him. He must see the consequences of the knowledge that he is mortal. He must never let go of this insight (Koestenbaum 1971: 264).

With this perspective, the thought of death gives us courage . If you admit you are going to die, you will no longer act out of fear, for you have understood the fear of death and you certainly can handle fears of symbolic death. To surrender to fear is based on the acceptance of a fraudulent promise: that of symbolic immortality. Nevertheless, the recognition of your ultimate death will not eliminate the pain involved in undertaking certain courses of action. What the realization will do, however, is to give you the courage and decisiveness to carry out decisions. The immediacy of death will lead to honesty with yourself, leading to the recognition that you have no choice but to be resigned to death and to focus all your energies on the creative reconstruction of the only existence you have.

With this recognition one will concentrate on essentials, avoiding useless details since they are often an excuse to avoid the real issues in life. This will give control, as eventual death will be perceived as an absolutely necessary aspect of human existence that helps to complete a plan for life. Life becomes a project with the point of termination at death. This prevents one from drifting into situations rather than creating them, and assists one in avoiding getting into a rut. Questions such as "What do I really want out of life?", "What is the purpose of my human existence?", "What will yield the highest fulfillment in life?" are ones we are all condemned to confront and that we must all answer for ourselves. These questions must be reevaluated continuously, with constant rededication to the decision much more important than the initial decision. Time cannot be wasted, and the individual must become a total realist, dispelling all illusions about life taught by our culture and recognizing life for what it is. Such an approach to life's problems may indeed be hard; however, in the long run it is the most successful approach, as it is the only realistic one available. The sooner one realizes the inevitability of this, the better for eventual happiness and fulfillment. Indeed, authentic success, decision, genuine happiness, and full meaning can be achieved only in light of the clear insight into the fact that all of us have been condemned to die.

The ten salutary consequences of death are summarized below (from Koestenbaum 1971: 269–271).

1. We cannot escape death—real or symbolic. We must construct our lives—daily actions as well as major plans—with the full and clear realization of this fact. We must accept, once and for all, without any reservations, misgivings, false hopes, repressions, or bitterness, the fact that we have been condemned to death. Then we can start living. By accepting this death we will neutralize an otherwise completely demoralizing and paralyzing fear.

2. Once we have recognized and admitted the inevitability of death, we are on the way to becoming courageous, fearless, and decisive. Whenever indecision or lack of courage is felt, we must remind ourselves that life will end for us and that the symbolic threat of death, often the cause of our indecision, will disappear because its basic fraudulence will have been made manifest.

3. By remembering the certainty and the finality of life, we immediately see the urgency of concentrating on essentials. We cut red tape, abandon excuses and procrastinations, and do not indulge in the luxury of wasting time.

4. Only through the constant awareness of death will we achieve integrity and consistency with our principles. Basically

there is no threat other than real or symbolic death. Once we have accepted this threat we will be well beyond fraudulent bribes and threats alike.

5. Those who know they will die waste no time in attacking the problem of finding meaning and fulfillment in life. The pressure of the thought of death is a persistent, nagging, and most effective reminder that we are coerced to make some sense of life, and that we must do it now. Those who have faced death adopt a no-nonsense approach to the business of living successfully.

6. Death makes it almost impossible to repress unpleasant but important realities. Death makes us honest and unable to accept excuses to postpone dealing with basic problems or to hide from ourselves and the reality of life.

7. The realization of death-of-ourselves leads to strength. To be strong means not to be intimidated by real or symbolic death.

8. To accept death means to take charge of our lives. Those who do are no fatalists; we do not feel strictured; we are the freest of anyone, with nothing holding us back but our own decisions. We have nothing to fear, nothing to be timid about, nothing to make us feel dependent, inadequate, or inferior, since we have conquered the ultimate threat.

9. The thought of death urges us to assume a total plan for life. Through the vitality of death we are able to see all events in life from the perspective of total existence. This enables us to perform tasks that otherwise might be boring, discouraging, or senseless.

10. The thought of death enables us to laugh off vicissitudes, pain, defeat, and disappointments. To take these too seriously suggests that we still harbor the hope that death may not be real after all and that perhaps we were meant to be immortal but have somehow missed our chance.

Conclusion: The Need For a Healthy Perspective

Death and dying *are* inevitable aspects of reality. To act as if this were untrue, or as if there were anything that we can do to change the situation, is to foster pathology that can reach the deepest levels. Consequently, our challenge is to recognize and accept this fact and to use it to enhance life and assist in providing its meaning. In this regard there must be a balance between the necessary amounts of anxiety and fear that therapeutically stimulate and motivate our actions, and the avoidance and distancing from death that prod us to care for ourselves and others. It is unrealistic to think that the fear of death can ever be totally eliminated, nor should it be, since the quest for life has an inherent component in it of not dying (Hoxeng 1980). Optimum amounts of denial and anxiety are necessary if we are not to be overwhelmed by our mortality or spend precious time denying it.

Nevertheless, this fear does not mean that we must want to die, or that we must always embrace it with complete acceptance. Indeed Feifel (1971) noted that the emotions of joy, love, and happiness are just as much a part of reality as dread and death. Evasion, avoidance, and denial of death all have a rightful place in our psychic economy. We have a legitimate need to face away from death. Under certain conditions this is absolutely healthy. It is the excessive camouflage and denial that must be assaulted because they lead to a falsification of our essence.

Lacking open communication about and examination of death and dying, it is highly probable that contemporary Americans will fall victim to those forces that remove death from its natural place in existence and rob them of the traditional resources used to cope with it. We know that what is discussed and openly addressed in the light of consciousness, and with the opportunity for examination in an environment of support, retains less power over us. It is less likely to lead to inappropriate ways of responding to death and dying such as denial, repression, exploitation, sensationalism, and romanticization. To the extent that death and dying are not affirmed as inevitable realities, are not integrated in and accepted as normal aspects of human discourse, pathological responses and magical thinking about the topics will occur. It has been well-documented in the field of mental health that repression leads to symptom formation. Honest and open address of feared topics diminishes acting-out behaviors, defensiveness, and psychiatric symptomatology. It liberates the energy that has been previously bound for more constructive efforts. Keeping death and dying taboo, or in any way quasi-taboo, will rob us of all the benefits that necessarily accrue to those who realistically face their mortality. Research findings and clinical observation bear this out. For example, children who are given inadequate information about death, or who are prevented from mourning, develop sequelae of all types of severity. Adults with unresolved grief experience all manner of symptoms and syndromes. Literature increasingly documents the importance of death education in providing individuals with resources to cope with these events. Those who have encountered such events have often articulated the wish that they could have had more instruction in and discussion about it in their families (LaGrand 1981).

We think we protect ourselves and others by not addressing dying and death. This ostrich mentality only leaves us to fall back on our own selves to explain these events and to cope with the intense feelings they generate within us. Then we not only lack the therapeutic benefits of incorporation of dying and death into our life view, but we also become more vulnerable to and are at a higher risk of developing pathologies resulting from inappropriate and unhealthy responses to these natural events. The irony is that a taboo is supposed to protect the individual; in this case it actually does quite the opposite.

References

Aires, P. 1974. *Western Attitudes Toward Death: From the Middle Ages to the Present*. Translated by P. Ranum. Baltimore: Johns Hopkins University Press.

Becker, E. 1973. *The Denial of Death*. New York: The Free Press.

Bowers, M., E. Jackson, J. Knight, and L. LeShan. 1964. *Counseling the Dying*. New York: Thomas Nelson and Sons.

Brantner, J. 1971. "Death and the Self." In B. Green and D. Irish, eds., *Death Education: Preparation for Living*, Cambridge, Mass.: Schenkman Publishing Company.

Bromberg, W. and P. Schilder. 1933. "Death and Dying: A Comparative Study of the Attitudes and Mental Reactions Toward Death and Dying." *Psychoanalytic Review* 20:133–185.

Feifel, H. 1959. "Attitudes Toward Death in Some Normal and Mentally Ill Populations." In H. Feifel, ed., *The Meaning of Death*, New York: McGraw-Hill.

Feifel, H. 1968. "Attitudes Toward Death: A Psychological Perspective." *Journal of Consulting and Clinical Psychology* 33:292–295.

Feifel, H. 1971. "The Meaning of Death in American Society: Implications for Education." In B. Green and D. Irish, eds., *Death Education: Preparation for Living*, Cambridge, Mass.: Schenkman Publishing Company.

Feifel, H. 1977a. "Death in Contemporary America." In H. Feifel, ed., *New Meanings of Death*, New York: McGraw-Hill.

Feifel, H. 1977b. "Epilogue." In H. Feifel, ed., *New Meanings of Death*, New York: McGraw-Hill.

Forster, E. 1962. "Aphorism." In W. Auden and L. Kronenberger, eds., *The Viking Book of Aphorisms*, New York: Viking Press.

Fowles J. 1964. *The Aristos*. Boston: Little, Brown and Co.

Freud, S. 1915. "Thoughts for the Times on War and Death." In *Standard Edition of the Complete Psychological Works of Sigmund Freud*. (Vol. 14). London: Hogarth Press, 1957.

Fulton, R. 1979. "Anticipatory Grief, Stress, and the Surrogate Griever." In J. Tache, H. Selye, and S. Day, eds. *Cancer, Stress and Death*, New York: Plenum.

Gillespie, W. 1963. "Some Regressive Phenomena in Old Age." *British Journal of Medical Psychology* 36:203–209.

Gordon, D. 1970. *Overcoming the Fear of Death*. New York: Macmillan.

Gorer, G. 1965. "The Pornography of Death." (1955) Reprinted in G. Gorer, *Death, Grief, and Mourning*. Garden City, New York: Doubelday & Company, Inc.

Harper, B. 1977. *Death: the Coping Mechanism of the Health Professional*. Greenville, S.C.: Southeastern University Press.

Hoxeng, D. 1980. "Fear of Death and Its Implications for Death Milieu Counseling." In B. Schoenberg, ed., *Bereavement Counseling—A Multidisciplinary Handbook*, Westport, Conn.: Greenwood Press.

Kalish, R. 1981. *Death, Grief, and Caring Relationships*. Monterey, Calif.: Brooks/Cole Publishing Company.

Kastenbaum, R. 1967. "The Child's Understanding of Death: How Does it Develop?" In E. Grollman, ed., *Explaining Death to Children*. Boston: Beacon Press.

Kastenbaum, R. 1977. *Death, Society and Human Experience*. St. Louis: C. V. Mosby.

Kastenbaum, R. and R. Aisenberg. 1972. *The Psychology of Death*. New York: Springer.

Killilea, A. 1980–81. "Death Consciousness and Social Consciousness: A Critique of Ernest Becker and Jacques Choron on Denying Death." *Omega* 11:185–200.

Koestenbaum, P. 1971. "The Vitality of Death." *Omega* 2:253–271.

Kübler-Ross, E. 1969. *On Death and Dying*. New York: Macmillan.

Lagrand, L. 1981. " Loss Reactions of College Students: A Descriptive Analysis." *Death Education* 5:235–348.

Lazarus, R. 1981. "The Costs and Benefits of Denial." In J. Spinetta and P. Deasy-Spinetta, eds., *Living With Childhood Cancer,* St. Louis: Mosby.

Lepp, I. 1968. *Death and Its Mysteries*. New York: Macmillan.

Leviton, D. and W. Wendt. 1983. "Health Education, the Denial of Death, and Global Well-Being." *Health Education* 14:3–6.

Lifton, R. 1975. "On Death and the Continuity of Life: A Psychohistorical Perspective." *Omega* 6:143–159.

Maddi, S. 1975. "Developmental Value of Fear of Death." Presented as part of a Symposium on "Fear of Death and Creativity," *American Psychological Association Convention*. Chicago.

Maslach, C. and S. Jackson. 1979. "Burned-Out Cops and Their Families." *Psychology Today* May, p. 59.

May, R. 1977. *The Meaning of Anxiety*. New York: W. W. Norton.

May R. 1982. "Anxiety and Values." In C. Spielberger, I. Sarason, and N. Milgram, eds., *Stress and Anxiety* (Vol. 8), Washington, D.C.: Hemisphere Publishing Corporation.

Murphy, G. 1959. "Discussion." In H. Feifel, ed., *The Meaning of Death,* New York: McGraw-Hill.

Neale, R. 1973. *The Art of Dying*. New York: Harper and Row.

Parsons, T. and V. Lidz. 1967. "Death in American Society." In E. Shneidman, ed., *Essays in Self-Destruction,* New York: Science House.

Pattison, E. 1977. *The Experience of Dying*. Englewood Cliffs, N.J.: Prentice-Hall.

Pine, V. 1984. "Perspectives on Dying and Death for the EMT." In S. Lewis and H. Weinman, eds., *Emergency Care Dynamics,* New York: Wiley.

Rando, T. A. 1981. "Concepts of Death, Dying, Grief and Loss" (Participant Manual). In U.S. Department of Health and Human Services, *Hospice Education Program for Nurses* (Publication No. HRA 81–27). Washington, D.C.: U.S. Government Printing Office.

Rando, T.A. 1984. *Grief, Dying, and Death: Clinical Interventions for Caregivers*. Champaign, Ill.: Research Press.

Rochlin, G. 1965. "How Younger Children View Death and Themselves." In E. Grollman, ed., *Explaining Death to Children,* Boston: Beacon Press.

Schoenberg, B. and R. Senescu. 1970. "The Patient's Reaction to Fatal Illness." In B. Schoenberg, et al., eds., *Loss and Grief: Psychological Management in Medical Practice,* New York: Columbia University Press.

Searles, H. 1961. "Schizophrenia and the Inevitability of Death." *Psychiatric Quarterly* 35:631–665.

Shneidman, E. 1971. "On the Deromanticization of Death." *American Journal of Psychotherapy* 25:4–17.

Shneidman, E. 1973. *Deaths of Man*. New York: Quadrangle//The New York Times Book Company.

Shubin, S. 1978. "Burn-out: The Professional Hazard You Face in Nursing." *Nursing 78* 8:22–27.

Simpson, M. 1979. "Social and Psychological Aspects of Dying." In H. Wass, ed.,

Dying: Facing the Facts, Washington, D.C.: Hemisphere Publishing Corporation.

Stephenson, J. 1985. *Death, Grief, and Mourning: Individual and Social Realities.* New York: The Free Press.

Vachon, M. 1978. "Motivation and Stress Experienced by Staff Working With the Terminally Ill." *Death Education* 2:113–122.

Verwoerdt, A. 1966. *Communication With the Fatally Ill.* Springfield, Ill.: Charles C. Thomas.

Wahl, C. W. 1959. "The Fear of Death." In H. Feifel, ed., *The Meaning of Death.* New York: McGraw-Hill Book Co.

Weisman, A. and J. Worden. 1975. "Psychosocial Analysis of Cancer Death." *Omega* 6:61–75.

Worden, J. 1982. *Grief Counseling and Grief Therapy. A Handbook for the Mental Health Practitioner.* New York: Springer.

Preamble: Since death and dying have traditionally been taboo topics in our culture, the logical means of combating the influences of repression, denial, exploitation, and sensationalism is through education. Education at all levels is indicated, beginning in kindergarten and continuing through courses for the mature adult and the aged. Training should be related, where appropriate, to all aspects and ramifications of death and dying, including loss and grief, care of the terminally ill, and recovery from bereavement—that is, to the discipline of Thanatology.

Principle 3: Education in Thanatology Is Necessary

3

Education in Thanatology

GARY J. GRAD and
STEPHEN V. GULLO

Since death and dying have been taboo topics in our culture, the logical means of combating individual and societal influences of fear and repression is through education. Education in thanatology at all levels is indicated, beginning as early as kindergarten and continuing through courses for mature adults and the aged. Training should be related, where appropriate, to all aspects and ramifications of death and dying, including loss and grief, care of the terminally ill, and recovery from bereavement, as well as the development of the capacity to deal with loss as a critical step in human maturation.

We will discuss education in its broadest context, relating to individuals of all ages as an aid to their coping with the painful and universal issues of death and loss. Such education must reflect individuals' cognitive and affective development as well as their life experiences. Interpersonal and educational perspectives are of equal importance and must be taken into account as well. In effect, loss, death, grief, and recovery may be presented educationally within the context of the life cycle as experienced by individuals cognitively and emotionally and as they relate to "significant" others and to their own lives.

Broadening our perspective to that of the life cycle allows us to consider those issues pertaining to death as part of a process that affects and influences individuals differently. Death may be conceptualized as an especially important experience along the change/loss continuum. Bowlby (1980) has observed that loss cannot be separated from (and is an integral part of) attachment. Separation has ramifications not only in terms of our feelings but also leads to changes in behavior. Death is the final separation and most significant example of loss as it pertains to our relationships with all living things, others, and ultimately ourselves. Perhaps Taylor has expressed this most poignantly:

> One can see loss and its sequelae demonstrated in a more primitive and fundamental way as a human response to all change, and to the growth process itself. Change implies abandoning one state for another; and we often react to this with quite violent denial, anger and protest, as well as with disorientation, fear and sadness. (1981:16)

Dealing with dying and bereavement therefore means touching upon some of the most powerful of experiences with which one can grapple. Death education, within this perspective, becomes not only a vehicle for understanding the phenomenon of death and its emotional effects, but also a significant educational tool geared toward enhancing our capacities for coping with the universal and continuing experiences we have daily with loss and separation. Ultimately death education leads in one direction—back to life and dealing with the inevitable trajectory of its course through loss and separation.

Societal Resistance to Death Education

Societal resistance to death education clearly can be seen as an expression of our general concern about death. Until very recently, death was most often seen as mystical and frightening. Kübler-Ross (1975) has referred to contemporary America as death-denying in light of our need to put death and the dying away from us in hospitals and to speak of the end of life in euphemisms. In such a society, it can be anticipated that those who advocate death education will be greeted as the proverbial messengers of bad news. History has demonstrated repeatedly the rewards such individuals have garnered. Denial and other previously noted mechanisms pertain not only to society as an amorphous body but also directly affect educators and the educational process.

Guidelines for death education, however meritorious they may be, are meaningless if society resists their implementation. Such resistance has been noted in research reports by educators and especially parents. For example, parents of young children, though feeling that teachers' self-development should be fostered and that they should take part in curriculum planning and interactions with children and parents concerning death, "expressed significantly less support than teachers for death education as a part of early childhood education. . . . Parents also exhibited a more protective attitude than teachers relative to children's questions and expressed concerns about death" (Crase and Crase 1982:61). Hence, we will attempt a pragmatic and functional approach in our recommendations.

To those who would raise the question of whether it is damaging to teach about death and dying, we state our position clearly and unequivocally: the question is not whether it is damaging to know about death, as we have no choice in this matter; all of us know about death. The question is *what* will we know about death and how will we cope with it. Human communication includes the nonverbal as well as the verbal. We have always had death education: silence has been the lesson we have taught. Silence often fosters confusion, fear, and anxiety, as well as other forms of maladaptation. We are not born with a fear of death; we learn it from the taboo of silence and fear transmitted by our families, friends, and society as a whole. Death education has as its goal clarification of individuals' ideas and feelings about death, as well as aiding the development of coping mechanisms aimed toward tolerating separation, loss, illness, and death.

The Developmental Perspective

Recommendations concerning death education must reflect developmentally based concepts and concerns about death. They must also be sensitive to life experiences, relationships with others, and the relationships between educators and students as well as between educators and parents.

One of the earliest, but still most often quoted surveys of children's perceptions of death, was done by Nagy (1948). She identified three stages of development in children's concepts of death. Those less than five years of age saw death as a reversible and altered form of life where vital functions such as sleeping and breathing were maintained. The dead person might be seen as having gone away and living elsewhere. The main issue here seems to be that of separation. Children in the second stage, ages five through nine, saw death as final and awful, related in its occurrence to rules and behaviors such as good and bad, and as a personified image, death-man or skeleton-man, that comes to get one. For those over nine, death is a process obeying laws relating to wearing out or becoming dysfunctional.

More recent researchers (Plank and Plank 1975 and Kane 1979) have questioned the personification notion. Contemporary researchers and authors have correlated death-concept formation with Piaget's theory and stages of intellectual development. Kane (1979) has noted that in Piaget's stage of pre-operational thought (ages 2–7), when the child focuses on single dimensions of similar objects at a time and reversibility has not been achieved, death is defined as real, separation occurs, the deceased is immobile, and fantasy may produce death (death wish, anger produces death). In Piaget's second stage (ages 7–11), manifested by ability to think about the whole and its parts, death is specific, concrete, irrevocable; it produces, and is produced by, dysfunction and may be caused by internal and external agents (old age, weapons and accidents, respectively). Finally, in Piaget's third stage of formal operations (age 11 and up), the child begins to extrapolate on its thinking, thinks beyond reality and considers the possibilities of what might occur versus reliance on the actual. The child in this stage treats death more abstractly. Koocher's (1974) views are also correlated with Piagetian theory. Children in the three phases possess first primarily magical thinking about death (as noted previously). Later they think about how death comes about and, in the final of the three stages, they think about death as occurring after bodily systems wear out (as per Nagy for those over nine).

Gullo and Plimpton (1983) have elaborated the developmental point of view still further. Children under three are terrorized by the notion of separation, while those three to six still remain fearful of the separation involved, as they see it, in death. They feel that the dead are in another state, still capable of returning to life, and that this state may be a form of punishment. As their concepts of causality and finality cognitively evolve, children six to ten begin to recognize death as final and universal. Death is personified and externalized. By 10 or older, the child's conceptualization of death's meaning begins to parallel that of adults. Death becomes an inevitable part of the life cycle. The adolescent understands the reality of death's finality. While there is cognitive awareness and understanding, adolescence is also a time of focus on separation from parents and the achievement of individuation, newly achieved strengths, appearance, sexual identity, and future goals. Newly found intellectual capacities may be used to deal with some of the anxiety occasioned by thoughts of one's mortality at a time of excitement and plans for the future. Adolescent defenses often push death to the background as a distant and at times almost improbable reality. Adolescence is the time of death-defying behavior and illusion—that while death will claim us eventually, it's not going to be today! It is clear to us that death becomes even more real and complexly related to our lives, feelings, and relationships as we age. It takes on personal significance most readily as we are forced to deal with the deaths of friends, family, siblings, and children.

A Curriculum Model for Death Education

While there have been many attempts to develop thanatology courses for different age groups and in different settings, certain principles of general application have arisen. Warren (1982) notes that a thorough knowledge of the pupils is especially important in death education because of the sensitive nature of the topic, that "in addition to demographic and other background factors, there is scope to consider the present position of a student in relation to death and dying—what meanings he or she attaches to these notions and how these are integrated with other aspects of the total personality" (p. 25). He notes that for students within a group as well as for the instructor's relationship with the group, it is important that there be at least some sharing, for example, in meanings of the concepts of death and experiences with death.

Another guiding principle for death education is that in the context of the age, developmental level, and setting within which one works, exposure to a wide variety of experiential and didactic components appears necessary to acquire and enhance the variety of coping capacities pertaining to the self and others (Bugen 1980). Primary school students might well respond to education focusing mainly on general life cycle issues and experiences. Children and early adolescents may profit greatly from dealing with death in "safe" and more indirect ways such as children's books and stories or discussions of the deaths of plants, pets, and adults. Popular movies and television programs noted as leading to anxiety may also be fruitfully discussed. College students might well make use of education including the epidemiology of death, fundamentals of human grief, aspects of crisis intervention, the process of dying, the topic of children and death, and religious and parapsychological views of death. Community resources for prevention and coping with illness, separation, and death as well as constraints to their use may be discussed. Experiential components including attitudes exploration, visits to funeral homes, listening to the terminally ill and bereaved, etc. have also proven useful. Maintenance of small group structure throughout a course for college age students and older individuals might, as well, aid students' awareness of the use of support groups to foster coping.

Seeking parental aid in structuring programs for younger children may bring about greater acceptance of such programs. An informational seminar and orientation for parents may be most helpful. Parental fears and anxieties may then be made more visible and might be dealt with (Crase and Crase 1982). Communication with parents during the educational process aids the process and might provide some parental education in thanatology as well. Finally, it has repeatedly been noted that positive results of death education are hard to measure, especially immediately after the course is completed (Murray 1974; Shoemaker et al. 1981). Perhaps change in this area, rooted in personal development, family interaction and societal perspectives, may arise only slowly. Courses aimed at specific areas of death education, however, may have more immediate facilitating results (Shoemaker et al. 1981).

Though most authors, as noted, have divided conceptions of death into three to four phases, our suggestions are divided into six major sections: preschool children, those five to eight, preadolescents (nine to twelve), early adolescents, later adolescence and college (sixteen through the end of formal education), and adulthood (table 3.1). This six-stage format seems to fit better not only the cognitive and emotional development of children, adolescents, and adults but also their educational experiences and opportunities, as well as their life experiences and relationship patterns.

As noted, preschool children see death as irreversible, as a kind of separation or going away whereby the important person will never return. They may well, as is quite common, become very frightened if parents even "go away" for an evening out. Separation may also be associated with loss of love and fear that the person who leaves does not love the child and will never return. Going to sleep may become frightening and difficult if parents are away, or if losses occur. Even in the best of circumstances, however, death does have an impact on the lives of children of these ages through the death of flowers, plants, pets, and so forth. The most important issues are to clarify for the child what the occurrences actually are (vacations, business trips, divorce of parents, deaths) and whether separations are, in fact, permanent or temporary. The child may not fully understand these ideas, but at least misinformation may be avoided. Support and reassurance are appropriate with clarification of the types of separations from important others as well as situations like

Table 3.1 Human Development and Conceptions of Death

Developmental Period	Conceptions of Death	Personality Needs and Concepts	Educational Needs
1. Preschool	Irreversible separation	Loss of love	Determination of extent of separation and feelings through discussions with important others
2. Early School Years: 5–8	Death personified, death-man	Death due to wrong-doing or as punishment, irreversible	Life cycle discussion (plants, pets, etc. in school) and have settings, reassurance, and guilt; alleviate with discussion of other feelings.
3. Preadolescence: 9–12	Death as a wearing-out or dysfunction	Internal or external agents cause death	Reality oriented discussion includes current events and elaboration of feelings at home and school
4. Early Adolescence	Death as part of life cycle, more realistic and frightening due to personality needs	Separation, individuation, functional capacity, strength and attractiveness	As per 3, but with greater elaboration of feelings like fear, helplessness, and depression
5. Late Adolescence and College	Retention of death's reality, but less frightening	Less need to defend oneself against fear of death as more stable concepts of self and others and realistic capacities develop	Curriculum focusing on death and dying, suffering of dying person and loved ones, religious any parapsychological aspects, support groups, agencies and institutions
6. Adulthood	As per Stage 5	Death as an event that will occur to self, family, and friends	As per 5, but with groups specific to personal experience

the death of pets. Appropriate responses of sadness, tearfulness, anxiety, concern, and anger may be shared and discussed. Education for children of these ages is primarily personal and one-to-one between the important adult and the child. Central concepts are the varieties of separation and ability to experience feelings without being overwhelmed and becoming dysfunctional.

We have considered ages 5–8 as a group having similar ideas about death (Nagy 1948). At this age, children are in their early school years and also at the end of the Piagetian phase of irreversibility. Death is personified and magical. Death is seen as occurring for a reason, and the reason may well have to do with wrongdoing, guilt, and punishment. Death education at home continues as with younger children, but children of this age may well want to talk about the loss of pets and unfortunate accidents. Rituals like the burial of pets may be requested. These rituals are part of our societal means of handling death, loss, and the grieving process. They may well allow the child to begin to understand upset and sadness within societal norms which, though at times ritualized, also allow sharing with others. Experiencing and controlling feelings may be aided by the child's "taking care of" the dead and loved pet. If a loved person dies, some children may want to attend the funeral; generally it is a good idea to follow the child's lead. Parents are often fearful of the open casket; this may be discussed directly with the child to aid decision-making regarding attendance.

In school, natural science becomes the forum for investigating the life cycle cognitively and, to some extent, emotionally. "Show and Tell" and similar story-telling techniques may also occasionally focus on death and loss, not as planned events but as children decide to discuss their experiences. Death education focuses on greater understanding of life-cycle issues. While focus on life-cycle issues aids in teaching the natural qualities of life, change, death, and separation, experimental techniques, as noted, focus on concomitant feelings such as fear, sadness, guilt, and helplessness.

The nine- to twelve-year-old age group may well have difficulty focusing on feelings. Cognition and personality style have become more stable. Death may be seen in more functional terms as, for example, a wearing out. While some of the same means as noted for handling issues of separation, loss, and death with younger children may be useful at home, school can focus even more intensely on life-cycle issues by more overt mention of death as a universal experience and termination for all forms of life. Group discussions may be helpful if, for example, school pets die or a tragedy occurs in the community that is well-known to the pupils. Children naturally, at this time, may watch more true-to-life television and go to movies with themes of loss and separation, let alone death, which may then also be discussed. It should be made clear that children of this age, although intensely curious, may be, as noted, very reluctant to talk about upsetting events. They are often deeply touched by issues of separation, divorce, and death. Discussion of books, television, and movies decreases the fear and anxiety that may go relatively unnoticed. Transient hyperactivity, nervousness, sadness, and even persistent sleep problems and difficulty in separation from parents (like going to school) herald the ways in which children of these ages may react to losses and separation.

The 13- to 15-year-old is emotionally at the beginning of separation from home and personal individuation. Considerable denial of mortality may be part of this period of development, and is often accompanied by omnipotent fantasies of the future based on the adolescent's focus on attractiveness, sexuality, strength, increased functional capacities, and greater sense of time. Sex differences in coping, whether viewed positively or not, become more prevalent, with the usual attempts by boys to conceal feelings and by girls to heighten experiences and emotions. Adolescents of these ages continue to be more fruitfully approached through handling openly the common home events of separations, losses, and deaths, while school foci begin to elaborate on basic feelings and individual and group discussion of separation, loss, fear, helplessness, depression, and death. Cognitively, adolescents of this age may be better able to understand aspects of death and dying such as bodily change and suffering, which may become part of life-cycle education as related to humans as well as animals.

There is considerable overlap between adolescents 16 and

over and adults. Chiefly, adult education can incorporate more life experiences with separation, death, and dying into the educational experience. People of these ages can take part in formal education along the lines previously noted (Bugen 1980–81). Thanatology finally becomes more of a discipline unto itself than one constituted of parts enmeshed in general life-cycle issues and experiences related to death. People of these ages have a greater capacity to experience empathy with others and to be more sympathetic and helpful as well. They may have actual experiences with death and the dying, and they are also cognitively more capable of dealing with issues of an ethical nature such as death with dignity and quality of life. As noted, course work on specific issues should be incorporated with experiential education and group discussion. The course, if the group size is reasonably small, may even act to provide a place where feelings and possible coping mechanisms relating to loss, suffering, illness, dying, death, and grieving may be elaborated. The adult enters, if not in terms of time at least in terms of experience, an accelerating period of actual losses and deaths. As we have noted, even education of children may aid parental education in thanatology as they consider their children's education. Personal encounters with death and one's own health raise further issues of quality of life and death with dignity. Groups of an experiential nature for individuals who are undergoing or have undergone separation, loss, and death may lower anxiety, allow expression and sharing of feelings, and foster coping mechanisms. These groups can be held in a variety of settings including colleges, religious facilities, and even senior citizen centers. Such groups may increasingly work with people with similar life experiences.

Summary

Education in thanatology provides a reasoned alternative to the "education of silence" that has long surrounded death in our schools. How interesting a commentary on the "great taboo" of our society it is that sex and drugs now find a ready place in the educational curriculum, while discussions of death are deemed inappropriate or are still forbidden. Truly the dying have become the pariahs or lepers of twentieth-century life. Our leper colonies are the impersonal hospitals where the dying are sheltered from our view and touch.

A curriculum model rooted in the cognitive and affective needs of six major developmental periods along the life cycle is advocated. We caution, however, that even the most perfectly conceptualized model will prove useless unless it is designed in conjunction with the sensitivities of parents and educators. No model will endure any longer than the support it can generate, for without this support models are only the theories of thanatologists rather than the realities of the school. We favor linking death education to the life sequences model wherein death is studied within the broader context of a life cycle or human development approach. One can start with inanimate objects and progress to animate objects, people, loved ones, and ultimately to ourselves. We also propose an emphasis on dealing with death and bereavement in terms of the development of coping skills to confront the continuing sequence of losses that are part of every human life. Even those adults who have never had a loved one die still must confront loss daily. As they reflect on their own lives, it is apparent that life is also constituted of a series of losses, starting in childhood with the breaking of a favorite toy and continuing to the death of a beloved pet, to the loss of friends and relatives through relocation, to the loss of more personal attributes such as our youth and youth's agility in the actual confrontation with death and its inevitable touching of everyone.

As thanatology has emerged as a discipline, there is now enough information and data to design a curriculum model not just to teach but to "touch"—to touch the cognitive understanding as well as the affective needs and fears of the individual and the larger society. Educators have long maintained that knowledge and exposure alter behavior and prejudice. The challenge of death education will be the ultimate test.

References

Bowlby, J. 1980. *Attachment and Loss* (Volume 3), London: Hogarth.

Bugen, L. A. 1980–81. "Coping: Effects of Death Education." *Omega* 11(2):175–183.

Crase, D. R. and D. Crase. 1982. "Parental Attitudes Toward Death Education for Young Children." *Death Education* 6:61–73.

Gullo, S. V. and E. H. Plimpton. 1983. "On Understanding and Coping with Death During Childhood: The Child's Dilemma and the Games He Plays." In S. V. Gullo, et al., eds. *Death and Children: A Guide for Educators, Parents and Caregivers*, pp. 79–92. Dobbs Ferry, N.Y.: Tappan Press.

Kane, B. 1979. "Children's Concepts of Death." *Journal of Genetic Psychology* 134:141–153.

Kübler-Ross, E. 1975. *Death, the Final Stage of Growth*. Englewood, Cliffs, N.J.: Prentice-Hall.

Murray, P. 1974. "Death Education and Its Effect on the Death Anxiety Level of Nurses." *Psychological Report* 35:1250.

Nagy, M. 1948. "The Child's Theories Concerning Death." *Journal of Genetic Psychology* 73:3–27.

Plank, E. N. and R. Plank. 1979. "Children and Death." In A. J. Solnit, ed. *The Psychoanalytic Study of the Child*, New Haven: Yale University Press.

Shoemaker, R. K., G. G. Burnett, R. E. Hesford, and C. E. Zimmer. 1981. "The Effects of Death Education Course or Participant Attitudes Toward Death and Dying." *Teaching of Psychology* 8(4):217–219.

Taylor, D. 1981. "Facing Death: Helping the Helpers." *British Journal of Projective Psychology and Personality Study* 26(2):13–20.

Warren, W. G. 1982. "Personal Constructions of Death and Death Education." *Death Education* 6:17–28.

Selected Bibliography (Additional)

Bernstein, J. and S. V. Gullo. 1977. *When People Die*. New York: E. P. Dutton.

Bowlby, J. 1973. *Attachment and Loss* (Volume 2) New York: Basic Books.

Morris, P. 1974. *Loss and Change*. New York: Pantheon.

Rumes, S. 1975. *Teaching Your Child to Cope with Crisis*. New York: David McKay.

Wolff, S. 1969. *Children Under Stress*. Baltimore: Penguin Books.

Preamble: While the medical profession is usually most intimately involved with care of the dying patient, a continuous program of education in Thanatology requires a multidisciplinary approach that unites nursing, social work, philosophy, psychology, psychiatry, and religion, as well as other professional and lay groups. The development of adequate programs in the sensitive areas of Thanatology requires services, training, and research workers.

Principle 4: Education in Thanatology Requires a Multidisciplinary Approach

4

Education and Patient Care in Thanatology: A Multidisciplinary Approach

JOHN G. BRUHN
and RAYMOND G. FUENTES JR.

Death and dying remain neglected topics in the education of health professionals. Curative and restorative medicine still provide the basic structure for the curriculum in most health professional schools. To discuss personal feelings about death or to learn about the care of dying patients and their families can be threatening, as the death of a patient is represented as a failure to cure or to heal. Students therefore learn early in their education that death is such a personal matter that it should not be discussed openly and freely, and since they see so few role models preparing terminally ill patients for death they also learn that dying patients are to be avoided and even referred. Much of the education of health professionals in thanatology and thanatological care is unspoken, but the message is strong nonetheless.

The professional's feelings about the death of a patient are often a heavy personal burden because the professionals do not know how to involve other members of the team or how to use one another's skills in dealing with the many issues surrounding death. Education about death and the care of dying patients and their families require the active participation of many disciplines.

Death Education—When to Begin?

Several articles have discussed the successes and problems in implementing death education courses in high school and college (Ayalon 1979; Rosner 1974; Ulin 1977). Although surveys of high school students have indicated a need for teaching about death and dying, especially during adolescence (Cappiello and Troyer 1979; O'Brien, Johnson, and Schmink 1978), there is little evidence that death and dying are routinely addressed in schools, even though no age is free from experience with death.

Concepts of death are developed in direct relation to age and by certain defined stages (Glicken 1978). Although these concepts often change as children grow older, their foundations have a lasting influence on what the concepts of death will be for adults (Koocher 1973; Zeligs 1974). The concepts of death that a child will develop depend on many conditions in the child's life, including mass media, adults' reactions to death, religious training, and firsthand experiences with death. In general, we leave death education to chance (much like sex education), to be derived from experience in growing up. It is not surprising, therefore, that children learn from an early age that attitudes, feelings, and behavior surrounding death should be denied and concealed.

Teachers' attitudes toward death are not different from the attitudes that are common to adults in Western culture, and many teachers do not want to become involved in teaching a subject with which they are not comfortable. Education about death, if it does occur in a formal way, is often left to the health educator (if the school has one available). Even health educators are not trained routinely in death education (Crase 1980). Indeed, not every teacher or health educator should be an instructor of death education. Competencies need to be established, as well as mechanics of quality control and an adequate support system, if qualified teachers of death education are to be trained.

Furthermore, there is no consensus about the knowledge that is essential to include in a course in death education. As a result, death education courses vary greatly in scope and depth of topics covered. Current events, instructor biases, previous experiences, and departmental philosophy often determine the focus of a death education course (Eddy et al. 1980). Health educators are active in recommending that education about death be included as a part of health education. As Russell (1977) stated, "by learning about death many people become more aware of the value of life." Attitudes about life and death, as well as identification of values and preparation for personal health, should be part of the development of the total person (Harris 1978; Hart 1976). At present in our society, this process does not usually begin until the high school years. The cultural barriers to beginning the process of developing the total person, including health behavior, as the person grows and develops are enormous. Some investigators, however, have made an effort to begin this educational process in preschool (Bruhn and Parcel 1981; 1982).

Death Education in Professional Schools

MEDICAL STUDENTS

Death education in health professional schools began about 1970. Kübler-Ross, a psychiatrist, was one of the pioneers in the effort to initiate discussion about death and dying in medical schools. She recalls, "Our main problem was with the physicians. They first ignored the seminar; later they refused to give us permission to interview their patients. They often became quite apprehensive or hostile when we approached them. Many colleagues said to me quite indignantly 'you cannot interview this patient. She is not dying. She may even be able to go home once more.' It was obvious that they missed the whole point of the seminar. . . . We could not convey to our colleagues that we are all dying—that we all have to face our finiteness long before we are terminally ill" (Kübler-Ross 1969).

Barton (1977) pointed out that education about death has been limited and poorly integrated into health care training. Health care professionals tend to learn about the management of the dying informally. Indeed, the absence of education in this area is powerful communication. It tends to perpetuate the attitude that death is a taboo topic.

A survey of instruction, in 1972, on death education in medical schools in the United States showed that of 83 responding schools, 42 had no formal educational program for medical students on the dying patient (Liston 1973). A similar survey carried out three years later by another investigator showed that of 107 schools responding, only seven had a full-term course in death and dying, 44 had a "minicourse," 42 had "a lecture or two" on the subject, and 14 schools had no formal courses (Dickinson 1976). A survey of the Canadian medical schools in 1979 reported similar results (Perez, Gosselin, and Gagnon 1980).

The structure, content, and timing of experiences in death education in medical schools is diverse. Barton (1972) emphasized the need for instruction about death and dying at all levels of the medical school curriculum, particularly in a small-group format that allows each student to "work through" and synthesize his attitudes toward death and dying (Barton et al. 1972). At one medical school, discussions about death, dying, and dissection were initiated during the first-year curriculum to deal with personal questions and emotions evoked by cadaver dissection (Marks and Bertman 1980).

Schools with larger enrollments have used lectures to discuss loss and grief; attendance was poor and attitude change was minimal (Bleeker and Pomerantz 1979).

Whether death and dying should be taught in the preclinical or clinical years of medical school (or both), which teaching methods are most effective, and how much curriculum time is needed require systematic development as well as definition of course content (Liston 1975; Smith, McSweeney and Katz 1980). There is some evidence to suggest that medical students who have taken an entire course on relating to dying patients and their families tend to communicate better with dying patients than do medical students who do not have a course or have had only portions of a course (Dickinson and Pearson 1977; Herman 1980). Although Geelhoed and Bowles (1977) endorsed the importance of death education, they emphasized that the student-physicians' responses to dying patients mirror their responses to their own deaths, and that the major purpose of such education should be to enable students to express and come to grips with feelings about their own deaths.

HOUSESTAFF

Kübler-Ross (1969) found that the difficulty of involving a physician in death education increased with the level of the physician's training.

A survey of housestaff who care for dying patients at a large medical center demonstrated that house officers are aware of their discomfort in dealing with dying patients and their families, but that they believe they do not avoid them. They strongly agreed with the use of the "no code" designation and believed the quality of life was the most important factor in making that decision. The house officer who has concerns about a dying patient is most likely to talk with another house officer. This survey highlighted the needs of housestaff for experienced resource people and for informal programs dealing with the care of dying patients (Scurry, Bruhn, and Bunce 1979).

Housestaff are not uniform in their needs or attitudes in

relating to dying patients. A survey of the graduates from five medical schools showed that female physicians tended to relate better to dying patients and their families than did male physicians (Dickinson and Pearson 1979a). This same survey found support for differences in attitudes toward terminally ill patients among different medical specialties. Among 15 medical specialists, oncologists were most likely to feel comfortable with a dying patient, were least likely to find treating a dying patient unpleasant, had the least difficulty telling a patient that he was dying, and believed that physicians refer dying patients to other physicians to avoid having to deal with their dying. Obstetricians-gynecologists, on the other hand, were the least likely to deal with dying patients and were the least open in dealing with them (Dickinson and Pearson 1979b).

Another study indicated that students who are attracted to surgery have less interest in discussing the topic early in their careers than other specialists (Blumenfield, Levy, and Kaufman 1979). On the other hand, psychiatrists and students interested in psychiatry favor more discussion of death in medical school (Gertler and Ferneau 1975). A study of residents in internal medicine indicated that they employ the same defense mechanisms as those displayed by patients, namely, denial, belief in afterlife, hope that they will be spared a long disabling illness, or morbid preoccupation with depression (to the extent that they expressed suicidal intent) if they were terminally ill (Rich and Kalmanson 1966).

In this vein, Livingston and Zimet (1965) pointed out that underlying values and attitudes are not formed during specialty training or during the years of professional service, but that they are present before medical school and are part of the personality. The medical student discovers the surgeon or psychiatrist or other specialist within himself, and the hand of his values and attitudes slips into the glove of his future vocation. Certainly, age and clinical experience can later modify attitude and behavior. For example, a recent survey indicates that attitudes toward death and dying among practicing physicians differ more by age (or clinical experience) than by specialty (Bruhn, Bunce and Scurry 1982). The differences found among specialists in studies of housestaff appear to diminish with age and clinical experience.

NURSING STUDENTS

Several efforts have been made to survey the attitudes of nursing students toward the care of dying patients, and to assess the effectiveness of different learning experiences in death education. A two-year survey of one class of students in the third year of a baccalaureate nursing program indicated that seminar discussion and direct care of a dying patient contributed most to attitude change (Martin and Collier 1975). In another study no differences were found in attitudes among a group of senior-level nursing students who took a course in death and dying and a group of their peers who did not take the course. Difference in attitudes about death and dying among the total group tended to be related to experience with a family death and a belief in a supreme being (Hopping 1977). A seminar for RNs and LPNs, in which they could become aware of their personal attitudes and behavior by simulating their own dying, was found to be an effective learning experience (Mills 1977). A course on death and grief did create a more positive attitude toward dying patients among nurses who worked in areas of the hospital where patients were at high risk of dying (Miles 1980). The common factor in all of these examples was that the nurses either had direct experience with a dying patient or a dying family member or had the opportunity to discuss their own feelings about dying. A statistically significant shift in attitude on a scale or test does not appear to be a meaningful way to assess whether a learning experience in death education has been successful. Indeed, this might be why attempts to measure death anxiety among nurses who have taken a course in death and dying have yielded mixed results (Yarber, Gobel, and Rublee 1981; Vargo and Batsel 1981; Laube 1977; Murray 1974).

ALLIED HEALTH SCIENCES STUDENTS

Allied health professionals may not be involved as intimately with dying patients as are physicians and nurses, yet they may become the ones to whom the dying patient or the family turns. Death education is a recent introduction into allied health curricula and is usually an elective course. Dietrich (1980) has proposed guidelines for introducing a course in death and dying to allied health professionals. She proposed that course content should be integrated into the entire curriculum, that the course should be team-taught and should involve a mix of students from different disciplines, and that the course content should be tied to clinical experience. A need exists for preparation of instructors to teach such a course. Dietrich (1980) advocated workshops for potential instructors that would involve exploration of personal feelings about death and exploration of course content, teaching techniques, and methods for evaluating students.

An increasing number of occupational therapists are being requested to work with patients dying with cancer, emphysema, and other illnesses. Therapists are generally unprepared to assist the patient and members of the family in adjusting to a fatal illness, and expectations of occupational therapists have not been clearly defined (Gammage, McMahon and Shanahan 1976; Oelrich 1974). One innovative program at UCLA has a training program for nonclinicians (defined as people who lack traditional credentials and who have not completed professional training). These nonclinicians provide a link between the dying person, the family, and health professionals, as visitors, counselors, listeners, and volunteers. Their training includes didactic lectures and a practicum, with both individual and group clinical supervision, over an 18-month period. The trainees work in a variety of settings, some for pay and some as volunteers through church or friendship networks (Harris 1980).

What is striking in a review of literature about death education in health professional schools is the general absence of a multi- or interdisciplinary approach involving faculty or students. Nonetheless, most authors emphasize the complexity of death education, because it involves so many different perspectives: social, psychological, biological, religious, and ethical. If death education is to be realistic, a multidisciplinary framework is needed. Ideally, instruction would be interdisciplinary: course content would be integrated and team-taught, rather than presented by a parade of instructors through the course (often with no total commitment) as is typical in many multidisciplinary courses (Bruhn 1980).

A Multidisciplinary Framework for Death Education

Various goals have been expressed in recommendations that health-professions students be taught about death and dying and several curricular formats have been proposed. Most of these proposals, however, have been aimed at a single discipline. For example, Bloch (1975, 1976) has outlined goals for teaching medical students, and Dietrich (1980) has modified these goals for allied health science students. We propose here a content for death education for all health professionals that would integrate and encompass knowledge, attitudes, and experience.

The variety of strategies for learning that could be used in a death education course span the continuum from formal or didactic modalities to informal or experiential ones (table 4.1). What is important is that learning experiences about death and dying should include a blend of all these varieties. They can be either voluntary or required, depending on the goal or expected outcome of the learning experience, and learning about death and dying should not be limited to a specific year or period in the education of a health-professions student. Although the curriculum may not permit time for formal education, voluntary learning experiences can always be offered, and students encouraged to take advantage of them. If the faculty or mentors do not encourage the students to pursue a subject, students assume that it is unimportant.

One concern in a multidisciplinary approach to death education, which is sure to be raised by educators, is the different educational preparation of medical, nursing, and allied health students. This mix of different preprofessional preparation, however, actually offers an advantage. As a consequence of exposure to only peers, similar in age, experience, and professional goals, health-professions students reinforce existing attitudes rather than learn to appreciate new views, opinions, and options.

The structure and content in death education does not fit nicely into the usual lockstep curriculum of most health professional schools. Indeed, the reason for not including death education is that

Table 4.1 A Multidisciplinary Learning Strategy in Death Education For Health Professionals

DIDACTAC		*EXPERIENTIAL*
Knowledge	Attitude	Experience
• View videotapes or films demonstrating techniques of communication and counseling • Hear lectures by a variety of persons on aspects of death and dying • Take electives in death education with students from different disciplines • Read general and special literature, including novels dealing with death and dying • Participate in values clarification course	• Observe several health professionals talk with dying patients • Seek out a role m odel who has contact with terminal patients • Participate in informal, small-group discussions with peers • Participate in panel discussions of a specific aspect of the care of dying patients or analyze a case history • Talk with persons with different religious and cultural beliefs about death • Write your own epitaph and reflect on its meaning as to lifestyle and behavior in a group • Observe behavior of health professionals when a patient has died • Attend interschool, interdepartmental workshops • Enact role-playing and role reversals • Interview family members of a recently deceased person	• Talk with a dying person and their family • Work with a team of health professionals • Take trips to anatomy laboratory, autopsy room and mortuary • Simulate the experience of dying • Work in a nursing home or hospice • Talk with children and adults of different ages about death • Work in intensive care or coronary care unit • Observe preparation of patients for surgery • Attend a funeral • Observe group therapy with terminal patients

"there is no room for it" in an already overloaded curriculum. If death education is to be viewed as an important part of total patient care, it must be offered in a variety of ways, at various times, and to a spectrum of health professionals. Elective courses are a start, but they are not the answer. Electives ensure only that those students who are already interested in death and dying will have the option to learn more about it. If attitudes and behavior are to be modified, the knowledge base in all health-professions curricula needs to be greater. If health professionals learn together, the probability that they will work together might be increased, especially in those grey areas of health in which they share responsibility and their unique skills.

A format in which death education would fit readily is any curricular structure that focuses on normal growth and development or uses the life cycle as a structure to discuss human behavior. Death and dying should not be separated out as a special topic or elective, for then it is treated as an anomaly or a specialty when, in truth, it is normal, common, and universal. How and when death and dying are offered as learning experiences will establish an attitude for students before they hear a word of the content. It is not enough that we offer "something" regarding death and dying. "Mini-courses" and electives convey a message about how health professionals regard the subject of death and dying. A multidisciplinary approach to death education is the direction we must go toward in the future if the care of dying patients is to be part of health care.

Impending Death as a Process

The knowledge of impending death is the beginning of a new process in the lives of many people. The dying patient, the family, and the staff experience psychological and somatic reactions when they learn that a patient will die. The symptoms include somatic distress, feelings of guilt, hostile reactions, and the loss of previous patterns of conduct. Terminal illness takes a heavy toll from every person involved in the life of a dying patient. More specifically, individuals experience an "anticipatory grief reaction," which occurs when an announcement is made of an impending death. These reactions may range from loss of control to outward calm and resignation (Binger et al. 1969). In their study of the emotional impact of terminal leukemia on children and their parents, Binger et al. found that parents experienced symptoms and feelings of physical distress, depression, inability to function, anger, hostility, and self-blame during the first days or weeks after hearing about the terminal illness. Lindemann (1944), in his well-known study of bereavement among the survivors of the Coconut Grove fire in Boston, described the acute grief syndrome as including a feeling of tightness in the throat, shortness of breath, an empty feeling in the abdomen, lack of strength, exhaustion, loss of appetite, and a subjective expression of "tension" or "mental pain." The component of grief that is considered to be more psychological in nature includes feelings of an altered sensorium, guilt feelings, a sense of separateness from other people, a sense of unreality, and intense preoccupation with thoughts. Some persons begin to act in a formal manner in order to prevent offense to others as a result of their irritability and anger. These reactions occur in family members, as well as in other persons who have shared in a significant way in the life of a dying patient; health professionals are not excluded from this group.

It is interesting that although Americans have become more sensitive to the need of humanizing the poor, the mentally ill, and persons who have been denied their human rights in other countries, we still experience difficulty in perceiving the dying patient as a person (Woodward 1978). The announcement of impending death immediately creates new constructs in the minds of patients, families, and caretakers. New roles begin to develop. The terminally ill begin to feel that they will be shunned because of their new status (and, in fact, some are). They begin to fear not only death but also the separation from their families and the health staff that may occur first. More than death itself, dying patients seem to fear the loneliness and isolation that may come, and their initial reactions of denial, complaining, fault-finding, and anger may alienate some people who have little experience with dying persons.

Most dying patients are aware that dying from a terminal illness is commonly associated with pain, growing helplessness, altered consciousness, and other infirmities, independent of the manifestations of specific disease (Noyes 1967). This awareness manifests itself in varied ways, depending on patients' maturity, their religious or philosophical understanding of life and death, and the way others are relating to them. The patients will experience the feeling of helplessness, because death is the one event over which they have no control. So, as patients face their fate they may begin to become more dependent, as if saying, "I am helpless now; you [the doctors, the nurses and family] take over." This dependency may cause others to withdraw, for it reminds them of their own mortality. This dependency threatens even health professionals, for it challenges their feelings of control or power and (on a subconscious level) feelings of omnipotence. This threat creates difficulty in maintaining equanimity when health professionals care for and relate to terminal patients (Artiss and Levine 1973). Often, the family and staff expect more than the patient can provide; their ultimate wish is that the patient not die and, thus, the patient is expected to be strong and courageous.

Care of the Patient

Because impending death is a taboo topic in our culture, terminally ill patients become nonpersons. Consequently, they are not only stripped of their personhood, but also subjected to the assumption that their sense of reason or intellect has gone. They are stripped of their integrity and any decision-making role and are discouraged from feeling and expressing needs, wants, fears, and concerns. In essence, impending death becomes translated somehow into "dead" or "no longer alive." But dying patients are not yet dead. They realize their condition before the professionals tell them. In fact, many become tutors to the nurses and doctors who care for them.

Nevertheless, dying patients do have such specific fears as

bodily deterioration and loss of family and friends. They fear separation and the cessation of being (Shah and Reese 1978). So, how can we assist patients who are to die to do so with dignity and humanity?

Physical care is obviously important, particularly easing physical pain and suffering. It is important to ease the mental distress of dying patients when their illness is linked to physical pain (Sacerdote 1968). Sacerdote advocated the use of hypnosis, which serves as a useful form of therapy in the relief of pain and other physical symptoms, and also as an important tool for communication between dying patients and their environment. He further stated that such a therapist, aware that he is giving the patient intense emotional support as well as minimizing the discomfort of pain, will himself have less anxiety. Hypnosis, which assists in the technical part of medicine, is joined by the psychological aspect of medicine—the art of medicine. Health professionals who are qualified to use hypnosis can provide a needed human source of faith, hope, assistance, and mental well-being. Hypnosis, according to Erickson (1959), can become a psychological modality in the treatment of painful terminal illness.

Hypnosis is not the only recommended approach nor does it replace other medical procedures. Rather, it is one adjunct to treatment that can be used to meet the patient's overall needs. In helping the patient, the question is no longer the treatment of the illness itself, since the patient is dying. Hypnosis does not deprive the patient of the privilege of knowing that he is alive, as do some sedatives, analgesics, and narcotics. Hypnosis also allows patients and relatives to continue optimal contact with each other. This mode of intervention may sometimes be used alone as a means of pain control, so it possesses a special value at both psychological and physiological levels (Erickson 1959).

Stop *treating* the illness and start *caring* for the patient is perhaps the most important concept to adhere to when providing treatment to the terminally ill. Patients go through a series of behavioral, cognitive, and affective experiences upon learning that they are going to die. Their reactions can include renunciation, affirmation, alteration of reality, and depression, rage, paranoia, and euphoria (Artiss and Levine 1973). As death approaches, however, they may psychologically come to accept the reality of dying (Kübler-Ross 1969).

Before the acceptance stage is achieved, how can health personnel care for dying patients and assist them? Whatever the age of the dying person, several authors agree that honesty and truthfulness are important among caregivers (Vernick and Karon 1965; Popoff 1975; Friedman 1970; Binger et al. 1969). As stated previously, patients are usually aware of their impending death (Noyes and Travis 1973). Once the reality is shared, all persons involved, including the patient, can give up some of their defensiveness and relate to one another in a sincere and helpful way.

Attitude Toward the Dying Patient

Patients who are dying are most reasonably served by a *caring* attitude rather than a *curing* attitude (Wagner and Goldstein 1977). In order to be able to adopt a caring attitude, health professionals must accept the idea that death does not represent defeat, but rather a progression and an opportunity for growth and increased awareness, for the patient and for others. Dying patients want others to continue to relate to them as people. Health professionals and family members must be able to reach out to the patient with simple acts, such as establishing good eye contact and showing a sincere interest in them (Greishaw 1980). As a dying nurse taught her students in the management of the terminally ill, one must not forget that the patient remains to the end worthy of life and worthy of our greatest care (Sommer 1975).

Patients may begin to be treated as "socially dead" long before they are "biologically dead," so it is important to assure them that they will not be neglected and isolated and that all will be done to provide them comfort. The health personnel can reassure the patients that relief from pain will be provided and that they will not be abandoned (Pett 1979). They must also let the patients know that their concerns are shared and understood and that personnel are willing to talk about them, although the patients need not be pressured into active, open discussion. They will begin to communicate when they are ready.

Each person reacts to impending death in a way that is consistent with individual personality and past experiences, the current crisis, and the particular meaning or special circumstances associated with the impending loss. Therefore, in order to be helpful, health professionals must try to get to know each patient and to ascertain as clearly as possible the individual's philosophical, religious, or personal view of life and death. The health staff should also learn about the patient's current burdens and concerns and personal sources of emotional support (Vande Creek 1980).

Patients must feel they are safe and in an environment they can trust—one that will allow them to ask any question and to feel confident that they will receive an honest answer. Once patients begin to communicate openly and verbalize feelings, fears, concerns, and wishes, they must be provided the time they need to continue to communicate freely. Inability to discuss their areas of concern can exacerbate their feelings of loneliness, depression, and helplessness.

Helping patients to mourn their impending death involves allowing them to experience the pain of realizing what they must leave behind. This psychic pain is inevitable, and should not be alleviated by injections or pills, but by a deep and open relationship, sustained in the present, that will divert attention away from excessive nostalgic dwelling upon the past (Pett 1979).

Patients' acceptance of death is sometimes easily recognized by certain dramatic changes in their pattern of communication. In fact, there is virtually nothing left to talk about, so conversation becomes meaningless (Artiss and Levine 1973). It is this silence that communicates to those who will continue to live that the patient is ready to die. This silence also says that our presence is the most comforting aspect for the patient. This silence serves as the transition from existence to death.

Care of the Family

It is also important to learn about the family: Who are the individuals who are most important to the patient? The personal experiences of one of the authors in working on a burn unit has made him aware of the complexity of the system called "family or loved ones." The "family member" is not always a blood relative, and may even be someone not considered a member of the traditional family. The persons whom dying patients consider important and from whom they will require the most support may be the health personnel caring for them. Once the family is defined, its members will require help in coping with their impending loss.

Family members, like patients, appreciate frankness and honesty (Binger et al. 1969). In this study, several families stated that the major source of help to them was direct, clear, and truthful information about the impending death of a loved one. Family members who had received information piecemeal described the anxieties provoked by unanswered questions.

To be truthful and honest with a family about a dying patient is difficult and uncomfortable for most people. The health professional must realize, however, that when the people who are important to the patient request information about their loved one, they usually are not asking for technical medical data. They would like an attentive ear. They need someone to listen as they express guilt and their own anger, confusion, and fears of death. The loved ones want to begin their mourning even if the death has not yet occurred. This anticipatory mourning should not be discouraged, as it may lessen the shock when death occurs. The initial mourning or first responses from the family usually include confusion, denial, or disbelief. The family members lose a sense of direction or purpose and may not know what to say or where to turn. This is an important time, as the family must be supported and guided.

Because of the busy schedules of all health professionals, a joint meeting before telling the family is of benefit so that specific members of the health team can spend sufficient time with the family. At this point, the family is very sensitive and vulnerable and would be distressed further if health personnel spent only brief moments with them during this crucial period. Each individual family member needs to have adequate time with the health personnel, because people tend to react differently, depending on their own personalities and their individual strengths and weaknesses. Chaplains may be especially helpful during this period.

It is preferable that the professional who informs the family of the impending death of a loved one be someone who has a positive, trusting relationship with the family members—someone who will be able to accept the family's unpleasant reactions. Expressions of hostility and anger against God, religion, or the medical staff are not uncommon and the informant is obviously in a position to receive much of the displaced anger. The family members should not be restrained from crying or emotional expressions; it is necessary to let them see that such reactions are acceptable. Pett (1979) stated that if their manifestations of distress should become embarrassing or disturbing to the rest of family, it is better that they be guided to some more remote place to work through their grief.

If a mental health professional is not part of the health care team working with the family and patient in which the grief reaction is intense, one should be summoned. The proper psychological management of grief reactions may prevent prolonged and serious alterations in the person's social adjustment (Lindemann 1944; Wagner and Goldstein 1977). Lindemann has suggested that over-reaction as well as under-reaction of the bereaved must be given attention, because delayed responses may occur at unpredictable times. The family members who experience severe reactions must be assisted professionally in accepting the pain of the bereavement. They need to review their relationship with the deceased or dying patient, and need to become acquainted with the alterations in their own modes of emotional reaction. Fears of insanity, fears of accepting the surprising changes in feelings, especially hostility, may need to be worked through professionally.

Sedatives, tranquilizers, or antidepressant medications should generally not be given even though family members often request them. The undue chemical tranquility can impede the necessary course of grief (White and Gathman 1972).

In order to help the grieving person, health professionals must be familiar with and understand the process of grief. The grief process should be allowed to occur and should not be impeded so that the natural course of the grief syndrome is altered. Although it is important to learn the proposed specific states of grieving (Kübler-Ross' five psychological stages of dying: denial and isolation, anger, bargaining, depression, and acceptance), an individual may manifest these stages out of sequence or may not experience all of them. It is important to respect the uniqueness of individuals and to provide a supportive, nonthreatening environment for those working through their grief reactions.

Binger et al. (1969) proposed helping grieving families by means of a team approach, which includes physicians and mental health personnel. (In the burn unit previously mentioned the health care team includes a nurse or any health professional who has established a special relationship with the family or patient.) Meetings need to be open-ended and the team needs to be prepared to respond to the technical and medical questions, as well as to the psychological discomforts of the family. The team conferences are useful in allowing the team to know the family better and giving the family an opportunity to know the entire health team. Expressions of feelings are encouraged, and the conference is not used to give advice or to provide direction. The primary purpose of team conferences with families is for the staff to become sensitive to the family needs. This also allows families to learn that the health professionals are not only concerned about the medical aspects of the illness, but are engaged with them as human beings who are facing a crisis. Families are reassured that efforts to help them will be steady and continuous.

Care of Health Professionals

The director of the aforementioned burn unit asked one of the authors to assist her in working with a new resident who had experienced the death of a patient. Her sensitivity and caring for both the patient and the resident made the loss less traumatic for the caregivers. Not only were family members mourning the loss of the patient, but the physicians, nurses, and other health personnel were experiencing similar feelings of loss and helplessness. Death had once again become a reality.

Health professionals are not proof against establishing significant relationships with their patients nor are they immune to the emotional reactions that everyone experiences as a result of death. Death reminds the health staff of their own mortality and of the feelings of loneliness and isolation resulting from the experience of death (Sonstegard et al. 1976).

Patients who know they are going to die seem to have an advantage that health personnel do not. Patients usually have the time to ponder, to deny, to grieve. The staff, however, are busy going on to the next patient, never able to stop long enough to look at or experience their feelings or to think or talk about them. Everyone is busy taking care of the patient, a formidable and respectable task indeed, but in the focus on the patient, other people significant in the patient's life are often forgotten or ignored—the family and staff. Curiously, it is often the patient, who already has a significant job ahead in coping with impending death, who has to take time to assist others in their own grieving.

Many professionals are becoming concerned about the inadequacy of means to help staff cope with death and dying. Several have advocated that staff members be allowed to work through the deaths immediately. Health personnel need an opportunity to express fears and emotions if they are to avoid suppressing them (Cundey 1981). Support from other colleagues is essential when a staff member has lost a patient through death (Summers 1979). The staff members must be allowed the time to talk, listen, and share experiences with one another during times of loss, just as they need to be permitted to take the time to share feelings with their dying patients. Health professionals are rewarded for their technical competence, but they must also be rewarded for their ability to share their feelings and to address their own and their patient's psychological needs. There is pain in doing this, but as Terrill (1978) stated,

"Only when nurses (and other health professionals) willingly risk the discomfort will they learn to be comfortable with dying."

Summers (1979) suggested that health professionals have a place away from the immediate work area where they can sit together and express personal feelings in confidence. It has also been suggested that someone in authority, who is able to listen or to arrange for necessary help, needs to be available during difficult moments, such as the time of the death of a patient.

At our university hospital, two psychologists are available to members of the burn team when their tasks of caring for severely ill patients become overwhelming. Individual members may seek out the assistance of the psychologists, and on occasion informal get-togethers have addressed such issues as patient deaths or near deaths. Tears and feelings are allowed at these informal meetings, and the burdens of the health personnel are minimized as they are encouraged to work through the grief. The danger of not allowing health personnel to grieve properly is that inappropriate defensive strategies may be developed to alleviate the uneasiness associated with terminal care. These strategies may involve minimizing the time that health professionals spend with the patient, maintaining social distance from the patient, and controlling the content of conversation with the patient (Stoller 1980). Stoller listed two types of death-related conversations that are especially difficult to handle. The first involves dying patients in the context of suspicion-awareness, in which they do not know but suspect that the hospital staff believe them to be dying. The second involves patients in a context of open-awareness in which they wish to discuss aspects of their impending death.

Many students in health fields, particularly medical students, experience the phenomenon of death in their training in an impersonal manner as they are exposed to a cadaver in anatomy or pathology laboratory. This meager and relatively inappropriate introduction to death and dying is not adequate to prepare the beginning student to deal with the highly charged event of death. What seems to occur is that the attitude actually acquired or reinforced in many students is one that serves defensively to maintain an emotional distance between them and dying patients (Olin 1972).

There are ways to assist health professionals in their work with dying patients and to prepare them to deal with the emotional impacts of death and dying. Several authors speak of the importance of fostering staff sensitivity not only to dying patients and their families but to their own emotions (Burkhalter 1975; Marie 1978; Durlak and Burchard 1977).

Several programs have been described, which have such goals as sensitizing participants to important psychosocial aspects of terminal illness, grief, and bereavement and providing them with an opportunity to examine and share personal feelings regarding death. Multidisciplinary teaching teams are used, which include nurse, physician, psychologist, and chaplain. The combination of lecture-discussion and experiential techniques has been used with successful results (Durlak and Burchard 1977).

At the Holy Cross Hospital of Silver Spring, Maryland, a thanatology coordinator has been employed, whose role is to develop and implement special educational programs. This person assists nursing, technical, dietary, housekeeping, and other personnel in learning to respond to the needs of the terminally ill patients and their families. A 13-week, two-hour-per-week course that covers the topics of death and dying as well as bereavement is offered to the staff of the hospital. Guest speakers from various fields are used: physicians, consumer advocates, social service specialists, clergymen, and funeral directors. The course emphasizes learning to listen and respond to the spoken and often unspoken needs of dying patients and their families, building a trusting relationship, and helping dying patients to tie up loose ends during their last days (Marie 1978).

Others such as Olin (1972) have suggested that direct experience with dying patients is essential in helping health professionals deal with the psychological aspects of death and dying. He also advocated that students work with a family who has lost a loved one to learn firsthand about the mourning process. It is also important that the students be allowed time to discuss with faculty their experiences and feelings while caring for dying patients and the families.

The health personnel are no exception. These individuals also require care, support, and a trusting and open environment as do dying patients and their families. If we assist the health care team to cope adequately with the emotional impacts of death, and to accept ultimately its inevitability, we provide dying patients and their loved ones, in turn, greater understanding and acceptance as they face the patient's progression into death.

References

Artiss, K. L. and A. S. Levine. 1973. "Doctor-Patient Relation in Severe Illness: A Seminar for Oncology Fellows." *New England Journal of Medicine* 288:1210–1214.

Ayalon, O. 1979. "Is Death a Proper Subject for the Classroom?: Comments on Death Education." *International Journal of Social Psychiatry* 25:252–257.

Barton, D. 1972. "The Need for Including Instruction on Death and Dying in Medical Curriculum." *Journal of Medical Education* 47:169–175.

Barton, D., J. M. Flexner, J. Van Eys and C. E. Scott. 1972. "Death and Dying: A Course for Medical Students." *Journal of Medical Education* 47:945–951.

Barton, D., ed. 1977. *Dying and Death: A Clinical Guide for Caregivers*. Baltimore: Williams and Wilkins.

Binger, C. M., A. R. Ablin, R. C. Feuerstein, J. H. Kushner, S. Zoger and C. Mikkelsen. 1969. "Childhood Leukemia: Emotional Impact on Patient and Family." *New England Journal of Medicine* 280:414–418.

Bleeker, J. A. C. and H. B. Pomerantz. 1979. "The Influence of a Lecture Course in Loss and Grief on Medical Students: An Empirical Study of Attitude Formation." *Medical Education* 13:117–128.

Bloch, S. 1975. "A Clinical Course on Death and Dying for Medical Students." *Journal of Medical Education* 50:630–632.

Bloch, S. 1976. "Instruction on Death and Dying for the Medical Student." *Journal of Medical Education* 10:269–273.

Blumenfield, M., N. B. Levy and D. Kaufman. 1975. "Current Attitudes of Medical Students and House Staff Toward Terminal Illness." *General Hospital Psychiatry* 1:306–310.

Bruhn, J. G. 1980. "Death and Dying in the Life Cycle: An Educational Model for Health Professionals" In B. Schoenberg et al., eds. *Education of the Medical Student in Thanatology*. New York: Arno Press.

Bruhn, J. G. and G. S. Parcel. 1981. Current Knowledge About the Health Behavior of Young Children: A Conference Summary. University of Texas Medical Branch at Galveston, December 1, 1981.

Bruhn, J. G. and G. S. Parcel. 1982. "Preschool Health Education Program (PHEP): An Analysis of Baseline Data" *Health Education Quarterly* (in press).

Bruhn, J. G., H. Bunce and M. T. Scurry. 1982. "Texas Physicians' Attitudes

Toward Death and Dying." *Texas Medicine* 78:62–66.

Burkhalter, P. K. 1975. "Fostering Staff Sensitivity to the Dying Patient." *Supervisor Nurse* 6:54–59.

Cappiello, L. A. and R. E. Troyer. 1979. "A Study of the Role of Health Educators in Teaching About Death and Dying." *Journal of School Health* 49:397–399.

Crase, D. 1980. "The Health Educator as Death Educator: Professional Preparation and Quality Control." *Journal of School Health* 50:568–571.

Cundey, B. 1981. "A Time of Stress." *Nursing Mirror* 152:23–24.

Dickinson, G. E. 1976. "Death Education in U.S. Medical Schools." *Journal of Medical Education* 51:134–136.

Dickinson, G. E. and A. A. Pearson. 1977. "Death Education in Selected Medical Schools as Related to Physicians' Attitudes and Reactions Toward Dying Patients." *Annual Conference on Research in Medical Education* 16:31–36.

Dickinson, G. E. and A. A. Pearson. 1979a. "Sex Differences of Physicians in Relating to Dying Patients." *Journal of the American Medical Women's Association* 34:45–47.

Dickinson, G. E. and A. A. Pearson. 1979b. "Differences in Attitudes Toward Terminal Patients Among Selected Medical Specialties of Physicians." *Medical Care* 17:682–685.

Dietrich, M. C. 1980. "A Proposed Curriculum on Death and Dying for the Allied Health Student." *Journal of Allied Health* 9:25–32.

Durlak, J. A. and Burchard, J. A. 1977. "Preliminary Evaluation of a Hospital-Based Continuing Education Workshop on Death and Dying." *Journal of Medical Education* 52:423–424.

Eddy, J., R. St. Pierre, W. Alles and R. Shute. 1980. "Conceptual Areas of Death Education." *Health Education* 11:14–15.

Erickson, M. 1959. "Hypnosis in Painful Terminal Illness." *American Journal of Clinical Hypnosis* 1:117–121.

Friedman, H. J. 1970. "Physician Management of Dying Patients: An Exploration." *Psychiatry in Medicine* 1:295–305.

Gammage, S. L., P. S. McMahon and P. M. Shanahan. 1976. "The Occupational Therapist and Terminal Illness: Learning to Cope with Death." *American Journal of Occupational Therapy* 30:294–299.

Geelhoed, G. W. and L. T. Bowles. 1977. "Fear of Dying." *Journal of the American Health Care Association* 3:45–49.

Gertler, R. and E. Ferneau. 1975. "The First-Year Resident in Psychiatry: How He Sees the Psychiatric Patient's Attitudes Toward Death and Dying." *International Journal of Social Psychiatry* 21:4–6.

Glicken, M. D. 1978. "The Child's View of Death." *Journal of Marriage and Family Counseling* 40:75–81.

Greishaw, S. 1980. "My, These Are Beautiful Flowers." *American Journal of Nursing* 80:1782–1783.

Harris, A. P. 1980. "Content and Method in a Thanatology Program for Paraprofessionals." *Death Education* 4:21–27.

Harris, W. H. 1978. "Some Reflections Concerning Approaches to Death Education." *Journal of School Health* 48:162–165.

Hart, E. J. 1976. "Death Education and Mental Health." *Journal of School Health* 46:407 –412.

Herman, T. A. 1980. "Terminally Ill Patients: Assessment of Physician Attitudes Within Teaching Institutions." *New York State Journal of Medicine* 80:200–207.

Hopping, B. L. 1977. "Nursing Students' Attitudes Toward Death." *Nursing Research* 26:443–447.

Koocher, G. P. 1973. "Childhood, Death and Cognitive Development." *Developmental Psychology* 9:369–375.

Kübler-Ross, E. 1969. *On Death and Dying*. New York: Macmillan Publishing Co., Inc.

Laube, J. 1977. "Death and Dying Workshop for Nurses: Its Effect On Their Death Anxiety Level." *International Journal of Nursing Studies* 14:111–120.

Lindemann, E. 1944. "Symptomatology and Management of Acute Grief." *American Journal of Psychiatry* 101:141–148.

Liston, E. H. 1973. "Education on Death and Dying: A Survey of American Medical Schools." *Journal of Medical Education* 48:577–578.

Liston, E. H. 1975. "Education on Death and Dying: A Neglected Area in the Medical Curriculum." *Omega* 6:193–198.

Livingston, P. B. and C. N. Zimet. 1965. "Death Anxiety, Authoritarianism and Choice of Specialty in Medical Students." *Journal of Nervous and Mental Disease* 140:222–230.

Marie, H. 1978. "Reorienting Staff Attitudes Toward the Dying." *Hospital Progress* 59:74–76, 92.

Marks, S. C. and S. L. Bertman. 1980. "Experiences with Learning About Death and Dying in the Undergraduate Anatomy Curriculum." *Journal of Medical Education* 55:48–52.

Martin, L. B. and P. A. Collier. 1975. "Attitudes Toward Death: A Survey of Nursing Students." *Journal of Nursing Education* 14:28–35.

Miles, M. S. 1980. "The Effects of a Course on Death and Grief on Nurses' Attitudes Toward Dying Patients and Death." *Death Education* 4:245–260.

Mills, G. C. 1977. "Nurses Discuss Dying—A Simulation Experience." *Journal of Continuing Education in Nursing* 8:35–40.

Murray, P. 1974. "Death Education and Its Effect on the Death Anxiety Level of Nurses." *Psychological Reports* 35:1250.

Noyes, R. 1967. "The Dying Patient." *Diseases of the Nervous System* 28:790–797.

Noyes, R. and T. A. Travis. 1973. "The Care of Terminally Ill Patients." *Archives of Internal Medicine* 132:607–611.

O'Brien, C. R., J. L. Johnson and P. D. Schmink. 1978. "Death Education: What Students Want and Need!" *Adolescence* 13:729–734.

Oelrich, M. 1974. "The Patient With a Fatal Illness." *American Journal of Occupational Therapy* 28:429–432.

Olin, H. S. 1972. "A Proposed Model to Teach Medical Students The Care of the Dying Patient." *Journal of Medical Education* 47:564–567.

Perez, E. L., J. Y. Gosselin and A. Gagnon. 1980. "Education of Death and Dying: A Survey of Canadian Medical Schools." *Journal of Medical Education* 55:788–789.

Pett, D. 1979. "Care of the Terminal Patient: Grief in Hospital." *Nursing Times* 75:709–712.

Popoff, D. 1975. "What Are Your Feelings About Death and Dying?" (Part 1) *Nursing 75* 5 :15–24.

Rich, T. and G. M. Kalmanson. 1966. "Attitudes of Medical Residents Toward the Dying Patient in a General Hospital." *Postgraduate Medicine* 40:A127–130.

Rosner, A. C. 1974. "How We Do It: An Interdisciplinary Approach to Death Education." *Journal of School Health* 44:455–458.

Russell, R. D. 1977. "Educating About Death." *Health Education* 8:8–10.

Sacerdote, P. 1968. "Involvement and Communication With The Terminally Ill Patient." *American Journal of Clinical Hypnosis* 10:244–248.

Schachter, S. C. 1979. "Death and Dying Education in a Medical School Curriculum." *Journal of Medical Education* 54:661–663.

Scurry, M. T., J. G. Bruhn and H. Bunce, III. 1979. "The House Officer and the Dying Patient: Attitudes, Experiences and Needs." *General Hospital Psychiatry* 1:301–305.

Shah, D. K. and M. Reese. 1978. "Living With Dying: A Good Death." *Newsweek* May 1, pp. 54–55.

Smith, M. D., M. McSweeney and B. M. Katz. 1980. "Characteristics of Death Education Curricula in American Medical Schools." *Journal of Medical Education* 55:844–850.

Sommer, C. 1975. "Four Distinctive Views of the Dying Patient: Managing Terminal Care of Herself." *RN* 38:37–38.

Sonstegard, L., N. Hansen, L. Zillman and M. K. Johnston. 1976. "The Grieving Nurse." *American Journal of Nursing* 76:1490–1492.

Stoller, E. 1980. "Effect of Experience on Nurses' Responses to Dying and Death in the Hospital Setting." *Nursing Research* 29:35–38.

Summers, D. H. 1979. "Care of the Terminal Patient (Part 8): Staff Support." *Nursing Times* 75:790.

Terrill, L. A. 1978. "The Clinical Specialist in Oncology and the Dying Patient." *Journal of Neurosurgical Nursing* 10:176–179.

Ulin, R. O. 1977. *Death and Dying Education.* Washington, D.C.: National Education Association.

Vande Creek, L. 1980. "How to Tell the Family That the Patient Has Died." *Postgraduate Medicine* 68:207–209.

Vargo, M. E. and W. M. Batsel. 1981. "Relationship Between Death Anxiety and Components of the Self-Actualization Process." *Psychological Reports* 48:89–90.

Vernick, J. and M. Karon. 1965. "Who's Afraid of Death on a Leukemia Ward?"

American Journal of Diseases of Children 109:393–397.

Wagner, J. and E. Goldstein. 1977. "Pharmacist's Role in Loss and Grief." *American Journal of Hospital Pharmacy* 34:490–492.

White, R. B. and L. T. Gathman. 1972. "The Syndrome of Ordinary Grief." (Unpublished paper) Department of Psychiatry and Behavioral Sciences, The University of Texas Medical Branch at Galveston.

Woodward, K. L. 1978. "Living with Dying." *Newsweek* May 1, pp. 52–61.

Yarber, W. L., P. Gobel and D. A. Rublee. 1981. "Effects of Death Education on Nursing Students' Anxiety and Locus of Control." *Journal of School Health* 51:367–372.

Zeligs, R. 1974. *Children's Experience with Death.* Springfield, Ill.: Charles C. Thomas.

Preamble: Dying patients should neither be abandoned nor exploited. They are entitled to the same respectful care as those patients who are expected to fully recover. They should be given, where this is appropriate, information about their illness and treatment, and know that they have the right to refuse treatment. Confidentiality should always be respected. Care should be responsive and considerate and should always be given by qualified personnel.

Principle 5: Dying Patients Have Human Rights That Should Be Respected

5

The Rights of the Dying Person

BERNARD E. ROLLIN

Just as human language, in all of its infinitely variegated manifestations, must rest upon a syntactic skeleton, so too human action, in all of its bewildering complexities, individual and social, must rest upon a moral skeleton—a set of notions of right and wrong, good and bad, just and unjust. That the moral basis of action is rarely recognized, even more rarely articulated, and almost never critically examined bespeaks the human tendency to ignore fundamental presuppositions in favor of pressing pragmatic concerns. But the inevitable price of ignoring our moral axioms is failure to recognize the incoherences and inconsistencies with which they are invariably riddled, and thus to generate individual action and social policy that are rationally indefensible.

In the hodgepodge of societies conveniently lumped together as "Western democracies," perhaps the fundamental moral keystone is the notion of the individual human being as the primary locus of moral value and concern. So basic is this notion to our moral foundations that societies that do not embrace it are viewed with a mixture of fear, incredulity, and loathing—witness, for example, virtually any college student's response to a first encounter with Plato's *Republic*. Totalitarian societies, which view the society as the fundamental object of value and individuals as dispensable components thereof, are literally the stuff of nightmares to atomistic, individualistic, and democratic man. Human society is viewed as a mixture rather than a compound—a bag of marbles rather than an organism. Human freedom is seen as absence of constraint rather than obedience to a rational order or greater good. The sort of sentiment epitomized in the SS dictum "my freedom is my obedience," which in fact expresses a clear and deep axiom of nonindividualistic societies, is seen as incomprehensible and vicious doubletalk. Freedom is seen as being allowed to go to hell in your own way, not having your journey interrupted "for your own good."

Given the viewpoint that sees only the individual human being as an ultimate or intrinsic object of value who ought to be viewed and treated "always as an end, never merely as a means," in Kant's phrasing, even the very fact of social life becomes morally problematic. Man is seen as restricted in society, "chained" according to Rousseau, not actualized as the Greeks thought. Yet man must live with other men, so some society is inevitable in order to mediate, protect, adjudicate, and make decisions on matters pertaining to the welfare of all. But even here, the object of the exercise is not to submerge the individual any more than is absolutely necessary, and not to reify "society" into an entity with a life of its own. Group decisions are made by counting benefits to individuals; only such a decision procedure can possibly be fair. The common good is seen simply as the sum of the individual goods, or the individual preferences.

As fair as this procedure seems, the moral problem it creates is glaring. What of those individuals whose interests, concerns, and desires do not converge with those of the majority? Are they simply to be submerged under the duly reckoned weight of the common good? If so, what has happened to the individuality of the individual as the ultimate locus of value and concern? And if such submersion is morally unacceptable, how can it be prevented while still allowing for some such notion as the common benefit?

This is, of course, a problem that has never been wholly solved. But the steps towards its solution, which are exemplified in the American political system, reveal much about our moral presuppositions. In this tradition, the individual is unequivocally the basic locus of moral concern. It is recognized that decisions about the common good can suppress the good of the individual whose interest and beliefs are not in accord with the general welfare. The notion of basic rights provides a partial solution of this dilemma. Rights are protections for certain essential aspects and concerns of individual human beings in those cases where there is a conflict with the common good, general benefit, or general consensus, and where it would be expedient to disregard the individual. Rights serve as protective fences around those aspects of human nature that are considered to be essential to functioning as a person. We consider all human beings to be worthy of equal consideration and equal legal protection because we consider all human beings to be objects of intrinsic value. We protect the right to free speech, free assembly, free worship, and so on because we consider reason, speech, sociality, and belief to be essential features or interests constitutive of human nature. And this is no mere rhetoric—these rights are legally guaranteed and their protection often extracts great social cost in money, time, effort, convenience, and general welfare (Dworkin 1977).

Let us consider two examples. When the American Nazis wished to rally in Skokie, Illinois, considerations of general welfare and majority inclination alone would have unequivocally prohibited them from speaking: no one wished to hear them; the ideas they espoused aroused painful emotions and memories in members of the community; the danger of violence was great; the costs in police protection, business and traffic disruption, and ill-feeling were significant. Nonetheless, they were allowed to speak, since free expression is seen as a fundamental right to be protected at virtually all costs. A second example comes from medical and scientific research on human beings. The laws that protect human subjects are long and detailed. And even if it might be of immense social benefit for physicians to test therapeutic agents on a relatively small group of prisoners or derelicts or other powerless and socially disvalued minorities, still and all we feel that their intrinsic value as human beings and their correlative right to be protected from involuntary invasive use outweighs even the great potential benefit their coerced use might bring. In sum, our moral and legal systems rest upon a presupposition that the human individual possesses intrinsic value, which in turn suggests rights that should be legally codified and protected even when there is a utilitarian cost to society as a whole in doing so.

The above discussion serves as a necessary precondition for dealing with the set of moral problems surrounding the dying person. Insofar as a dying person is obviously a person, this moral schema provides the conceptual framework for adjudication of such issues. By the same token, it is extremely important to stress that the position outlined above is an ideal, shorn of the myriad sociocultural and economic vectors that constrain and blunt its application. It is well-known that the framers of this ethic in our political history owned slaves and, despite the commitment in this ethic to the intrinsic value and dignity of all citizens, the institution of slavery endured for almost 100 years after our independence. Human beings are far from totally rational, and rational ideals are blunted when confronted with the pressures of expediency, economics, superstition, tradition, and prejudice. Thus we should not be surprised to find our laws, social policies, and popular sentiments to be fraught with inconsistencies and incoherences. Just because a society has a coherent underlying ethic does not mean that the implications of that ethic have been thought out or followed through for a wide range of cases. For example, the ethic outlined above would seem to entail that decisions concerning sexual morality and behavior be left to the discretion of the individual so long as that behavior is not directly harmful to others. Yet, in point of fact, it is only relatively recently that such an ethic has even become socially respectable, and our laws in many places still forbid "unnatural intercourse." Our laws and policies on sexual behavior are heavily influenced by tradition, religion, time-honored taboos, and ignorance.

As in many other respects noted earlier in the discussion of death education, similar problems arise in discussing the basic areas of sex and death. The logical unpacking of our fundamental ethic as it applies to death and dying and its rational implementation have been stymied by a whole host of considerations that must be called nonrational. One powerful force among these are avoidance reactions to anything having to do with death. People would rather not think about such "depressing" subjects. Other forces militating against open moral progress in this area are the powerful religious traditions that have very specific injunctions on death and dying, and that exert strong political influence, as they do in sexual matters as well. One very obvious example illustrating this notion is the widespread "truism" that individuals do not own their own lives, that only God has the right to decide when a life may be terminated. As a result of these sorts of pressures, these sorts of hard ethical problems have been pretty much avoided throughout our history. Thus, for example, in the few cases of individuals who have been prosecuted for "mercy-killing," the deep ethical issues have often been sidestepped by courts declaring the person "not guilty on the grounds of temporary insanity" (Backer, Hannon and Russell 1982). In this way, the courts have not had to deal with the hard ethical questions of the right to death.

As a result we find ourselves in a strange position. The technological advances that have direct and immediate impact on death, dying, and the prolongation of life have increased exponentially, yet our moral thought in this area not only has failed to keep pace with this advance, but also has not even been clear about fundamental questions that are independent of technology (Veatch 1976). One such question concerns the right to decide when to terminate one's own life. Historically, suicide has been frowned upon by society, and has even been viewed as a criminal act. In Britain, suicide was a felony until 1961 (Stengel 1965:63). Aside from the obvious pragmatic silliness involved in criminalizing suicide, it is also clear that such legislation, like the legislation mentioned earlier directed at prohibiting certain "unnatural" sexual activity, reflects the strong influence of religious tradition, a tradition that is inimical to the exercise of certain rights in taboo areas like sex and death, and which exercises a powerful force in limiting them. While an enlightened judiciary serves as an effective counterforce to such special-interest moral traditions and serves to some extent to define social morality (as in the civil rights cases of the last decades), its attitudes inevitably reflect both directly and indirectly the social awareness of and attitudes toward the issues in question. Thus, no court could order something, however enlightened, that was totally unacceptable to everyone in society. And in decisions such as those dealing with obscenity, which involve tests like "standards of the community," the influence of the level of moral awareness in society is again invoked. Thus, since even fundamental legal/moral rights must always be filtered through someone's interpretation at some point in history, the cash value of these rights, especially in difficult cases, will always reflect the level reached by "the social mind," not necessarily the majority, but at least those who articulate such issues for the society.

Thus, it is of primary importance that the social dialogue on such difficult issues as death and the rights of the dying be guided by reason rather than by custom, emotion, taboo and superstition. Happily, in recent history, the mass media have exposed a major portion of the population to relevant issues and to the dialectic required for their resolution. But more must be done to lay bare and to publicize the intricate moral issues that demand solution. And thus any discussion of such an issue as the rights of the dying patient must bring us back to the rational ideal that follows from our most basic moral principles. It is only by articulation of such an ideal that society knows in which direction to aim. And without clear enunciation of such ideals, as Plato pointed out, society becomes the greatest sophist or false teacher, and such indefensible moral principles mentioned earlier as "only God has the right to make a life and death decision" or "whatever physicians say goes" move in to fill the moral vacuum and serve as a basis for social decisions. For, as we saw early in our discussion, moral commitments are inescapable.

What, then, does our ideal social morality tell us about the rights of dying persons? In the first place, as mentioned earlier, it must never be forgotten that the dying person is still a person—still a full object of moral concern. We are, after all, all of us mortal—

what we call a dying person is an ordinary person who as become all too tragically conscious of that fact. And the fundamental right of any individual who is an object of moral concern is the right to be treated as an object on a par with all other such objects by anyone who is a moral agent (Rollin 1981). This right, a precondition for all other rights, may appear to be too obvious to mention. Yet all too often dying persons are not granted this right, and the fact that they are moral objects is eclipsed by the fact that they are dying.

In another paper, I have discussed this problem as it specifically pertains to the dying aged (Rollin 1983). Much of the argument presented there is relevant to our current discussion. Given the reductionistic, scientistic, mechanistic, and atomistic path that medicine has taken in the twentieth century, it is not surprising that physicians have tended to think of their task in terms of repairing bodies and keeping them alive, and to forget that a person is more than a body. The greatest progress in contemporary medicine has grown out of hard science—biochemistry and molecular biology—and thus there is a seductive tendency to see medicine as essentially a hard science. Social, cultural, idiosyncratic, and moral dimensions of a person—features essential to being a person—come to be seen as irrelevant to the task of medicine, or as mystical or metaphysical, and therefore outside of the physician's purview. Thus physicians too often treat illnesses as bodily malfunctions and see no need to be more than polite and competent applied scientists. A great deal has, of course, been written about the tendency of physicians to forget that patients are persons and to designate patients by such locutions as "the kidney in room 422," "the osteosarcoma," "the gomer." What is interesting to medicine as a science are the repeatable, universal features of bodies, not the individuality of persons. Hospitals and hospital garb suppress even external manifestations of individual uniqueness (Rollin 1979).

To these vectors, militating in favor of eclipsing the fact that a sick person is an individual object of moral concern, are added additional ones that apply to dying persons. Any person who is terminally ill, who is dying, who has no hope of recovery, for whom there is nothing that medical science can do is likely to be seen as a defeat of medical science, as an embarrassment to the physician, as a counter-example to and mockery of his raison d'être. So many physicians have nothing to say to dying patients because they have nothing to do for them. One extraordinary example of this was provided to me by an eminent medical researcher whose daughter was interning at a major medical center. She was sitting up with a dying patient, holding his hand, when an attending physician burst in and, in front of the patient, rebuked the young house officer for wasting time on a patient who is dying anyway! The physician/scientist is not professionally equipped to provide what the dying need most—a reaffirmation of their uniqueness, worth, and the intrinsic value—a glorification of that uniqueness before it is forever extinguished.

Thus modern medicine militates against physicians who treat dying persons as unique objects of moral concern and intrinsic value and eclipses that most basic right to such treatment. But physicians are not alone in ignoring this right. In a society where exposure to death is severely limited, where many people have never seen a dead person or even a dead animal, where language sugar-coats the fact of death, where youth is glorified and praised above age, death is a bogeyman to be ignored and forgotten. We are uncomfortable even around sick people—how well we can all remember standing around hospital rooms even with close friends and family who were ill and finding nothing to say. All the more so with the dying, who remind us of our own mortality and of our ultimate impotence in the face of death, who strike at the heart of our defenses. So we ignore them, broadcast our discomfort to them in a million ways, make visits of obligation, and engage in the most inauthentic conversation—what Heidegger calls "idle chatter"—and prattle to them of the likelihood of rain when they most desperately need authentic communication. And so the fundamental right to being treated as an end in itself is eroded, and with it are eroded a whole array of human interests that follow in its wake—speech, social interaction, friendship.

The preceding discussion demonstrates how insidiously even the most basic, self-evident right can be eroded on the level of individuals. This example is especially illuminating because it is so clear. Presumably, no one will consciously deny that dying persons are full objects of moral concern, yet so few of us are psychologically able to practice what we fervently believe.

The situation is a good deal less theoretically transparent when we come to discuss other rights of the dying. We have so far emphasized only a moral truism—that inasmuch as dying persons are persons, they enjoy all the rights that any person should enjoy. The question obviously arises as to whether there are any special rights that logically must accrue to dying individuals because they are dying. (Compare the question of whether members of minority groups ought to enjoy special rights of the sort provided by affirmative action programs.) Much of the discussion in this area has focused on the question of whether the dying have a special right to choose their own death, be it by termination of heroic medical procedures or by some positive action such as drug overdose. This discussion has generated a veritable Talmud of issues and distinctions in the medico-ethical literature. Ought a dying, conscious, rational adult person be allowed to request cessation of heroic medical treatment? Ought such a person be allowed to request a painless death, a "good death," if the alternative is a slow, painful, financially and emotionally burdensome one? Are there morally relevant differences between cessation of treatment (passive euthanasia) and active inducement of death, say by barbituate overdose (active euthanasia) if either has been requested by a rational patient? Can such a decision ever be rational? What of dying persons who are not now rational or conscious? What if they have left a "living will"—i.e., at some point, when rational, indicated a desire for passive or active euthanasia? And what if they have not? Must all heroic efforts at prolongation of life be expended? Or can someone else make the decision for them (involuntary euthanasia)? If so, who? And are not all forms of euthanasia fraught with social dangers owing to the potential for abuse and so on?

These questions become increasingly pressing as the technological armamentarium that allows us to keep the body alive under more extreme conditions grows more and more formidable. A voluminous and valuable literature exists that explores all sides of these questions, something we clearly cannot do within the confines of this essay. But perhaps we can cut through some of the tangles that have grown up around the heart of the basic problem, which I state as follows: Does a dying person in full possession of his rational faculties have the right to choose the time and manner of his own death so long as he does not thereby endanger others?

I shall approach this question by first addressing the more general question of whether the logic of our moral concepts entails that all individuals have a right to choose death freely without being constrained against such choices by society; in short, whether human beings have a right to suicide. For simplicity, let us stipulate from the outset that we are talking about rational adult individuals in full command of their faculties.

The first point to realize is that, traditionally, no such right was in fact recognized. The common law condemned suicide, and until very recently attempting to commit suicide was a criminal act throughout the United States (Battin 1982). This position, however, reflected the influence of religious beliefs that only God has the right to make such decisions, and cannot be seen as a logical consequence of the ideal social morality developed early in this essay. The common-law condemnation of suicide was also based in the secular moral principle that a king has an interest in the preservation of all his subjects, a notion that could also be applied to a commonwealth and its citizens, but one that again must be weighed against the moral ideal of individual rights (Campbell *v.* Supreme Conclave Improved Order Heptasophs, 66, N.J.L. 274, 1901).

What then, does this morality imply about suicide? Is there a right to dispose of one's life? What arguments can be invoked against such a right? In the first place, our original hypothetical case of a rational adult committing suicide could and has been questioned. Surely, it is argued, no one seriously considering suicide could possibly be rational. Life is so good that anyone even considering suicide must be viewed as insane and hence irrational, and therefore not a full bearer of rights. This is in fact the tack that has characterized contemporary medicine. As Szasz (1977) has pointed out, "it is difficult to find a 'responsible' medical or psychiatric authority today that does not regard suicide as a medical and specifically as a mental health problem." Thus suicide became conceptually connected with irrationality and madness; it becomes logically impossible to be sane and suicidal. Thus it is absurd to say that one can have a right to suicide, since the people "choosing" suicide are in effect doing nothing of the kind, since they are too disturbed to choose. Thus it becomes reasonable to choose for such people, and to constrain and "cure" them of this mental illness.

In many of his writings, Szasz has made a powerful case against the coherence of talking about "mental illness," especially when such talk is used to justify infringement on a person's basic rights, as it is, for example, in the case of involuntary hospitalization of the mentally ill. And society as a whole has grown more and more skeptical of diagnoses of mental illness that rest on no clear empirical criteria and provide an escape hatch ("innocent by reason of insanity"), allowing people to avoid the consequences of criminal action. (It is often remarked that if one wishes to commit murder, one is well advised to do it as brutally or in as bizarre a manner as possible, since one is then clearly mentally ill and thus immune to punishment.) In any case, one need not reject the entire concept of mental illness in order to cast doubt upon its cogency when applied to suicide. For it is surely not logically absurd to suggest that there are cases where it is not unreasonable for a person to choose death. We do not, for example, dismiss as psychotic people who chose to die rather than live under Nazi domination, hurt another human being, give up their beliefs, or betray their country. We do not condemn as insane people who fall on a grenade or give up their place in a lifeboat. In fact, we eulogize such people and call them heroes and martyrs, not psychotics. We do not suggest that Nathan Hale was in need of psychiatric attention when he regretted having but one life to give for his country. The point, in more philosophical terms, is this: We do value life and value it highly, but there are other things which, in at least some cases, we value more highly. This is enough to show that one can be sane and yet choose death. So we may dismiss the claim that anyone who chooses suicide must necessarily be mentally ill. Even if one does believe in mental illness, one needs independent evidence other than the mere fact of choosing suicide to make such a diagnosis.

Let us return to our original case. If a rational person wishes to die, does he have a right to do so? One might suggest that he does not because it is against his own best interest to make such a choice. But this will not do, for two distinct reasons. First of all, this is partly an empirical claim. It may indeed be against a person's best interest to choose to die, but it may in fact not be—it depends on what he values and on how accurate his predictions are. Second, even if it is against his own interests, the moral principles outlined earlier militate against forcing people to do things "for their own good." In our society, the fundamental right of liberty means freedom to make one's own choices, not forced obedience to what is right. We do not, for example, feel that we have the right to prohibit people from choosing a career at which they cannot possibly succeed, or force them to refrain from dangerous activities. Freedom means being allowed to make one's own mistakes, unless one is thereby directly harming others. And this prohibition against hurting others is meant to exclude the sort of harm wrought by shouting "fire" in a crowded theater, not the sort of damage done by preaching communism in a Midwestern community. By the same token, you are not free to drive where you choose because you may hurt others. But if you choose to try to jump your car over a 300-foot chasm on your own property, that is your own business. Finally, it is not at all clear that there is an objective meaning to the phrase "a person's best interests" besides what he in fact chooses in accordance with rational applications of his own values.

Insofar as the rational choice of suicide directly affects only one's own life, it is hard to see why the individual ought to be any less free to choose it than to choose a career. My life is, after all, *mine,* and certainly the limiting case of freedom of choice over that life is the choice to end it. One might try to argue against the right to suicide by suggesting that suicide threatens the fabric of society, but this is highly implausible. By such reasoning, one can (and governments have) essentially erode all sorts of basic rights. One can imagine a case where a given individual's suicide would result in grave danger to the society as a whole—for example if the potential suicide had concealed a nuclear device in a major city and was killing himself to make sure that it would never be found—but such cases are so extraordinary as to be irrelevant to our main discussion.

One might also argue that one has no right to suicide for the same reason that one has no right to murder—that life is intrinsically valuable, and no one ever has the right to take it. Such an argument, which is surprisingly common, either collapses into a theological one or is highly implausible. In the first place, suicide is logically no more like murder than masturbation is like sexual intercourse. In both cases the results are the same, but the actions are logically distinct. In suicide I am killing myself, not another. Thus I have chosen for myself certain values that are more important than life; that is a far cry from doing it for someone else who may not share my values and has not made the choice. And in those cases where A, knowing that B has a rational wish to commit suicide, helps B to do so (say because B is paralyzed and thus cannot reach the pills but would if he could, and so A hands him the pills), the action is surely B's suicide, not B's murder by A. "He who acts through another," says a principle of law, "acts through himself."

It is therefore quite difficult to generate a rational, cogent moral argument against the right to suicide, at least in the case of those individuals for whom we have reason to believe that suicide is a rational choice. And, as mentioned earlier, such a rational choice can proceed from a variety of rational sources, ranging from a desire to save a friend to a basic decision that one has gotten all one can out of life or that one's life is meaningless. And from this comes the crux of our argument: If there is a general right to suicide for all rational human beings, there is a fortiori a right to suicide in the case of dying persons who, as we saw earlier, are obviously just a subclass of human beings! If *any* person has a right to choose his own death, then a dying person must also have such a right.

There are, furthermore, other considerations that strengthen this presumption in the case of dying persons, especially those whose illness involves suffering, pain, humiliation, dependence, or degradation, loss of autonomy, a sense of being burdensome to others, a fear of financial ruin, and so on. As we said earlier, a variety of values may acceptably and rationally be weighed heavier than life, and surely the above mentioned concerns would count as such values. As I have pointed out elsewhere (Rollin 1981), we have very undeveloped moral intuitions or principles about the value of animals in our society, yet virtually all of us feel that it is monstrous to keep alive a suffering animal whose pain is intractable. We rightly condemn someone who insists on "prolonging the animal's agony." If we feel so strongly about animal life, why then do we hesitate to extend the same logic to human life, especially when the person rationally and articulately expresses the desire to die? In my book on animal rights, I pointed out that the right to live one's life in accordance with one's nature is more important than mere protoplasmic existence—a dog kept alive by mechanical devices, unable to actualize its "dogness" is not being treated morally (Rollin 1981:59ff). But the same is true of a person and even more so. For whereas there is always some skeptical doubt that can be generated in the case of the dog ("does he really want to die?"), it is impossible to doubt the desire of persons who repeatedly plead for death. We are not making the choice for them—they have chosen to value something else over an extra month or year of questionable existence. It is perfectly rational not to wish to suffer beyond a certain point, not to wish to be a lingering burden to family, not to wish to deteriorate, not to wish to have to rely on others to perform even the most basic biological functions. And for all of the preceding arguments, we must therefore affirm that a fundamental right of dying persons, at least of rational dying persons, is the right to choose the time and manner of their own death.

The obvious question that of course arises in the face of such a position is the question of when a person is "rational." It has, for example, been suggested that an individual suffering great pain can never be said to be rational. But this is again a vestige of the argument discussed earlier that no one choosing suicide can possibly be rational. Independent, well-established tests of rationality are regularly employed societally to determine such questions as competence to stand trial or to write a will. Granted that these tests are not foolproof, and furthermore that the whole question of rationality constitutes a deep and vexing philosophical problem, there is no special problem in the case of the dying individual—we use the same sort of criteria for rationality that we employ anywhere else. And we certainly ought not assume a priori that any given decisions, even those made under very taxing conditions, are inevitably nonrational.

But what of the cases, surely quite frequent, where the dying person is *not* rational, either by virtue of illness, medication, or coma? Obviously, the concept of the right to die that we have developed is not germane here, since we have linked the concept with the notion of rational choice. Let us start with the case of people who have at some time been rational. It seems plausible to suggest that such people—most of us—give some prior thought to these questions. It is thus a good idea to build into the fabric of our social institutions some such notion as "the living will." In such a document, to be drafted when a person is of sound mind and body, the individual stipulates his wishes concerning treatment, care, prolongation of life, administration of painkillers which may be life-shortening, use of heroic measures, and so on. In this way, just as every person in society ought to have a will indicating disposition of property, so too each person should, after due reflection, stipulate choices concerning life and death.

Harder cases arise regarding such nonrational people as the comatose, the retarded, the demented, children and so on. Here, of course, our model of the right to decide on one's own life or death by rational choice breaks down, and one must look elsewhere for resolution of the issue. And clearly no simple answer exists for all such cases. Interestingly enough, one may learn here from analyses of the moral status of animals. From a philosophical point of view, there do not seem to be morally relevant differences between nonrational humans and at least the "higher" animals. One apparent difference, of course, arises out of the fact that, legally, animals are property—either private property or community property—and nonrational humans are not. But this difference is only apparent for, as I have argued elsewhere, there is no rational and moral justification for seeing animals as property if we do not so see people (Rollin 1981:67ff). The law here reflects human self-interest (as did laws allowing slavery) and religious bias (as did much public morality regarding slavery), not the rational consequences of our ethic.

In any case, as we mentioned earlier, we generally feel that it is immoral to prolong the life of a suffering, terminally ill animal. This intuition does not always reflect the interests of human beings, since very often pet owners, for example, would like to keep the animal alive at all costs for the sake of their own egos or emotional needs rather than out of concern for the interests of the animal. Yet we feel that such a desire is unjustified, for the animal cannot possibly be happy or even comfortable if it is paralyzed, constantly suffering, or unable to control its bodily functions. In such cases, the animal is not actualizing its nature or *telos;* a dog that is totally paralyzed and in constant pain is experiencing mere protoplasmic existence, and not realizing its "dogness." As we saw earlier, the whole notion of rights is based on what we consider to be essential to human beings, to their natures. If animals are also objects of moral concern, then we must look to their natures to determine their rights as well (Rollin 1981:52ff). In the case of nonrational humans, a similar logic must obtain.

Rights arise out of a sense that certain interests are essential to being a human person—speech, for example, and its protection as freedom of speech. Similarly, animal rights should be deduced from our knowledge of an animal's interests, growing out of its nature. (Penning veal calves so that they cannot move is an obvious example of such a violation of a right growing out of an animal's nature.) By the same token, the rights of nonrational humans must be constructed in the same way, with consideration of their essential interests and of what it takes to satisfy these interests and to make them happy kept paramount in our moral deliberations. And if we keep this concept in mind, our deliberations concerning termination of life for nonrational humans will be made conceptually easier. Is the individual in such pain that he cannot live the sort of life that his nature determined before his illness? Is the individual similarly incapacitated by paralysis, or seizures, or coma? The point is that decisions or termination of life must morally be decided in each case by appeal to the interests of the patient, not by considerations of convenience to society, family, and so on. Thus is the notion of rights as a protection of the individual preserved even when one cannot oneself press for these rights or when one is nonrational.

It remains now to consider some of the traditional distinctions that have been brought to bear in these discussions and to locate them within the context of our analysis. A traditional pair of distinctions is drawn between active and passive euthanasia and voluntary and involuntary euthanasia. In passive euthanasia, treatment is withheld from a patient. In active euthanasia, a person is injected with a lethal drug or actively killed in some other way. In voluntary euthanasia, the patient chooses to die; in involuntary euthanasia, someone else makes the choice. Putting the distinctions together, we may recognize four cases of euthanasia: active voluntary, active involuntary, passive voluntary, and passive involuntary. In passive voluntary euthanasia, the rational patient requests that medical treatment be discontinued, respirators be unplugged, and so on. The moral justifiability of such cases follows from our previous discussion. In active voluntary euthanasia, the rational patient requests that some positive measure be taken to terminate his life. Our earlier discussion has implied that when a person is essentially taking his own life with another person acting as his agent, this also morally counts as suicide. Legally, however, the case is murkier, as the law does not recognize the morality of such actions, and technically the act would be murder, not suicide. In actual practice, as mentioned earlier, the legal system has tended to duck the hard moral issues by appealing in many cases to temporary insanity.

One reason for social conservatism on active voluntary euthanasia is, of course, the potential for abuse. Once we allow the killing of people by other people, we have opened a Pandora's box. While this is indeed an important concern, it is not as acute in voluntary active euthanasia as in involuntary. For it would seem quite possible to set up legal safeguards to ensure that a person is indeed choosing to die. In general, it seems difficult to sustain a clear distinction between active and passive voluntary euthanasia. If the patient chooses to stop medication, that is passive; if he chooses to request an overdose of painkiller, that is active. Where, we may ask, is the difference that makes a difference? If he could, he would get the drug himself; since he can't, he requests that the physician or someone else do it.

Both forms of involuntary euthanasia are more problematic, since they do not involve the patient's choice, except in the case of a living will, in which case the situation may be construed as voluntary. There is, of course, no justification for involuntary active or passive euthanasia for a rational person who has not chosen to die. For nonrational humans, the case is more difficult. It is necessary to use the criteria we discussed earlier concerning the interests of the patient. Here it would seem that passive involuntary euthanasia would be most plausible—on the basis of irreversible coma, for example, we choose to shut down a respirator. Active involuntary euthanasia is most problematic for, unlike the voluntary cases, where the distinction between active and passive blurs, there does seem to be a major difference here, since we are actively killing people who have not indicated a desire to die, and this could indeed be subject to abuse (the "wedge argument"), as occurred in Nazi Germany (Veatch 1976:86ff). It certainly does not behoove society to permit what is generally perceived as killing. Since we have no solid peg analogous to the rational patient's decision to die upon which to hang our act, it is best to err on the side of caution.

To what extent are the ideals we have delineated actualized in the law? It appears that there is an increasing tendency toward legal codification of some of the principles we have enunciated. In the first place, suicide has been increasingly decriminalized (Battin 1982), though not so much out of a recognition of the rational person's right to choose death as out of increasing dominance of the medical-psychiatric model of the suicide as a sick person who cannot help himself. According to some legal theorists, there is indeed a constitutional right to suicide (Sullivan 1980). (The law would of course not grant such a right to an incompetent person.) Similarly there is strong legal support for the right of rational adult patients to refuse treatment and, correlatively, of course, for the right to refuse heroic treatment (Battin 1982). The law also recognizes increasingly in both case law and statute the need to take seriously "living wills" and statements that people have made about prolongation of heroic measures before the person's becoming incapacitated (Battin 1982; Backer, Hannon, and Russell 1982:192–193). In the case of nonrational persons, the courts have rightly been more cautious. But as indicated by the recent cases of Karen Ann Quinlan, who was irreversibly comatose for years, and Joseph Saikewicz, who was severely retarded and terminally ill, courts have looked to the interests of the patient in allowing for termination of treatment and thus for passive involuntary euthanasia (Matter of Quinlan 355A. 2d 647, 1976; Superintendent of Belchertown F. Saikewicz, Mass., 370 N.E. 2d 417, 1977). Hospitals routinely, of course, make decisions concerning passive euthanasia in terms of cessation of treatment

(Backer, Hannon, and Russell 1982:p 187). The case of Saikewicz is especially relevant, since to permit the withholding of treatment from the nonrational patient was granted on the grounds that such treatment would have led to great suffering by the patient. In terms of active involuntary euthanasia, the law has wisely remained very conservative. Thus it appears that, in the main, the law and public policy are moving closer to the ideal moral analysis we have outlined in our discussion. We may hazard a guess that such progress has been in large part a function of the degree of social discussion, mass-media coverage, and awareness of these issues that has grown up in the past three decades.

It remains for us to consider one more question concerning the rights of the dying person—do patients have the right to know the truth about their condition, as others, especially physicians, see it? Certainly it is a general moral principle that people (at least rational adults) should be told the truth. It is often said that dying people constitute a special case, since the truth can be harmful, demoralizing, and actually accelerate their deterioration. On the other hand, it is argued, dying people most of all must know the truth, since they need desperately to get their affairs in order. Both of these arguments are beside the basic point. The fact is that, given the ethic we have argued for in this essay, control over one's own life must be seen as the fundamental right of any rational human being. As stated earlier, this ethic is incompatible with decisions being made for one's own good against one's will. Thus the kind of paternalism that suggests that the truth be withheld from a person because "it might hurt him" is incompatible with the fundamental right of individuals to be in command of their own lives. It is, in fact, incompatible with any serious concept of primacy of the individual.

A solution must be sought not in concealing the truth from patients, but rather in the manner in which truth is conveyed. In the first place, it is imperative that authentic communication be established between physician and patient. Second, the physician must be ever on guard to the performative dimensions of his pronouncements. Diagnosis and prognoses should not be sentences. Given the Aesculapian authority of physicians, a statement like "you have six months to live" made by a physician can be like the statement "you are sentenced to six months" made by a judge—it can be self-fulfilling. For this reason, the physician must strike the difficult balance between doom-saying and false hope. And the best way to do this is to present the facts of the situation as accurately as possible in language the person can grasp. Such an effort is time-consuming, but morally inescapable. And a physician should also recall that no physician possesses sufficient knowledge to time exactly the course of an illness. Statements like "you'll be dead in six months" are as unacceptable scientifically as they are morally.

We have attempted to survey, very briefly, a number of questions that concern the rights of the dying person. Such an activity is of great importance, for it must inevitably sharpen our sensitivity to the issues and questions involved. Even those who hold different moral positions from those expressed here can benefit by dialectically confronting an alternative position. Moral concern for the rights of dying persons is not esoteric moral theorizing. It is a precondition for responsible social policy, moral progress, and, in the face of exponentially proliferating biotechnology, of the very existence of a moral order commensurate with our level of technological sophistication. It is also an investment in our own futures for, much as we would deny it, in the final reckoning we are all dying persons.

Patients' Bill of Rights

The American Hospital Association presents a Patient's Bill of Rights with the expectation that observance of these rights will contribute to more effective patient care and greater satisfaction for the patient, the physician, and the hospital organization. Further, the Association presents these rights in the expectation that they will be supported by the hospital on behalf of its patients, as an integral part of the healing process. It is recognized that a personal relationship between the physician and the patients is essential for the provision of proper medical care. The traditional physician-patient relationship takes on a new dimension when care is tendered within an organizational structure. Legal precedent has established that the institution itself also has a responsibility to the patient. It is in recognition of these factors that these rights are affirmed.

1. The patient has the right to considerate and respectful care.

2. The patient has the right to obtain from his physician complete current information concerning his diagnosis, treatment, and prognosis in terms the patient can be reasonably expected to understand. When it is not medically advisable to give such information to the patient, the information should be made available to an appropriate person in his behalf. He has the right to know by name the physician responsible for coordinating his care.

3. The patient has the right to receive from his physician information necessary to give informed consent prior to the start of any procedure and/or treatment. Except in emergencies, such information for informed consent, should include but not necessarily be limited to the specific procedure and/or treatment, the medically significant risks involved, and the probable duration of incapacitation. Where medically significant alternatives for care or treatment exist, or when the patient requests information concerning medical alternatives, the patient has the right to such information. The patient also has the right to know the name of the person responsible for the procedures and/or treatment.

4. The patient has the right to refuse treatment to the extent permitted by law, and to be informed of the medical consequences of his action.

5. The patient has the right to every consideration of his privacy concerning his own medical care program. Case discussion, consultation, examination, and treatment are confidential and should be conducted discreetly. Those not directly involved in his care must have the permission of the patient to be present.

6. The patient has the right to expect that all communications and records pertaining to his care should be treated as confidential.

7. The patient has the right to expect that within its capacity a hospital must make reasonable response to the request of a patient for services. The hospital must provide evaluation, service, and/or referral as indicated by the urgency of the case. When medically permissible, a patient may be transferred to another facility only after he has received complete information and explanation

concerning the needs for and alternatives to such a transfer. The institution to which the patient is to be transferred must first have accepted the patient for transfer.

8. The patient has the right to obtain information as to any relationship of his hospital to other health care and education institutions insofar as his care is concerned. The patient has the right to obtain information as to the existence of any professional relationships among individuals, by name, who are treating him.

9. The patient has the right to be advised if the hospital proposes to engage in or perform human experimentation affecting his care or treatment. The patient has the right to refuse to participate in such research projects.

10. The patient has the right to expect reasonable continuity of care. He has the right to know in advance what appointment times and physicians are available and where. The patient has the right to expect that the hospital will provide a mechanism whereby he is informed by his physician or a delegate of the physician of the patient's continuing health care requirements following discharge.

11. The patient has the right to examine and receive an explanation of his bill regardless of source of payment.

12. The patient has the right to know what hospital rules and regulations apply to his conduct as a patient.

No catalogue of rights can guarantee for the patient the kind of treatment he has a right to expect. A hospital has many functions to perform, including the prevention and treatment of disease, the education of both health professionals and patients, and the conduct of clinical research. All these activities must be conducted with an overriding concern for the patient, and, above all, the recognition of his dignity as a human being. Success in achieving this recognition assures success in the defense of the rights of the patient.

References

Backer, B., N. Hannon and N. Russell. 1982. *Death and Dying: Individuals and Institutions*. New York: Wiley.

Battin, M. P. 1982. *Ethical Issues in Suicide*. Englewood Cliffs, N.J.: Prentice-Hall.

Dworkin, R. 1977. *Taking Rights Seriously*. Cambridge: Harvard University Press.

Rollin, B. E. 1981. *Animal Rights and Human Morality.* Buffalo, New York: Prometheus Books.

Rollin, B. E. 1983. "Nature, Convention, and the Medical Approach to the Dying Aged." In M. Tallmer et al., eds., *The Life-Threatened Elderly.* New York: Columbia University Press.

Rollin, B. E. 1979. "On the Nature of Illness." *Man and Medicine* 4:157.

Scotto, J., et al. 1977. "Cancer Prevalence and Hospital Payments." *Journal of the National Cancer Institute,* August.

Sobel, H. J., ed. 1981. *Behavior Therapy in Terminal Care.* Cambridge, Mass.: Bellinger.

Spiegel, H. and D. Spiegel. 1978. *Trance and Treatment: Clinical Uses of Hypnosis.* New York: Basic Books.

Stengel, E. 1965. *Suicide and Attempted Suicide.* London: Macgibbon and Kee.

Sullivan, A. 1980. "The Constitutional Right to Suicide." In M. Battin and D. Mayo, eds., *Suicide: The Philosophical Issues,* pp. 29ff. New York: St. Martin's Press.

Szasz, T. 1977. "The Ethics of Suicide." In R. Weir, ed., *Ethical Issues in Death and Dying,* New York: Columbia University Press.

Veatch, R. 1976. *Death, Dying, and the Biological Revolution.* New Haven: Yale University Press.

Preamble: While the circumstances surrounding dying vary greatly, the care of dying patients should give emphasis to their psycho-social as well as to their physical needs. In usual circumstances, patients should be entitled to a relatively pain-free death, and with the maximum maintenance of control of self and self-esteem—in short, since death with dignity often seems hardly achievable, the goal to be sought should be death with as few indignities as possible.

Principle 6: An Ultimate Ideal in the Care of Dying Patients Should Be That of Death Without Indignity

6

Death Without Indignity

CAROL FARKAS
and MATTHEW LOSCALZO

Death with dignity has been described as the goal for care of terminal patients. Accepted too literally, it could become another burden upon them and their families. Actually, the thesis developed in this paper is that the ideal in the care of the dying patient should be that of death without indignity. This goal should be helpful both to patients and to society's feelings regarding a more acceptable view of death.

Minimal indignity may not be easy to attain for terminal patients, who have been stripped of many of the indices by which they previously defined themselves: family, job, social, and community roles. The sense of prior roles is lost and with it a sense of control. Part of the issues revolve around the individuals' attempts to maintain integrity as psychological, social, and spiritual beings. Central to the psychosocial aspects, however, are the physical symptoms with which the patients must contend. In fact, "the number one predictor" of good "emotional adjustment is a low level of discomfort," as noted by Elizabeth Kübler-Ross (1975:83). Indeed, it is this fear of discomfort, primarily pain, that cancer patients fear even more than death. Cassell has aptly stated (1982): "Suffering is experienced by persons, not merely bodies, and has its source in challenges that threaten the intactness of the person as a complex social and psychological entity."

Health Care Professionals' Words That Diminish the Ideal of Death Without Indignity

It is ironic that the health care staff can add to the distress experienced by patients by such innocuous means as choice of words. We discuss "aggressive treatment" with patients, but how do they perceive this term, which seems suggestive of a battleground upon which a war is now being waged? (Messina 1982). It can be reassuring for some patients but frightening to others, so it requires explanation.

"Active treatment" is the better term, since it encompasses the concept of treating the entire human being. The patient becomes a partner in the effort, which is focused upon attaining maximal quality of life, while discarding the concept of life or death, success or failure.

Often we use incorrect terms in defining success and failure and again burden the patient inappropriately. We sometimes speak of a patient who "failed a protocol" when treatment has been ineffective. Actually, patients do not fail protocols; nor do protocols fail patients. If we eliminate the word "fail," the patient is protected from feeling guilty about somehow not "passing" the test. Even acronyms commonly used to refer to specific chemotherapeutic regimens could be perceived by patients in a negative or positive manner. It is important to be aware that a word may not be perceived by patients as it is perceived by us.

Communication and Caring for the Terminally Ill

Hope is eternal and natural. Human beings have the ability to prepare realistically for death while retaining a measure of hope. How to nurture rational hope is important for life and health. It is not necessarily what is said but how it is said (Cangello 1962). It is important to be truthful, since the relationships that the patient depends on require trust. Patients do perceive the discrepancies between how people speak and how they behave (Wortman and Dunkel-Schetter 1979). Bok (1978) has noted that often when people are less than truthful they are acting on the assumption that this "will be beneficial, perhaps prevent harm, or support fairness or prior obligation"; those who are not truthfully informed often do not share this moral view. According to Bok, "Many lies to those who are very ill, for example, are taken by the liars themselves as understood and accepted by all involved, whereas those thus lied to have agreed to nothing of the sort" (1982:88). The patient involved in such a contract is usually not a partner in its initiation or development.

Several studies have substantiated that the overwhelming majority of healthy individuals, when questioned, state that they would want the truth about a fatal illness (Cassem 1978a, 1978b; Caughill 1979; Radabough and Radabough 1982). It is essential that persons working with terminally ill patients be comfortable with handling information about illness. Staff discomfort may lead to their spending less time with critically ill patients out of fear that questions concerning their illness may be asked. For the patient and family "what could be more upsetting, more anxiety producing, than an evasive health professional?" (Truscott 1982). In fact, we know patients are aware of their precarious physical condition, even though they do not discuss it. We cannot "protect" patients from truth; we can, however, alienate them from any meaningful contact when we shy away from discussions with them. The staff person who permits this to happen repeatedly is not performing an essential role in caregiving. The perception of consistent verbal and nonverbal messages across all channels allows patients to establish trust, reduce their anxiety level and die interacting with others rather than isolated from them. This may be what is meant by death with dignity (Klagsbrun 1977; Radabough and Radabough, p. 46; Sanes 1979; Summers 1982). At the time of greatest need for contact, the health care staff has an important role in preventing the indignity of isolation.

The Interdisciplinary Team's Role

If a patient is to receive appropriate and concerned care, the talents of a coordinated health care team must be employed. The team should be composed of at least the following: the primary physician, who is responsible for overall coordination and plan of care; other physicians from appropriate specialties; the primary nurse, who will remain as a consistent figure; and finally clinical nursing specialists, social workers with expertise in areas of mental health and symptom control, a dietitian, and a member of the clergy. Psychiatric consultation should be available. Each discipline makes its own contribution. When one member of the team monopolizes the patient, the result is distorted communication within the team, which in turn causes fragmentation of care which, when inevitably sensed by the patient, may produce anger, frustration, and fear (Lansky et al. 1976). Families find the patient's emotional responses contagious and may exhibit similar reactions.

Patients usually choose the member or members of the team to whom they relate best. The team's task is to facilitate this opportunity. Not infrequently, a patient may choose a team member who would not on the surface seem to be of comfort to him (Battin 1983; Craytor 1979; Jaffe 1980; Sanes 1979).

The Patient/Family Unit in Crisis

In attempting to comfort and support the patient one should not lose sight of the family, which requires the same degree of concern. The family must be included in all phases of caring for the patient. In order to know how the patient is adapting at any given time it is necessary to know how the patient has reacted in the past. Who knows better the intimate needs of the patient? Families are vital to such understanding, providing information about the religious and cultural context in which the patient has lived.

According to Baldwin, "patients have a right to have their sociocultural backgrounds understood in the same way that they expect their physical and psychological needs to be recognized and understood" (1982). Any life-threatening diagnosis or chronic illness precipitates disequilibrium in the family system. Murray concludes "that the attitudes of patients approaching death are a function of interweaving factors—the psychological maturity of the person, the kinds of coping techniques available to him, variables of religious orientation, age, socioeconomic status, the severity of the organic process and the attitudes of physicians and significant people in his environment" (1982).

Acute stress mobilizes family and friends into rapid action in an attempt to alleviate the stress. They become focused on the goal of the patient's survival, sometimes forgetting self and the need for maintenance of homeostasis within the family. As stressful and anxiety-provoking as the acute situation may be, it is time limited: the patient dies, stabilizes, or improves, often in a matter of weeks. Aspects of chronic situations present a different picture. The family must maintain balance in which the long-term future is unknown. Families have described this period as if it were an indeterminate prison sentence. Control has been transferred to the unseen illness. Support systems, rapidly mobilized and active during the acute phase of illness, often fade away as illness persists. This process is clear when one counts the decrease in the number of cards and flowers sent as the patient requires more frequent and lengthy hospitalizations. The impact can have a negative impact on every level of family functioning.

As the disease progresses, both patient and family may feel increasingly isolated. The networks families relied on for their livelihood and social interaction, as well as a reference against which they judged their behavior and attitudes, slowly dissipate. At this most disruptive time, the vulnerable family is faced with the additional task of integrating the health care team into its unique structure. It is crucial that communication channels, both within the family and the health care system, remain open.

Psycho-Financial Considerations

In recent years much attention has been paid to the financial and emotional costs of cancer. For example, it is estimated that in 1976 direct medical costs for cancer exceeded 30 billion dollars. Furthermore, when one considers only hospital, physician, and burial costs, the average cost per family was $27,718. It has been estimated that the direct costs were only 20 to 30 percent of the total costs. Cancer Care, Inc. (1972–1973) studied 115 families in the New York City area who had a family member living with cancer. Though only 3 percent were uninsured, six months after death of the patient over one-third of the families were still in debt. The median cost of the illness was 2.3 times the median income, and 84 percent of the families incurred costs in excess of 25 percent of the median income. In order to finance these additional debts, educational plans were deferred or cancelled, life insurance policies were cashed in, and loans were taken out. Life styles and future plans were severely and negatively altered.

Although there is extensive literature on the medical cost of cancer, there is a paucity of information and research on the subject of nonmedical, or out-of-pocket, expenses. In their reports, Cancer Care listed "unanticipated costs" (those expenses not usually covered by insurance companies) as including medical, homemaker, housekeeper, special diets, special clothing, nurses, blood transfusions, psychiatric treatment, modifications of dwelling, nursing home, child care, personal care of patient, home attendant, domestic, patient laundry, transportation, special treatments, food for household help, etc. (1972–1973; 1973).

A figure that is often not taken into account is the income lost when the patient has been the primary wage earner in the family. The American Cancer Society (1978) reports that income lost by the patient alone due to disability is estimated to cost the country between 15 and 25 billion dollars each year and this is a 1977 statistic. This figure does not include additional income and productivity lost by family members who care and provide for or visit the patient. Presently there are no published data on this figure.

One of the few studies on the nonmedical costs of cancer were reported by Lansky et al. from the University of Kansas Medical Center (1979). This study requested that families keep a weekly log of nonmedical expenses. One-half of the families reported that 25 percent of their weekly income was going for nonmedical expenses. The point is correctly made that out-of-pocket expenses must be paid immediately and are rarely reimbursable. Therefore, the posthumous outstanding debt of the patient may be directly related to these unreimbursable expenses. The largest categories were for transportation, food, and miscellaneous items. The four main variables of nonmedical costs were: level of care (terminal phase of illness necessitates increased level of care); performance status (patients who are terminal generally perform at a markedly reduced level, scoring below 50 on the Karnofsky Scale); family size; and distance from hospital. The level of care appeared to be the most significant variable for each category of expense, except for lodging. In general, expenses increased with family size and extra financial pressure was experienced by single-parent families. Although no single family experiences all of the above nonreimbursable expenses, many of these concerns are felt to varying degrees by most families.

When we consider the meaning of money in our society, we can better understand what it means to be suddenly vulnerable after prior security. In many families financial solvency is closely related to emotional well-being. Money contributes to equilibrium within the family system in a society that equates money with success, freedom, pride, power, alternative of options, accomplishment, and especially control. In addition to the indignity of loss of health the increasing financial burden renders the family virtually impotent. When the aspirations and savings of a lifetime have been depleted and the patient has become dependent on the health care team, an increasingly undignified self-image and vulnerability may ensue for the family as well as the patient. The need to maintain control over one's life is shared by patient and family member alike.

The social worker can do little to protect the patient and family from the financial realities. Nevertheless, the social worker can assist the family system in engaging appropriate financial resources: religious, community, state, and federal agencies. It is essential for patients and family members to know that there are members of the health care team who are able to assist them in understanding their often complex insurance policies and to discuss with them the many changes within the family structure caused by the reality of financial crisis. Even the best social work services and financial counseling cannot locate resources where none exist. But what can be provided is continuing professional support and guidance that can assist families to cope to the best of their ability.

Since many patients have previously retired or are forced to do so by their own illness or that of a family member, they are often dependent on sparse and inadequate medical insurance coverage for most or all of their medical needs. The financial strain on this population can often put their life's work, savings, and promise of a pleasant retirement in serious jeopardy. Quite often the surviving spouse is forced to seek lodging with a family member, and this can have a devastating impact on the host family, who may not have the resources, or the space, to accommodate the new addition to the household. Furthermore, for the surviving spouse who is compelled to enter such a situation, the perceived role within the family may be permanently changed. An independent elderly person may be expected to passively follow rules in an adult child's home in an effort to become integrated into it.

During the course of the disease there appears to be a process in which there is a parallel depletion of financial and emotional resources. Four psycho-financial phases are noted here. They should be evaluated as an entire process, rather than as single unrelated events.

The first phase, *Naïve Acceptance* usually occurs at the time of diagnosis or recurrence. The attitude of the family is that money cannot be considered at this crucial time. All is focused on the survival of the patient. This is often a time of great faith and trust in the health-care institution.

In the second phase, *Renegotiation for Health* (or: money *is* an issue), the disease continues to take its course. If the illness is arrested, the patient and family are spared the more dramatic financial effects of long-term illness. Should the disease continue on, however, the family experiences increasing depletion of resources as various methods of treatment are employed. It is usually at this time that both medical and nonmedical bills combine with loss of work days to heighten anxiety. Financial issues begin to become increasingly important to the family. Concomitant with this may also be rising feelings of ambivalence and frustration toward the patient and institution. The patient often experiences an increasing sense of guilt, helplessness, and fear of abandonment.

Solvency vs. Insolvency, the third phase, is the point where the family painfully accepts the reality of their financial limits: going along with protocols and further investment of resources does not necessarily ensure a successful outcome. The best they can hope for, in many cases, is to buy time and this does not always mean time of good quality. This realization often binds the family and the patient in a sense of helplessness. Each feels he has let the other down; all feel a loss of self-esteem. Patients tend to feel guilty over the amount of money and attention they continue to require, and families are forced to consider the law of diminishing returns.

Family members are often exhausted, seesawing in a state of ambivalence—grieving for the anticipated death and denying it will come. At a time when they are most in need of support they have depleted their own inner resources and have nothing left to give to each other. Then the anger felt toward those mates and relatives, perceived as "unhelpful" or "not understanding," becomes apparent. This phase is also a time when each of the family members is experiencing the same emotions and trying to maintain personal equilibrium as well as that of the family unit. It is a time when appropriate recognition of the dynamics can help to prevent further deterioration.

Patients and family members now may need to seek additional financial assistance, from relatives, friends, and supportive social agencies. They may for the first time feel dependent on others for their support. For many families this is a repudiation of their life's work and an assault on their integrity as they are faced with the task of having to reorder the priorities of their financial expenditures.

In the final phase, *Resolution: Balancing the Budget,* families may be able to accept the reality of what they can provide for the patient or they may become overwhelmed with guilt at not being able to do enough. Acceptance of the death of the patient is for some a painful but inevitable reality, bringing about a sense of relief. For others it brings an exacerbation of anger toward the patient for depleting them of necessary resources without offering anything in exchange. Death is viewed as desertion. If the pre-illness relationship was one-sided, and the patient seldom gave to the spouse who would survive, the remaining debts may engender anger. The surviving spouse may re-experience the past deprivations and feel that even death does not end the demands he or she had always responded to. If the relationship was healthy, the remaining spouse will usually work through the ambivalence around separation and loss and make an adaptive adjustment.

The Emergence of Innovative Approaches

The more we try to understand terminal illness as a chronic condition with acute crises, the more we recognize the need to intervene in ways that are consistent with the patient's ever-changing needs. We need to go beyond what the person is feeling or fearing and to demonstrate that there are areas within the control of the individual. When reasonable options can do no harm, e.g., special diets or vitamin therapy, they increase the patient's sense of optimism and feelings of being in control. It is necessary, however, to stress that traditional therapy should be continued. There is never a reason for physicians to say "there is nothing further we can do." Attempts to control symptoms and offer supportive care keep patients from feeling abandoned.

Interventions need to be tailored to patients' needs and not to any one theoretical framework. Behavioral medicine is a new modality for ameliorating a range of symptoms associated with medical illness (Agras 1982; Baldwin 1982; Melamed and Siegel 1980; Pomerleau 1982; Pomerleau and Brady 1979; Redd and Andrykowski 1982; Redd et al. 1979). Included among the behavioral techniques are desensitization, reinforcement, extinction, relaxation, distraction, biofeedback, and hypnosis. They have been used with promising results in patients with terminal illness for the amelioration of anxiety, pain, and phobias.

The primary focus of behavioral intervention is on behavior and in areas over which patients can be taught to experience some control. Even greatly debilitated patients are able to benefit from successful behavioral intervention by their increasing sense of control and competency. The authors were able to teach an adolescent in the Special Care Unit to allow his family to assist him in entering a hypnotic state by visualizing a baseball scene in which he was on the pitcher's mound, "a little bit above it all." The patient and family were able to share this experience effectively until the patient's death to alleviate the patient's pain and temper the parents' sense of helplessness.

Behavioral techniques, primarily relaxation/distraction and systematic desensitization, have been successfully used in a variety of medical settings for control of anticipatory nausea and vomiting as side effects of chemotherapy (Burish and Lyles 1981; Kutz et al. 1980; Morrow et al. 1982; Morrow and Morell 1982; Nesse et al. 1980; Redd and Andrykowski 1982). An increasing number of behavioral techniques in the treatment of pain have also been reported in the literature (Barber and Adrian 1982; Barber 1963; Cangello

1962; Chong 1968; Crasilneck and Hall 1973; Erikson and Rossi 1979. Foley 1979; Fordyce 1976; Hendler 1961; Hilgard and Hilgard 1975; Kerr 1981; Livingston 1978). Another area of intervention involves uncomfortable and/or painful medical procedures, e.g., suctioning, injections, lumbar puncture. The anxiety levels of some patients approach phobic proportions in reaction to specific medical treatments. Desensitization and other anxiety-reducing techniques can often increase control and ameliorate the discomfort involved in these procedures (Spiegel and Spiegel 1978).

The impact of these techniques is just beginning to be felt in the care of the terminally ill. What we have learned from them is that by employing behavioral techniques in an appropriate manner, the patient is able to learn skills that can increase his sense of competence and control. The father of a 16-year-old boy expressed it best when he said "Thank you for giving me back my son!" after his son was taught to control painful muscle spasms through hypnosis.

The Developmental Process

"Everything comes to him who waits—among other things, death" (Bowlby 1980). For the patient, the dying process is composed of at least two separate but interdependent processes: the accelerated decline of organ function and the completion of a psychosocial life-cycle. Death is much more than a mere biological shut-down of organ systems.

Just as the proper dosage of narcotics in the control of pain is the dosage that works in eliminating it, so the proper interventions are those that allow the patients and families to cohere as a unit and to feel confident in their ability to shoulder the burden of illness and the fear of death. The psychosocial phases of the life-cycle, as proposed by Erikson (1959), can be an extremely helpful guide. They include: Trust vs. Mistrust, Autonomy vs. Shame and Doubt, Initiative vs. Guilt, Industry vs. Inferiority, Identity vs. Identity Diffusion, Intimacy vs. Isolation, Generativity vs. Self-Absorption, Integrity vs. Disgust.

During the earlier life cycle stages children lack experience to comprehend death, but are aware when they are seriously ill. Before five years of age, death is perceived as a transient state from which one can return. At about five years the increasing awareness of the finality of death is manifested by separation anxiety. The lack of boundaries between child and parent is experienced by both as highly stressful. Each is perceived as an extension of the other.

During the latency period open communication concerning the illness is of paramount importance. The anxiety over separation is reduced when both child and parent share the same information.

During adolescence, increasing separation is a normal process, although an ambivalent one. Increased awareness of the diagnosis can produce greater stress in the relationship between adolescent and parent (U.S. Dept. of Health and Human Services). The young adult may be acutely aware of the finality of death. Social disruption and isolation from valued peers occur as medical considerations increase. There is little chance to affirm ego-identity; developmental tasks are severely compromised. The adolescent may be at risk for regression as dependency on the parents is necessary for care. A double-bind, which will have an impact on the child's sense of dignity, may be created. The adolescent may be unable to complete separation and the parents, having to relate to an adolescent with the needs of a much younger child, may further hinder their child's development.

During marriage and/or parenthood the needs of the spouse and child transcend self-need and fear of death. The patient may perceive himself as abdicating his role within the family if care for self takes priority over the immediate needs of a child or spouse. The person's ability to fulfill his developmental task as a parent and spouse is greatly undermined and may engender much guilt and lead to self-absorption. Dignity at this stage of development is dependent upon the maintenance of the family's integrity and the patient's role within it.

Middle age is a period of reassessment. It is a time of taking stock of one's accomplishments in anticipation of collecting the rewards. A diagnosis of terminal disease at this time in the life-cycle may be perceived as the ultimate untimely loss. The goals of life seem just barely out of reach. The myths of Damocles. Sisyphus, and Tantalus seem all too intimate. The threat of being cut down in the prime of life becomes reality.

The aged person, having witnessed the loss of family members and friends, is more familiar with death. Death can be seen as the ultimate loneliness or as the end to it, depending on the person's situation and life experiences. Although during this period death is anticipated as a near reality, most elderly are in no hurry to arrive at its doorstep. It is a misconception that the elderly will or should accept death placidly. Culture will greatly influence how one accepts death at any age, but in no way should one interpose his own value system upon another. The elderly also have a right to mourn the loss of those who will survive them, communicate their fears and concerns, have their wishes respected, and have available appropriate medical and psychological treatment regardless of age.

Options for Care

People once died in their homes, surrounded by family. Death was a family affair, a sad but accepted conclusion to life. Families shared with and supported each other, and the role of the health care professions was one of emotional support to the family. Today, death takes place in the hospital (Cassileth and Donovan 1983).

Rapidly expanding technological advances began the process of extending life, sometimes without a concomitant increase in its quality. This brought a host of moral, social, ethical, and financial issues to light. Simultaneously, care of the dying patient was more often assumed by strangers, the health care providers. Many acute diseases became chronic conditions. The family was given a secondary role and was increasingly alienated from the treatment process. Technology brought not only increased costs to hospital care, but also diminished sensitivity to the whole person. The risk for patients to become their diagnosis was enhanced.

In Great Britain, after 1945, the stage was set for a new public awareness. The British demanded from their health care professionals a return to concern for the entire individual, a holistic approach to care. There was a need to balance treatment of disease with support of the emotional life of the patient and family. Hospice, a concept of care for the dying, was the fruit of this ideology.

The word "hospice" is derived from a medieval place that served as a sanctuary for travelers on a long, difficult journey (Markel and Simon 1978). Hospice programs deemphasize what we now consider traditional hospital-based care and emphasize care focused on control of symptoms and psychosocial support to the patient/family in the most appropriate setting. An interdisciplinary team, working full-time, and organized on the basis of a nursing care model, is available to follow and provide all necessary elements of care, usually in a home and sometimes in an in-patient setting.

In August of 1982, the United States Congress passed the Bill to Amend Title XVIII of the Social Security Act to Provide for Coverage of Hospice Care under the Medicare Program, after showing projected savings of over $100 million to the Medicare program during the five years immediately following passage (1981). The legislation took effect in November 1983, a compromise date arrived at between the House and Senate, and is being reviewed for cost effectiveness at the time of writing. This bill affects only Medicare-eligible patients with a terminal prognosis of six months or less and who will accept only palliative treatment.

The Hospice movement generated an interest in home care. Home care is similar to hospice care in its philosophy and attitude. The primary difference is that the patient in home care need not carry a terminal prognosis.

Care at home is possible for most patients as a result of technological advances that have made it more feasible to provide such care. Requirements are: the patient/family's desire and ability to maintain the patient at home; the health care team's ability to provide active support and assurance to the family that optimal care is possible in the home; the around-the-clock availability of this care; and a realistic catchment area. The home care team must be able to provide or to educate the family or significant others to provide: pain and symptom control; continuous medical and psychosocial assessment; coordination of care; education in caregiving techniques and anticipation of patient needs for family members; counseling resources for patient and family; realistic goals for the family; assistance to families in organizing their time and sharing responsibilities (Prichard et al. 1979; Rosenbaum and Rosenbaum 1980).

The backlash against hospital care has resulted in a view of home care that is often unrealistic and romantic. It is difficult, physically, emotionally, and financially. Nonetheless, psychological and emotional growth can occur for both patient and family and it tends to lessen, on the part of the family, the sense of alienation, helplessness, hopelessness, and guilt.

The type of care and the setting in which it is to be provided should be determined by the needs of the patient and the family. Home care is not a panacea. The choice of the place for the delivery of care should be based on the patient's need and the most appropriate way to satisfy it, not on the system's needs and resources.

The best time to prepare for death is while it remains a philosophical issue rather than a near reality. Caine (1974) makes a strong case for choosing one day when families ought to review together financial matters: where stocks, vault keys, bank books, insurance and other policies, bonds, valuables, deeds, records, etc., are kept. We also feel that this is an appropriate time to talk about long-range planning for the family. Included within this is planning for the conclusion of life: wills, living wills, as well as the type of funeral desired and burial plans. Substituted judgment is always a poor second to open communication of an individual's personal desires.

Summary

Providing the opportunity for a person with terminal illness to live without indignity and die in comfort, and to enable the family to survive with peace of mind requires an effort of complex commitment. This chapter covers some, but by no means all, of the areas that must be considered if humane and appropriate care is to be provided. The emphasis has been on the need for sensitivity to the impact of treatment protocols on the patient/family unit. Of primary importance is the multidisciplinary team that initiates and maintains communication among patient, family, and staff. The patient and family have inherent strengths that can be maintained and, at times, maximized when treatment plans are tailored to the individual family unit's needs.

Our brief review of the use of behavioral medicine presents a new type of intervention. Appropriate intervention requires a knowledge of the developmental stage of the patient and the family. An attempt has been made to summarize some of the developmental milestones necessary in making an effective care plan.

Living is a process of which death is a part. The process of dying can be a time of sharing and of reflection on how the family has lived and will continue living after the death of the loved one. With the appropriate knowledge and help of the interdisciplinary team, and with the acceptance of flexible methods of care, the ultimate ideal of death without indignity is possible.

References

Agras, W. S. 1982. "Behavioral Medicine in the 1980's: Nonrandom Connections." *Journal of Consulting and Clinical Psychology* 50:797–803.

American Cancer Society, *1978 Cancer Facts and Figures,* New York, 1977.

Baldwin, A. 1982. "Cultural Awareness in Professional Education." In E. Polusny et al., eds. *Nursing and Thanatology,* New York: Arno Press, p. 85.

Barber, J. and C. Adrian. 1982. *Psychological Approaches to the Management of Pain.* New York: Brunner/Mazel.

Barber, T. X. 1963. "The Effects of Hypnosis On Pain." *Psychosomatic Medicine* 25:303–333.

Battin, M. P. 1983. "The Least Worst Death: Selective Refusal of Treatment." *The Hastings Center Report* 13(2):12–16.

Bok, S. 1978. *Lying: Moral Choice in Public and Private Life.* New York: Pantheon Books, p. 86.

Bowlby, J. 1980 *Attachment and Loss.* New York: Basic Books.

Burish, T. G. and J. N. Lyles. 1981. "Effectiveness of Relaxation Training in Reducing Adverse Reactions to Cancer Chemotherapy." *Journal of Behavioral Medicine* 4:65–78.

Caine, L. 1974. *Widow.* New York: Morrow.

Cancer Care, *Annual Report 1972–1973.*

Cancer Care. 1973. *The Impact, Costs and Consequences of Catastrophic Illness on Patients and Families.* New York, New York.

Cangello, V. W. 1962. "Hypnosis for the Patient with Cancer." *American Journal of Clinical Hypnosis* 4:215–226.

Cassell, E. J. 1982. "The Nature of Suffering and the Goals of Medicine." *New England Journal of Medicine* 306:1476–1480.

Cassem, N. 1978a. "Treatment Decisions in Irreversible Illness." In T. P. Hackett and N. H. Cassem, eds., *MGH Handbook of General Hospital Psychiatry,* pp. 562–575. St. Louis: C. V. Mosby.

Cassem, N. 1978b. "The Dying Patient." In T. P. Hackett and N. H. Cassem, eds. *MGH Handbook of General Hospital Psychiatry,* pp. 300–316. St. Louis: C. V. Mosby.

Cassileth, B. R. and J. A. Donovan. 1983. "Hospice: History and Implications of the New Legislation." *Journal of Psychosocial Oncology* 4:60.

Caughill, R. E., ed. 1979. *The Dying Patient.* Boston: Little, Brown.

Chong, T. M. 1968. "The Uses of Hypnosis in the Management of Patients with Cancer." *Singapore Medical Journal* 9:211–214.

Crasilneck, H. B. and J. A. Hall. 1973. "Clinical Hypnosis in Problems of Pain." *American Journal of Clinical Hypnosis* 3:263–273.

Craytor, J. K. 1979. "Working with Dying Patients and Their Families." In E. R. Prichard et al., eds. *Home Care Living With Dying,* pp. 37–59. New York: Columbia University Press.

Erikson, E. 1959. *Identity and the Life Cycle.* New York: International Universities Press.

Erikson, M. H. and E. L. Rossi. 1979. *Hypnotherapy—An Explanatory Casebook.* New York: Irvington Publishers.

Foley, K. M. 1979. "The Management of Pain of Malignant Origin." In H. R. Tyler and D. M. Dawson, eds. *Current Neurology,* 2:279–302. Boston: Houghton Mifflin.

Fordyce, W. E. 1976. *Behavioral Methods for Chronic Pain and Illness.* St. Louis: C. V. Mosby.

Hendler, V. 1981. *Diagnosis and Nonsurgical Management of Chronic Pain.* New York: Raven Press.

Hilgard, E. R. and J. R. Hilgard. 1975. *Hypnosis in the Relief of Pain.* Los Altos, Calif.: William Kaufmann.

Jaffe, L. 1980. "Death Education: The Use of Terminal Candor in System Change." *Advances in Thanatology* 5(1):1–26.

Kerr, F. W. L. 1981. *The Pain Book.* Englewood Cliffs, N. J.: Prentice-Hall.

Klagsbrun, S. 1977. "Communication in the Treatment of Cancer." *American Journal of Nursing* (May):944.

Kübler-Ross, E. 1975. *Death: The Final Stage of Growth.* Englewood Cliffs, N.J.: Prentice-Hall, p. 83.

Kutz, I., J. Z. Borysenko, et al. 1980. "Paradoxical Emetic Response to Antiemetic Treatment in Cancer Patients." *New England Journal of Medicine* 303:1480.

Lansky, S. B., et al. 1979. "Childhood Cancer: Non-Medical Costs of the Illness." *Cancer* 43 (1).

Lansky, S. B., J. T. Lowman, et al. 1976. "A Team Approach to Coping with Cancer. In J. W. Cullen, et al., eds. *Cancer—The Behavioral Dimensions,* pp. 291–317. New York: Raven Press.

Livingston, R. B. 1978. *Sensory Processing, Perception and Behavior.* New York: Raven Press.

Lynch, J. J. 1977. *The Broken Heart: The Medical Consequences of Loneliness.* New York: Basic Books.

Markel, W. M. and V. B. Simon. 1978. *The Hospice Concept.* American Cancer Society, Inc., p. 3.

Melamed, B. G. and L. J. Siegel. 1980. *Behavioral Medicine.* New York: Springer.

Messina, E. 1982. *The Experience of Cancer.* Annual Conference, Cancer Care, New York, October 20.

Morrow, G. R., J. C. Arseneau, et al. 1982. "Anticipatory Nausea and Vomiting with Chemotherapy." *New England Journal of Medicine* 306:431–432.

Morrow, G. R. and C. Morell. 1982. "Behavioral Treatment for the Anticipatory Nausea and Vomiting Induced by Cancer Chemotherapy." *New England Journal of Medicine* 307:1476–1480.

Murray, P. 1982. "Thanatology Education for Nurses." In E. Poslusny et al., eds. *Nursing and Thanatology,* p. 73. New York: Arno Press.

Nesse, R. M., T. Carli, et al. 1980. "Pretreatment Nausea in Cancer Chemotherapy: A Conditioned Response?" *Psychosomatic Medicine* 42:33–36.

Pomerleau, O. F. 1982. "A Discourse on Behavioral Medicine: Current Status and Future Trends." *Journal of Consulting and Clinical Psychology* 50:1030–1039.

Pomerleau, O. F. and J. P. Brady, eds. 1979. *Behavioral Medicine: Theory and Practice.* Baltimore: Williams and Wilkins.

Prichard, E. R., J. Collard, et al., eds. 1979. *Home Care: Living with Dying.* New York: Columbia University Press.

Radabough, C. and T. Radabough. 1982. "The Nurse as Image Formulator." In E. Polusny et al., eds., *Nursing and Thanatology,* p. 46. New York: Arno Press.

Redd, W. H. and M. A. Andrykowski. 1982. "Behavioral Intervention in Cancer Treatment: Controlling Aversion Reactions to Chemotherapy." *Journal of Consulting and Clinical Psychology* 50:1018–1029.

Redd, W. H., A. L. Porterfield, et al. 1979. *Behavior Modification: Behavioral Approaches to Human Problems.* New York: Random House.

Rosenbaum, E. H. and I. R. Rosenbaum. 1980. "Principles of Home Care for the Patient with Advanced Cancer." *Journal of the American Medical Association* 24(18):1484–1487.

Sanes, S. 1979. *A Physician Faces Cancer in Himself.* Albany, New York: State University Press.

Summers, D. H. 1982. "Nursing the Terminally Ill." in E. Polusny, et al., eds., pp. 64–70. *Nursing and Thanatology.* New York: Arno Press.

Truscott, J. P. 1982. "Why I Choose the Dying Patient." In E. Polusny et al., eds. *Nursing and Thanatology,* p. 13. New York: Arno Press.

U.S. Congress, House. 1981. *A Bill to Amend Title XVIII of the Social Security Act to Provide for Coverage of Hospice Care under the Medicare Program.* H.R. 5180, 97th Congress, 1st Session.

U.S. Dept. of Health and Human Services. 1980. *Coping With Cancer.* NIH Publication No. 80-2080, Sept.

Wortman, C. and C. Dunkel-Chetter. 1979. "Interpersonal Relationships with Cancer: A Theoretical Analysis." *The Journal of Social Issues* 35(1):120–155.

Preamble: Earlier formulations in Thanatology may have created the impression that terminally ill patients always know or always should be told they are dying. While patients differ greatly in their ability, need, or desire to acknowledge imminent death, the concept of "death without indignity" subsumes the right of patients to express, or not to express, their fears, hopes, gratitudes, and dissatisfactions about their fate. Therefore, absence of shared communication about dying should reflect the patient's choice or circumstances rather than the anxieties or impatience of caregivers and relatives.

Principle 7: Death Without Indignity Is Most Likely to Occur in an Atmosphere of Open Communication.

7

Death in a Context of Open Communication

ROBERT G. STEVENSON

The meaning of physician-patient communication is today so frequently taken for granted that we often forget how and why we arrived at this point. Looking at current practice in isolation from its origin may cause us to overlook possible alternative methods of dealing with the difficult situation that arises when working with a terminally ill patient. This chapter will examine the evolution and meaning of current patterns of physician-patient communication in that context and suggest how communication may aid in facilitating "death without indignity."

Doctor-patient communication in the face of terminal illness has gone through three distinct phases, all of which are reflected in both professional and popular literature. At first, physicians believed that the patient should be "spared" as long as possible. To avoid anxiety, to forestall emotional suffering, and to allow the patient to enjoy life, the physician would "carry the burden" alone, or perhaps share it with the patient's relatives. This phase ended in the 1960s with the studies of Glaser and Strauss (1965), Kübler-Ross (1969), and others, who pointed out that the patient knows more than the physician chooses to share. It was shown that many patients had accurate knowledge about their own situation despite attempts by health professionals to shield them, and that dissatisfied patients in most cases wanted more information, not less.

The second phase was seen throughout the 1970s and in the early 1980s. Following an intense but relatively short debate in professional journals, disclosure replaced denial as the standard pattern of communication. Physicians and nurses were certain that patients had to be given the whole truth about the situation so that they might deal more effectively with their own emotions and those of their loved ones and so that they might be better prepared to make necessary decisions when they arose. Denial on anyone's part became anathema. "Full disclosure" was seen as an absolute necessity in meeting professional responsibilities, both legal and humane.

Phase three represents an attempt by many to admit that there may not be only one right way to handle this difficult type of communication. Patients differ greatly in their ability, need, and desire to acknowledge imminent death. The concept of "death without indignity" includes the right of patients to express or not express their fears, hopes, gratitudes, or frustrations about their fate. A balance between the traditional patterns of the "paternalism" shown by staff and the "autonomy" that patients wished to exercise is finally emerging.

"Paternalism" dominated phase one and saw the medical staff do all that they could to further what they considered the best interests of the patient. This included making many key decisions because patients did not have the knowledge that there might, in fact, be other options. When information was imparted, the physician sought to control not only the message but also the entire situation surrounding its delivery. This type of total control was a trial for both patient and physician.

The second phase saw a sudden, and at times drastic, shift toward "autonomy." Patients were faced with an intellectual-emotional deluge of data they were expected to process so they might be better able to make many of the decisions that had previously been the responsibility of the medical staff. In some cases it almost appeared as if patients were being asked to take responsibility for decisions affecting their care in order to relieve the physician of this burden.

Out of the tension seen in this progressive balancing of paternalism and autonomy has come the model of a dynamic process of communication between physician and patient. If the physician is to allow patients to exercise their rights, one right that must be included is the right to "denial." While many patients want and need full knowledge of their situation, there are some for whom denial is the only coping strategy available. Increasingly, there are fewer "absolute" rules to guide the health care professional and each decision must rely on the trust inherent in the traditional doctor-patient relationship.

What Is Communicated

This area is often limited to a discussion of appropriate content. This usually consists of the nature of the illness, the contemplated treatment, possible side-effects, and the prognosis. However important these items of discussion may be, to start with them overlooks a major point. Communication is not a series of one-way pronouncements from doctor to patient.

The first item that must be communicated between doctor and patient is trust. Patients "trust" that physicians will respect them as individuals and use all their skills to help them in every way possible. If a doctor-patient relationship is based on financial and legal obligations, as some consumer advocates claim, then the technical expertise of the physician is all that matters. Few physicians and still fewer patients find this arrangement acceptable.

As human beings we require care and not mere maintenance. If this is to occur, physicians will need to listen to all the verbal and nonverbal communications they are receiving from their patients. After all, as Wilson (1975) pointed out, communication is *mutual* and in the give-and-take of this highly personal encounter people are more important than principles.

Once the importance of this bond of trust between physician and patient is established, attention can then be directed to what information should be communicated. Wilson (1975) stated that whatever is communicated, whether good or bad, must be the truth. Saunders (1976) pointed out that all we can give is the truth *as we see it*. That is a key point. No matter how objective we try to be, what we call "the truth" is almost always subject to interpretation. Different people, depending on their point of view, can see it in different ways. Might full disclosure cause problems as well as solve them? Such a fear has hindered communication in more than one instance. This is not a fear that the patient may lose hope or break down when faced with bad news. As Stedeford (1981) and LeRoux (1977) have stated, this rarely happens. Nevertheless, Stedeford (1981) has offered an example of needless emotional suffering caused by revealing an honest prognosis of the time left to a patient. While no one today advocates lying to a patient, there are many who would agree with LeRoux (1977) that this does not mean that one must state all the facts that are known.

The truth is often accepted only gradually by a patient. How else can we explain the need of a patient to hear the same news over and over again? Saunders (1976) pointed out that knowing the facts is not the same as believing them. Patients do not absorb at first all the information they are given. A variety of factors from anxiety to different cultural backgrounds can impair learning. In order to overcome this selective perception the physician must learn to *listen*.

Patients will communicate requests for the information they desire, including answers to both intellectual and emotional needs. Reinhold Niebuhr's famous "Serenity Prayer" has become popular with many patients who feel that it addresses their needs. It asks,

> God, give us grace to accept with serenity the things that cannot be changed, courage to change the things which should be changed, and the wisdom to distinguish the one from the other.

The philosophy in this short selection has been found beneficial by many facing life-threatening situations. However, it is often impossible for patients to sort out the information to do these things by themselves. Patients will communicate what it is they believe that they have heard. It is up to the caregiver to be alert enough to understand this communication when it occurs. If caregivers are preoccupied with *giving* information, the attempts of the patient to communicate may fall on deaf ears. Selective perception is not the province of patients alone. The caregiver might do well to employ something along the lines of Guerney's (1977) proposed "active listening" model, which uses techniques that can be easily acquired. More important than these techniques is the attitude of openness to what the other person is attempting to communicate that the model employs. In these communications, the physician as the professional in this relationship must assume more of the responsibility that the information exchanged is both accurate and truly addresses the needs of the patient. McIntosh (1974) and Stedeford both pointed out that when doctor-patient communication was blocked it was usually the fault of the physician. This breakdown in communication often occurred because the caregiver failed to ask *why* this communication was taking place, that is, to examine what each of the parties hoped to receive from it. As with "what" is to be communicated, "why" we are communicating often becomes another unexamined assumption.

Why Is It Communicated

Patients see their illness and impending death in many ways. Caregivers must be aware of what meaning these events have for each individual (patient or loved ones) with whom they communicate. For some, the approach of death is a challenge. They will summon all their resources to meet this test, and if they cannot win they can at least "fight the good fight." Others may see the situation as a series of losses to be accepted, each in its own turn, or as punishment (for some real or imaginary past misdeed) to which they must submit. The approach of death may be denied in several ways, as has been documented by Kübler-Ross (1969) and others. Nevertheless, death may even be seen as a release from a world that is seen as a "sea of troubles," a release toward which the individual may wish to hasten. To ignore these differences could have a negative impact on any doctor-patient communications.

While it is certainly true that the approach of death is merely a part of life, this type of generalization may not provide the type of insight needed by the caregiver. Physician, patient, and loved ones must constantly face a degree of uncertainty. In this society we often unrealistically demand certainty about the future. The uncertainty that accompanies illness can cause anxiety and may actually impair functioning of the immune system. Is this communication intended to diminish that uncertainty and, if so, for whom?

The patients or their loved ones are not the only ones who have difficulty dealing with uncertainty. The caregiver may have as much difficulty in dealing with the uncertainty of a given situation. It seems fair to ask to what extent this communication is intended as a relief for the physician or other caregiver. Are some communications with the patient intended primarily for the physician's benefit?

In the vast majority of cases patients want and appreciate knowledge about their condition, as Wilson (1975), Saunders (1976), Hinton (1980), Stedeford (1981) and numerous other researchers have shown. There is a danger, however, that what passes as communication may actually be a "dumping" of information on the patient. This serves the double purpose of making the patient bear a large measure of the responsibility for future decisions *and their consequences,* and of easing the physician's uncertainty about what information should be given to the patient. If all information is to be passed on, the *uncertainty* about what to communicate would be eliminated. This need not be the case in a particular communication, or even among a large number of physicians. However, the extremely emotional reaction on the part of some physicians when this question is raised suggests that it is indeed a point that should be considered.

Since there are few, if any, absolute rules about physician-patient communication beyond the legal requirement to secure "informed consent," physicians may have to accept that they will never have the certainty they might desire about what to communicate or why it is being communicated. Perhaps it will have to suffice to say that the "why" must lie with the needs of the individual patient. If physicians make every effort to meet the patient's requirements, no further rules should be necessary.

When physicians believe that they know what should be communicated and why, it may next be asked who should be a party to this communication?

Who Should Be Involved

Communications surrounding the terminally ill take on a three-way character. Lines of communication exist between professional staff and patients, between patients and concerned "others," and between these others and the professional staff. The study by Glaser and Strauss (1965) has become the model by which these lines of communication are most commonly described. They identified four "awarenesses" that can exist: open, closed, suspected, and that of mutual pretense. Open awareness, the one in which all three parties know of the patient's condition and prognosis and can speak freely about it, allows, of course, each of the parties the greatest freedom in communication.

The central figure involved in all of this communicating was the patient. With much of this important information, however, it was the patient who was often the last to know. In the best paternalistic fashion the staff and concerned others would try to spare the patient from any bad news. The patient's autonomy was almost nonexistent. After seeing the suggested benefits of open awareness for all concerned parties, a radical shift in focus occurred.

The patient was now given all the information that previously might have been held back, on the presumption that if patients were to assume this central role they would need all available information to make decisions about their own situations. It was argued that patients had a right to know their condition. By being fully informed they would not suffer the anxiety of uncertainty, and they would be better able (and more likely) to put their affairs in order. They would still be spared, if not the knowledge of their fate, then the uncertainty of being unable to anticipate possible future events or to evaluate future alternatives. The assumption behind this is that it is what the patient really wants and that the physician is bowing to the patient's autonomy.

Other studies indicate that these assumptions may be incorrect. Ley and Spelman (1967) asserted that cancer patients did not want to know their condition. As early as 1951, Shands said that only some limited knowledge should be shared with the patient. He believed in imparting only information specifically requested by the patient. Two decades later Bard (1970) came out in favor of passing on only that information that would facilitate the patient's cooperation in treatment.

Saunders (1976), drawing on her hospice experience, stated that it is not necessary for all dying patients to know they are dying. She stated that patients do not always welcome full disclosure and that harm can be done by unwelcome communication. For these patients denial has become an important, perhaps the only, coping mechanism.

The mechanisms we use in dealing with our problems are developed over many years and experiences. It does little good for caregivers to state that there are "better" coping styles if these cannot be employed by a particular patient. If denying is all that a patient has left, how can we assert that the patient "really" wishes to be told?

Hinton (1980) identified patients who concealed knowledge of their own condition from family and staff. They did not welcome "open awareness." This type of individual may be found at all age levels. Gullo (1985) has identified six coping mechanisms used by children facing life-threatening illness, one of which was the "death denier." He cautioned that the opinion of the caregiver regarding this style of coping was not nearly so important as the patient's need to use it. To use statistics in an attempt at forcing open communication on this type of patient does violence to the rights and dignity of the individual and in the long run may be of benefit to neither patient nor physician.

Stedeford (1981) examined the opinions of couples regarding the communications that they received about the condition of one of the partners. While many wished more information, others felt that they had been told more than they needed to know. The author concluded that this was because "the patient needed the defense of denial to cope with his anxiety." Other patients died without ever having discussed their illness, *as was their wish*. Whatever the opinion of the caregivers, the wishes of the individual patient were respected in these last cases. That, however, is not always the case.

Medical literature is replete with studies that cite the need to consider the social situation and personality of the individual patient in establishing guidelines for communication. Ginsberg (1949), Aitken-Swan and Easson (1959), and Wright (1960) have all supported this approach.

Nevertheless, actual practice tends to depart from this patient-centered theory, and that brings us back to the second assumption referred to above, namely, that communication is guided by the needs of the individual patient. Apparently, it is not the individual patient's need that determines communication but, as Glaser and Strauss (1965) and McIntosh (1974) have pointed out, the disposition of the individual *physician* to telling or not telling. Fitts and Ravdin (1953) found that roughly one doctor in three always or usually told patients about their conditions, while two out of three never informed their patients or did so only infrequently. The current percentages may have shifted from that early study, but if communication depends so clearly on the habits of the physician, then the needs of the patients are still not so important as physicians state they should be in determining communication.

Family members, traditionally informed before the patient, also have rights. Today patients may choose not to have family and friends fully informed, on the basis of the impact that such communication would have on the patients' coping mechanisms. Stedeford (1981) pointed out that some patients wished to be open with their families but, at the same time, wished to protect them from the bad news—a reversal of the traditional patterns. In this type of situation it is again the needs of the patient that should establish the ground rules for communication. The needs of important "others" are as real as those of the professional staff, but they are clearly secondary to those of the patient.

The theory of who should be involved in communication is clear. Patients, staff, and significant others should all be able to engage in open communication *as long as this communication meets the needs of the individual patient.* It is a practice that must be brought into line with this theory, with the patient replacing the physician as the central figure in determining who should be involved and to what extent.

How Does Communication Occur?

When caregivers have determined what they wish to communicate, to whom, and why, a new question arises: How should this communication occur? How information is communicated can not only affect the immediate reaction of the listener, but also set the tone for future communications. Included in the "how" of communication would be the way the information is given, and the setting used for this purpose.

In actuality, much of this is not consciously considered. This may explain some of the negative consequences, but an explanation is not an excuse. If there are choices that can be made by professional caregivers, and they are merely left to chance, the professional will have abrogated an important responsibility. To allow communications, which can be planned, to become a series of random, unrelated messages would be unprofessional indeed. This is not to say that doctor-patient communications cannot be spontaneous, or that all interaction must be "choreographed." Everything that can have an impact on doctor–patient communications, however, should be considered by the professional.

Clark and LeBeff (1982) described a five-part model of what they called the Tactics of Delivery: direct delivery, oblique delivery, elaborate delivery, nonverbal delivery, and conditional delivery.

Direct delivery involves telling the facts in a simple, straightforward manner. Whether this was seen as "cold" depended to a great extent on the personality of the deliverer. Oblique delivery involves setting the stage for the delivery of information, while allowing the receiver "escape routes" to avoid the information if he desires to do so. Elaborate delivery involves communication of every possible fact and with nothing omitted that has an effect on the situation. Nonverbal delivery conveys news by not saying anything. Body language and awkward silence are sometimes allowed to say as much as words might. Finally, in conditional delivery, the deliverer waits until the receiver provides appropriate clues to initiate the communication.

Of all the techniques, those most commonly used by physicians and nurses are elaborate and nonverbal delivery. Communications from medical professionals are often filled with what the layperson regards as incomprehensible jargon. Medical language has been used as a shield by those in the profession to protect them from unwanted expressions of emotion. Receivers are flooded with information (much of which is incomprehensible) while their ability to absorb anything is impaired by their understandable anxiety. Elaborate delivery meets the needs of the professional to communicate some information, but is not based in more than a marginal way on the needs of the recipient.

Nonverbal delivery uses paralinguistics to convey information that the deliverer is unable, or unwilling, to put into words. Patients and family know the area of concern as soon as they enter a doctor's office or a hospital. They must wait to see physicians (it is never the other way around), and they must go to the doctor's territory to ask for news. The patient is clearly not the one in charge in this situation. Finally, they search for clues in body language and facial expression. If they blurt out what they fear because of some nonverbal cue, it is they who have introduced this unfortunate news. The physician is absolved of the need to say it first.

An alternative is to use nonverbal communication, wherein the deliverer, say, can move around desks or tables. Information can be presented in a neutral atmosphere, or one where the receiver feels secure. If individuals are to be assisted in living the balance of their lives outside of the hospital, the house call is still appropriate and may be especially valuable in assisting in death without indignity. Even facial expression and body language can be employed with the needs of the receiver of the information in mind, rather than the fears or concerns of the caregiver.

The techniques described above have been developed by caregivers over time. The one a particular physician will choose is based as much on habit as anything else. If it is perceived as successful in one or more occasions it will likely become standard procedure. The physician thus comes upon a style almost by chance, choosing one according to the initial reactions of others. The same professionals who are so assertive in other areas do not assert their authority in this area, where it could perhaps be most effective.

Physicians and nurses have specific requirements regarding the way they would want information presented if they were the patients. These same requirements could serve as an effective starting point for the construction of a delivery technique based on the needs of patients and their loved ones. The hours devoted to conscious development of this technique would be well spent.

Summary

The main points of this chapter are that in the past physicians routinely chose to withhold certain information about their condition from terminally ill patients. This practice has changed as physicians have become aware that the majority of patients want and need much more information than they might have been given previously. This "open communication" works for the benefit of both physician and patient and can enhance the bond of trust between them that is so essential.

In this open communication it is the needs of the individual patient that are primary; those of the physician and concerned others are secondary. This is especially important when one is facing a situation involving terminal illness. Physicians must be aware that this order of priorities gives the individual patient the right to have open communication and also the right to *reject* it. To rule out a patient's denial (whether full or partial) as a possible coping mechanism would be to resubjugate patient autonomy to the paternalistic "certainty" of the physician as to the correct course of action.

When all of this is considered, it may then be stated that death without indignity is most likely to occur in a context of open communication.

References

Aitken-Swan, J., and E. C. Easson. 1959. "Reactions of Cancer Patients on Being Told of Their Diagnosis." *British Medical Journal,* 779–783.

Anderson, J. L. 1979. "A Practical Approach to Teaching About Communication with Terminal Cancer Patients." *Journal of Medical Education* 54:823–824.

Bard, M. 1970. "The Price of Survival for Cancer Victims." In A. Strauss, ed., *Where Medicine Fails,* Chicago: Aldine.

Clark, R. E. and E. E. LaBeff. 1982. "Death Telling: Managing the Delivery of Bad News." *Journal of Health and Social Behavior* 23:366–380.

Davidson, G. P. 1981. "Talking with the Terminally Ill: Grief and Care of a Particular Kind." *Australian Family Physician* 10:520–526.

Fitts, W. T., and I. S. Ravdin. 1957. "What Philadelphia Physicians Tell Patients About Cancer." *Journal of the American Medical Association* 165:901.

Ginsberg, R. 1949. "Should the Elderly Cancer Patient Be Told?" *Geriatrics* 4:101.

Glaser, B. G. and A. L. Strauss. 1965. *Awareness of Dying*. Chicago: Aldine.

Gluck, M. 1977. "Overcoming Stresses in Communicating with the Fatally Ill." *Military Medicine* 142:926–928.

Griffiths, J. 1979. "When a Patient Talks About Death." *Nursing Mirror* 149:35–37.

Guerney, B. 1977. *Relationship Enhancement.* San Francisco: Jossey-Bass.

Gullo, S. V. 1985. "On Understanding and Coping with Death During Childhood." In S. V. Gullo et al., eds., *Death and Children: A Guide for Educators, Parents and Caregivers,* Dobbs Ferry, N.Y.: Tappan Press.

Hinton, J. 1980. "Whom Do Dying Patients Tell?" *British Medical Journal* 281:1328–1330.

Hurley, B. A. 1977. "Problems of Interaction Between Nurses and Dying Patients: Certainty of Death." *Communicating Nursing Research* 9:223–235.

Krant, M. J. 1974. *Dying and Dignity: The Meaning and Control of a Personal Death.* Springfield, Ill: Charles C. Thomas.

Krant, M. J. and L. Johnston. 1977–78. "Family Members' Perceptions of Communications in Late Stage Cancer." *International Journal of Psychiatry and Medicine* 8:203–216.

Kübler-Ross, E. 1969. *On Death and Dying*. New York: Macmillan.

Kübler-Ross, E. 1975. *Death: The Final Stage of Growth*. Englewood Cliffs, N.J.: Prentice-Hall.

LeRoux, R. S. 1977. "Communicating with the Dying Person." *Nursing Forum* 16:145–155.

Ley, P. and M. S. Spelman. 1967. *Communicating with the Patient*. New York: Staples Press.

MacNamara, M. 1974. "Talking with Patients: Some Problems Met by Medical Students." *British Journal of Medical Education* 8:17–23.

Marshall, V. W. 1980. *Last Chapters: A Sociology of Aging and Dying*. Monterey, CA: Brooks/Cole.

McIntosh, V. W. 1974. "Processes of Communication, Information Seeking and Control Associated With Cancer: A Selective Review of the Literature." *Social Science and Medicine* 8:167–187.

Parkes, C. M. 1974. "Comment: Communication and Cancer—A Social Psychiatrist's View." *Social Science and Medicine* 8:189–190.

Saunders, C. M. 1976. "Care of the Dying 3: Should a Patient Know. . .?" *Nursing Times* 72:1089–1091.

Shands, H. C., et al. 1951. "Psychological Mechanisms in Patients with Cancer." *Cancer* 4:1159–1170.

Stedeford, A. 1981. "Couples Facing Death." *British Medical Journal* 283:1098–1101.

Webster, M. E. 1981. "Communicating with Dying Patients." *Nursing Times* 77:999–1002.

Wilson, J. M. 1975. "Communicating with the Dying." *Journal of Medical Ethics* 1:18–22.

Wright, B. A. 1960. *Physical Disability—A Psychological Approach*. New York: Harper and Row.

Preamble: The capacity of one person to form an affiliation with another carries with it the potential for grief and mourning when that affiliation or relationship is broken. These reactions can be observed even in the very young child. Thus, there is nothing unusual or abnormal about grief and mourning among relatives after the death of a loved person.

Principle 8: Grief Is a Normal Response to the Death of a Loved One

8

Grief Is a Normal Response to the Death of a Loved One

MARGOT TALLMER

In common parlance, grief is an intensely personal, deeply felt, natural sorrow occasioned by the loss of a highly important love object or an experience of traumatic misfortune. The sorrow accompanying grief is assumed to be painful but time-related, uncomfortable but necessary.

Within the relevant psychological literature, the concepts of bereavement, grief, and mourning are frequently assumed to be interchangeable. Professional definitions actually only refine and translate lay conceptions of these events and the human responses to them into less comprehensible language. For example, grief has been described as follows:

> The usual underlying process observed in the reaction to meaningful loss is mourning, and the subjective experience or feeling of the bereaved person is grief. The term mourning is used to describe the normal, adaptive, psychological healing processes that are initiated by the loss, and *grief,* to describe the subjective state that accompanies mourning.

Freud stated that the function of mourning "is to detach the survivors' memories and hopes from the dead. When this has been achieved the pain grows less and with it the remorse and self reproach." One of the primary functions of mourning is to permit the withdrawal of emotional attachment from the object and allow for attachments to new objects.

Grief is viewed as a process containing various emotional components (shock, disorganization, denial, desolate pining, despair, guilt, anxiety, aggression, resolution and reintegration) (Hodgkinson 1982).

Psychic pain attendant upon the work of mourning and mourning is the set of internal adaptations people make in the moderately brief period following the death of a significant person in order to integrate the changed reality they confront (Palombo 1981).

1. Mourning is a normal transformational adaptive process experienced by all people throughout history.
2. This mourning process has its own line of development, beginning in early life and reaching its maturity after adolescence when the psychic apparatus is fully developed.
3. The mourning process has evolved phylogenetically as an adaptive means of dealing with loss, disappointment, and change.
4. Bereavement, the specific reaction to the death of a meaningful object, is a sub-class of the mourning process (Pollock 1978:273).

Although a considerable part of this discussion will deal with the grief that follows the loss of a significant person, there are clearly other deprivations with the power to evoke grief reactions: loss of body parts, wealth, reputation, status, and the relinquishment of aspirations and fantasies. Lamentably few studies other than those by Fried (1962) and Marris (1974) have documented theeffects of losses other than death. Stillbirth, for example, has been accorded only slight scrutiny despite increasing evidence of intense grief reactions (Lewis and Page 1978; Kirkley-Best and Kellner 1982; LaRoche et al. 1982). Parents of impaired children are known to suffer extended, nonpathological grief reactions (Kornblum and Anderson 1982). The grief of those bereaved by the death of a loved one continues to attract the most frequent study, and the effects of spousal bereavement in older women have received particular attention.

Why has this group of bereaved individuals been studied so

often? Clearly, widowhood is an easily documented state, begun at a specific point in time. Futhermore, the wife's chances of being the surviving partner are far greater than the husband's. Women are sensitive and alert to the possibilities of widowhood, often rehearsing the situation with their friends. Except for deaths during wartime, widowhood is probably the most frequently occurring grief state in our society. Many of our theoretical notions about grief come from studies of widows.

Grief, then, is a normal, complex, active, expected process that proceeds apace like any other life-cycle phenomenon—backwards and forwards in discontinuous steps—but is, optimally, self-healing and limited in time, although often accompanied by an alteration of one's view of the world and one's social status. The internal representation of an environment that includes the lost loved object must be transformed to conform with the external reality of the loss. To be grieving in a normal fashion means to be unhappy. Psychological symptoms may include general subjective distress, depression, uncontrolled crying, loneliness, irritability, and debilitating anxiety. Tightness in the throat, shortness of breath, sighing, loss of appetite, loss of sleep and emotional waves lasting from twenty minutes to one hour may be physical manifestations of grief (Bugen 1977). Grief and mourning, in some form, appear to be universal phenomena, with culturally varied means of expression. Diverse groups have been observed to experience different, intense grief reactions. Grief rituals and behavior naturally vary considerably among ethnic and religious groups, but pain and distress are universally acknowledged and are met with strong community moves toward the bereaved. Groups that deny the experience of sorrow ("Samoans do not have such things," Ablou 1971) nevertheless make compensatory efforts toward survivors.

Theoretical Considerations

Freud did not greatly concern himself with the issue of grief, believing this to be an issue secondary to the more severe problems of melancholia and depression. In an attempt to differentiate normal grief (mourning) from morbid grief (melancholia), a distinction necessary for diagnosis and intervention, he characterized normal grief as a profound lack of interest in the environment (insofar as it was not directly connected to the deceased), an inhibition of activity, painful feelings of dejection, and an inability to adopt and relate to new love objects. Mourning was said to be a response to the loss of an important love object or to the "loss of some abstraction which has taken the place of one, such as one's country, liberty, an ideal and so on" (Freud 1959). Melancholia or morbid grief was marked by all of the above plus a lowering of self-esteem and ambivalent feelings toward the deceased, feelings not present in mourning. For Freud, grief work meant the painful, natural dissolving (decathexis) of each tie with the deceased.

Both Abraham (1949) and Fenichel (1945) assumed a lowering of self-esteem to be present in both mourning and depression. The degree of regression was the important distinction for Fenichel, with regression being assumed to be of greater dimension in depression than in grief. According to this theorist, the grieving process starts with the psychic introjection of the lost object. Feelings are then directed toward the mental image one has of the deceased. This process serves the griever as a buffering mechanism, enabling gradual relinquishment of the ties. (In passing, it may be noted that the adaptiveness of the slow, gradual letting-go espoused by Fenichel is in direct contrast to modern crisis intervention, wherein the bereaved is often enjoined to resume task-oriented behavior more quickly, leaving little time for this prolonged step-by-step loosening of the ties.)

It is significant that Freud, Abraham, Fenichel, and Melanie Klein—all psychoanalysts and all concerned with intrapsychic states of the individual—derived their notions about grief from pathological case studies. Of the major theorists, Bowlby (1980) alone studied mourning, albeit confining himself to children, and developed pioneering, stimulating ideas on attachment and loss in children. According to Bowlby, separation from the mother leads to three reactive stages: protest (separation anxiety), despair (grief and mourning), and detachment (defense). The reaction of anger is seen as central to loss. In further delineation and refinement, he posits four phases in mourning: (1) numbing; (2) the urge to recover the lost object; (3) disorganization and despair; (4) reorganization.

In the initial phase, numbing persists from a few hours up to a week. Most people are stunned for a while, carrying on activities in a rote, reflexive way. There may be breakthroughs of extreme emotion. In phase 2, there are vigorous efforts to recover the lost object; anger and weeping are adaptive, enticing the mother to return. Evidences of anger and resentment also indicate that the separation is not seen as permanent. During phase 3, this last bit of denial is no longer possible and despair and depression ensue. Self-regard is diminished and the world too is viewed as poor and empty (Solomon 1977). Familiar behavior patterns are no longer part of the response repertoire. Phase 4 incorporates the healthy reactions, with new behavior patterns developed for improved interpersonal relations.

Ambivalence is not a particular part of Bowlby's theories, for the connection with the lost person is seen as totally supportive and positive. Grief is explained in terms of separation anxiety, a very early childhood derivative, and its purpose is often not the psychoanalytic one, to detach oneself from the deceased, but rather to enhance the chance of reunion. Maintaining proximity is the aim, and behavior that has advanced that prospect in the past is evoked (Glick et al. 1974:8).

So far this discussion has developed from work based upon psychoanalytic thinking with a psychodynamic orientation. Empirical data have not been forthcoming to any great extent; generally, acute grief has not been examined in a laboratory setting, but rather has been detailed through reports of pathological case studies. Systematic observations describing normal grief are provided by Lindemann (1944), and Parkes (1972).

Observations of Grief Responses

Lindemann's widely cited work, which was derived from clinical experiences with bereaved survivors of the Coconut Grove fire in

Boston and has been a model for crisis interventions, dealt with persons whose lives were considerably changed by the event. He describes the acute reaction to bereavement, normal grief:

> The picture shown by persons in acute grief is remarkably uniform. Common to all is the following syndrome: sensation of somatic distress occurring in waves lasting from twenty minutes to one hour at a time, feelings of tightness in the throat, choking with shortness of breath, need for sighing, an empty feeling in the abdomen, lack of muscular power, and an intense subjective distress described as tension or mental pain (Lindemann 1944).

Solomon (1977) has noted methodological drawbacks to Lindemann's work: the criteria for normality were not delineated, only acute grief was examined, and a representative sample of persons who were grieving was clearly unavailable. Additionally, no description of his sample was provided other than that the loss resulted from a sudden violent death (Jacobs and Douglas 1979:167). Lindemann's predictions for recovery may have been sanguine, for grief work was said to be followed by improvement after only a few weeks.

Attention was drawn, however, to major themes in acute grief: somatic distress; initial denial; probable guilt (the bereaved person stresses minor omissions in behavior toward the deceased) and anger; an identification with the lost object. Abnormal grief is viewed as an exaggeration, in duration and intensity, of the symptons of normal grief with the additional presence of self-destructive urges.

Marris (1958) studied a group of 72 bereaved widows in London who were interviewed two years after their spouses' deaths. By and large, they viewed their present lives as futile and empty:

> They had in large measure withdrawn from earlier interests and social ties, many had become dependent upon their immediate families, and many seemed apathetic in relation to their immediate lives. Insomnia and loss of weight were frequent symptoms among them; about a third thought their health had been impaired (Glick et al. 1974:5).

In a later study, Parkes used this description by Marris to broadly characterize normal grief, despite the evident limitations of

Marris' work; that is, the use of retrospective data altered by time and memory loss; the exclusive dependence on a sample of women under the age of sixty; and possible bias in sample selection.

Parkes used Bowlby's and Engel's work, as well as that of Lindemann and Marris, to examine and analyze grief reactions. Engel, supported in his view by Bowlby, had compared grief to a pathological state—i.e.,disease, abnormal in the sense of total health: "the experience of uncomplicated grief also represents a manifest and gross departure from the dynamic state considered representative of health and well-being" (Engel 1961:20).

Parkes argued that grief reactions are functional mental disorders because of the resulting dysfunctionality and discomfort: "I know of only one functional psychiatric disorder whose cause is known, whose features are distinctive, and whose course is usually perdictable, and that is grief, the reaction to loss (Parkes 1971:6)."

Parkes then described normal grief:

> At first the full reaction may be delayed or there may be a period of numbness or blunting in which the bereaved person acts as if nothing had happened for a few hours or days up to two weeks—thereafter attacks of yearning and distress with autonomic disturbance begin. These occur in waves and are aggravated by reminders of the deceased. Between attacks the bereaved person is depressed and apathetic with a sense of futility. Associated symptoms are insomnia, anorexia, restlessness, irritability with occasional outburst of anger directed against others or the self, and preoccupation with thoughts of the deceased. The dead person is commonly felt to be present and there is a tendency to think of him as if he was still alive and to idealize his memory—the features are not typically so severe that they cause the patient to seek help from a psychiatrist, miss more than a fortnight's work, attempt suicide, or isolate himself to such a degree that he becomes unaccessible to relatives and friends.

Parkes (1972) believed that all bereaved persons exhibit the following list of behaviors:

1. Alarm, tension, and a high state of arousal
2. Restless movement
3. Preoccupation with thoughts of the lost person
4. Development of a perceptual set for that person
5. Loss of interest in personal appearance and other matters

that normally occupy attention

6. Direction of attention toward those parts of the environment in which the lost person is likely to be

7. Calling for the lost person

All except the first two items are part of the searching stage, the second stage.

According to Parkes, the pining or separation anxiety, a subjective acccompaniment of the alarm reaction, is demonstrated in restless hyperactivity that is purposeful to the extent that it aims at locating the missing person. One cannot easily admit to such irrational motives for restlessness and the behavior is often labeled aimless. Further, he suggested that the constant maintenance of a clear image of the deceased provides a continual perceptual set for reemergence, with such a set often leading to misperceptions as one scans the environment. An excited sighting or hearing of the deceased is all too common an experience. This constant imagery deprives mourners of energy for other tasks, as they try to occupy only the formerly shared territory between themselves and the lost love object. Clothing, furniture, and objects related to the deceased are retained and visits to the grave are frequent. Crying out for the deceased, the last item on the list, reflects impotence and evokes needed sympathy.

The mitigation stages consist of methods to assuage grief by sustaining the comforting feeling that the bereaved is present.

> That "searching" and "finding" go together is not surprising. A "sense of the continued presence of the deceased," "a clear visual memory of him," and "preoccupation with thoughts of him" were statistically associated; that is to say, widows with a strong sense of their husbands' presence also tended to recall them with greater clarity and to be preoccupied with memories of them. All these phenomena, which have been referred to as components of searching, are also components of finding. (Parkes 1972)

Clearly, these two concepts, searching and finding, are interrelated; one searches, pines, feels a presence, is comforted, realizes it is false, and recommences to pine. Other efforts at mitigation include denial, splitting, numbness or blunting, and eschewing all reminders of the deceased, even avoiding persons or environments that will evoke memories. At the same time there is a preoccupation with the events before the death—to understand, comprehend, classify, and try to fit the trauma into some orderly sense of the world. Anger and irritability seem to be part of the process of grieving; the bereaved reacts as if in a continual state of danger. Death is a punishment inflicted by cruel doctors, who have failed to make a correct diagnosis or prescribe treatment, or death is inflicted by God. Parkes' view of grief, then, is of bringing the external reality and inner world into agreement, with modification of the internal world accomplished only gradually.

To recapitulate, grief is a process marked by a progression of changes or phases: the first phase is a period of numbness; the second phase is characterized by separation anxiety, marked by preoccupying thoughts of the lost loved object along with the emotional factor of pining. Searching for the deceased is based on need to recover the lost person. Angry protest and crying are part of the phase. The above-mentioned numbness has been described in relation to children, and we certainly empirically witness such a phenomenon elsewhere—e.g., Lifton (1973) noted a process of psychic numbness and brutalization, a deadening of the senses, for soldiers in Vietnam.

Disorganization of behavior patterns as a result of apathy and despair mark the beginning of the next phase. As separation anxiety diminishes, so does anger. Feelings of depression are in evidence. As the depression diminishes and identification with the deceased appears, the bereaved person loosens the old and acquires new roles.

Much of Parkes' work agrees with Bowlby's observations. Parkes augmented the original sample of 43 by studying the psychiatric charts of 94 other subjects (1982). The phasic divisions are not so clearly defined as separate entities as one might surmise from the above outline; there is blending and overlapping. Others have suggested the existence of stages. Kavanaugh, for example, has identified seven: shock, disorganization, volatile emotions, guilt, loss and loneliness, relief, and reestablishment (1977). Kübler-Ross has accounted for the grieving process in five phases: denial, anger guilt, preparatory guilt, and the "goodbye" stage (1969). None of these must be experienced in their proper order, nor must all of them be experienced. But it is agreed that the loss sets off a progressive chain of reactions, not distinct in nature, but active and evolving, and in normal cases decreasing in intensity over time.

It is imperative to stress the adaptive, positive transformational aspects of the grieving process. No pathological phenomenon at all, grief offers the bereaved an acceptable coping mechanism, providing a temporary respite from the demands of everyday life. The length of time needed to adjust to a radically new lifestyle, to relinquish former bonds, and to adopt new ones will vary among individuals, but the process cannot be too telescoped without ensuing difficulties. "It is the progress of the course of grief that is the deciding factor and not necessarily the length of time it takes" (Hendin 1974:154). Thus time itself is a necessary but not sufficient factor; the outcome will depend upon the use of the time.

Certainly estimates of the temporal dimensions of grief vary considerably. Lindemann estimated that four to eight weeks are required for successful recovery. Marris extended the period, often indefinitely, and Parkes considered six months to be about average. Hardt (1978–79) adjudged eight months as appropriate. In general, although investigators set one year as the natural time for working through, with the second year as the upper limit, grief work time may take many years (Jacobs and Douglas 1979). The one-year limit is an obvious time allotment; during the course of the first 12 months, the griever goes through the first Christmas, first anniversary, birthdays, and the like.

The healing time depends upon survivors' age and sex and on their financial and social environments. The ability to adjust to a new environment, the degree of dependency and ambivalence in the relationship, the ease with which the grieving person deals with affect, and the support system offered to the bereaved are also important. The cause of death—sudden or after a long illness—may alter the grief process. A lengthy ailment may generate distinctive periods of acute grief, either at the time of the serious diagnosis or when the patient becomes aware of his terminality. Bereavement is also affected when the death occurs far from home as the risks are greater if survivors are not in their own residence. The reasons for the death may also play a part: was the deceased in any way responsible for the demise? We now see interesting grief reactions to death from AIDS. Victims are frequently viewed as being responsible for their illness: guilty because of participation in a different lifestyle, or punished because of promiscuous homosexuality.

The age of the dying person is another key issue in the time limits of expressed grief. Elderly persons are frequently, and mistakenly, viewed as having lived a reasonable length of time, and their departure is not seen as causing too much upheaval; the death of a young person is viewed as tragic. Thus, persons very much grieved by the loss of an elderly parent often are not accorded societal privilege to mourn, although the death may be traumatic for the survivor. The *type* and meaning of the relationships between the bereaved and the deceased are of *major* significance, however, no matter what the chronological ages may be. "The death of someone much loved does not cause intense grief if the relationship is no longer central to one's life. Married children, for instance, do not usually grieve deeply for the death of an elderly parent, though they may feel sorrow and miss him or her" (Parkes and Stevenson-Hinde 1982:196). This is because loss of meaning, not the loss of the love object, provokes grief.

In our discussion of the empirical data that are available in regard to grief, we noted that the observations made were largely confined to widowed older women. Since grief cannot be simulated in a laboratory experiment, data are based largely on self reports. Our ability to deal with children is due partially to the amnesic data available from adults, from inferential conclusions based on empirical data and observations of children, and from theoretical notions of childhood and adolescence.

Adults, however, vary much more from each other than children do, and pinpointing their responses to grief is more difficult than with youngsters. We have witnessed certain psychological responses, most of which have been delineated in the Bowlby and Parkes work. We have also considered the grief process in toto, examining both the bereaved's personality alterations and their affective bonds with the dead person. In one study on crib death (sudden infant death syndrome) (Rubin 1981), for example, the emotional ties to the deceased child remained as important parts of the mothers' lives, but the personality changes in the mother diminished over time.

What are these affects and personality changes that are experienced? The most commonly observed emotion, seemingly intrinsic to the grieving process, is the feeling of guilt—guilt proportional to the amount of felt hostility and death wishes toward the bereaved; and past evidences of mistreatment of the dead person—resentment, arguments, and the like—are paraded out for fresh review and add to the guilt. In certain circumstances, survivor guilt ("Why she and not me?") is also in evidence; as an example, concentration camp victims who often maneuvered to avoid death are beset by feelings of guilt for these strategies and do not wish to acknowledge strong drives toward survival. They also question why they were spared if they did nothing to ensure their safety. Parents lament that they lived when their children, so much younger, had to die. Guilt can also be evoked by the sense of relief and liberation the death releases; if the deceased had been a burden, psychologically or physically dependent over an extended length of time, the death may free the survivor from unwanted burdens. The relief can exacerbate guilt. The feeling of having been abandoned oftimes leads to expressed experiences of anger and hostility; when there is a depressive characteristic to the grief, it is related to anger (Jacobson 1957).

In summary, unconscious feelings include separation anxiety, ambivalence, guilt, and hostility, covert or expressed. Feelings of abandonment are a major threat to the self. Adjustment difficulties are increased when the ambivalence is relatively greater than acknowledged. Identification with the deceased is more difficult where hostility is felt or when the survivor is afraid to identify: for example, a mother's death is often harder for a daughter than for a son, as the girl does not want to identify with a female who has died early.

Coping with Grief

Because our knowledge of the biological and emotional effects of grief has only recently been expanded, methods for coping have been only minimally developed. Folk wisdom and custom have dictated how individuals can best be supported; we are now documenting observations and coping mechanisms. Naturally the ability to survive emotional crises or stress is enhanced by parents, friends, or others who are able to address the bereaved's needs, including the airing of conflicts and problems. The young, in particular, need to be able to verbalize their fantasies, feelings, and reactions.

The most important factor in dealing with grief experienced at any point in the life span is the sharing of grief with another person (Simos 1979). Furthermore, others can most importantly affect the outcome of the grief work. A perceived lack of support in the established social network is correlated with a poor outcome, and the perceptions and ratings of this nonsupportiveness are generally accurate. The accepted mourning rituals of the society, of course, also shape the response of the bereaved and the pattern of the grief.

According to Engel (1980–81) there is a certain autonomy to grief. As with the healing of any wound, this healing process follows a sequence, with longing, loneliness, rage, guilt, shame, challenge, and frustration elements in the process. An articulated understanding of the grieving process that is relevant to the particular person reinforces for the bereaved that his experiences are expectable and normal.

References

Ablou, J. 1971. "Bereavement in a Samoan Community." *British Journal of Medical Psychology* 44:329–337.

Abraham, A. 1949. "A Short Study of the Development of the Libido: Viewed in the Light of Mental Disorders." In *Selected Papers on Psychoanalysis*. London: Hogarth Press.

Achte, K. A. and J. Lonnquist. 1971. "Death and Suicide in Finnish Mythology and Folklore." *Psychat. Fenuca*, (Yearbook,) pp. 59–63.

Bowlby, J. 1963. "Pathological Mourning and Childhood Mourning." *Journal of the American Psychoanalytic Association* 11:500–541.

Bowlby, J. 1980. "Sadness and Depression." *Attachment and Loss*, Vol. 3. New York: Basic Books.

Bugen, L. 1977. "Human Grief—A Model for Prediction and Intervention." *American Journal of Orthopsychiatry* 4:196–206.

Cavenar, J. O., N. Butts, J. G. Spaulding. 1978. "Grief: Normal or Abnormal?" *North Carolina Medical Journal* 39:31–34.

Engel, G. E. 1961. "Is Grief a Disease?" *Psychosomatic Medicine* 23:18–22.

Engel, G. E. 1980–81. "A Group Dynamic Approach to Teaching and Learning About Grief." *Omega* 11:45–59.

Fenichel, O. 1945. *The Psychosomatic Theory of Neuroses*. New York: Norton.

Fortes, M. 1977. "Custom and Conscience in Anthropological Perspective." *International Review* PSA 4:127–154.

Frankel, S. and D. Smith. 1982. "Conjungal Bereavement Amongst the Huli People of Papua New Guinea." *British Journal of Psychiatry* 141:302–305.

Freud, S. 1957. "Mourning and Melancholia." (1917). In *Standard Edition of the Complete Psychological Works of Sigmund Freud,* vol. 14. London: Hogarth Press.

Fried, M. 1962. "Grieving for a Lost Home." In L. J. Duhl, ed. *The Environment of the Metropolis,* New York: Basic Books.

Glick, I. O., R. S. Weiss, and C. M. Parkes. 1974. *The First Year of Bereavement.* New York: John Wiley.

Goldberg, H. S. 1981–82. "Funeral and Bereavement Rituals of Kota Indians and Orthodox Jews." *Omega: Journal of Death and Dying.* 12:117–128.

Hardt, D. V. 1978–79. "An Investigation of the Stages of Bereavement." *Omega* 9:279–285.

Hendin, D. 1974. *Death as a Fact of Life*. New York: Warner Paperback Library.

Hodgkinson, P. E. 1982. "Abnormal Grief—The Problem of Therapy." *British Journal of Medical Psychology* 55:29–34.

Howard, A. and R. Scott. 1965–66. "Cultural Values and Attitudes Towards Death." *Journal of Existentialism* 6:161–171.

Jacobs, S. and L. Douglas. 1979. "Grief: A Mediating Process Between a Loss and Illness." *Comprehensive Psychiatry* vol. 20: pp. 165–176.

Jacobson, E. 1957. "On Normal and Pathological Mood." *Psychoanalytic Study of the Child.* New York: International Universities Press, p. 12.

Kavanaugh, R. 1971. *Facing Death*. Baltimore: Penguin Books.

Kirkley-Best, E. and K. R. Kellner. 1982. "The Forgotten Grief: A Review of the Psychology of Stillbirth." *American Journal of Orthopsychiatry* 52 (July): 420–429.

Kornblum, H. and B. Anderson. 1982. "'Acceptance' Reassessed: A Point of View." *Child Psychiatry and Human Development* 12:171–178.

Krupp, G. R. and B. Kligfeld. 1962. "Bereavement Reaction: A Cross Cultural Evaluation." *Journal of Religion and Health* 1:222–246.

Kübler-Ross, E. 1969. *On Death and Dying*. New York: Macmillan.

Laroche, C. et al. 1982. "Grief Reactions to Perinatal Death: An Exploratory Study." *Psychosomatics* 23:510–518.

Lewis, E. and A. Page. 1978 . "Failure to Mourn a Stillbirth: An Overlooked Catastrophe." *British Journal of Medical Psychology* 51:237–241.

Lifton, R. J. 1973. *Home from the War.* New York: Simon and Schuster.

Lindemann, E. 1944. "Symptomatology and Management of Acute Grief." *American Journal of Psychiatry* 101:141–148.

Marris, P. 1974. *Loss and Change.* New York: Pantheon.

Massamba, J. and R. Kalish. 1976. "Death and Bereavement: The Role of the Black Church." *Omega* 7:23–34.

Matchett, W. F. 1972. "Repeated Hallucinatory Experience as Part of Mourning Process Among Hopi Indian Women." *Psychiatry* 35:184–194.

Palombo, J. 1981. "Parent Loss and Childhood Bereavement: Some Theoretical Considerations." *Clinical Social Work Journal* 9:3–33.

Parkes, C. M. 1972. *Bereavement: Studies of Grief in Adult Life.* New York: International Universities Press.

Parkes, C. M. and J. Stevenson-Hinde. 1982. *The Place of Attachment in Human Behavior.* New York: Basic Books.

Pollock, G. H. 1961. "Mourning and Adaptation." *International Journal of Psychoanalysis* 42:341–361.

—— 1978. "Process and Affect: Mourning and Grief . . ." *International Journal of Psychoanalysis* 59:255–276.

Raphael, B. 1978. "Mourning and the Prevention of Melancholia." *British Journal of Medical Psychology* 51:303–310.

Rubin, S. 1981. "A Two-Track Model of Bereavement: Theory and Application in Research." *American Journal of Orthopsychiatry* 51:101–109.

Schoenberg, B. 1977. "Grief in General Practice." In R. Wittkower and H. Warnes, eds. *Psychosomatic Medicine,* pp. 67–74. New York: Harper and Row.

Schoenberg, B., I. Gerber, A. Wiener, A. H. Kutscher, D. Peretz, and A. C. Carr, eds. 1975. *Bereavement: Its Psychosocial Aspects.* New York: Columbia University Press.

Simos, B. G. 1977. "A Time to Grieve." New York: Family Service Association.

Solomon, H. 1977. "Grief and Bereavement." *International Journal of Social Psychiatry* 3:211–222.

Spiegel, D. 1981. "Vietnam Grief Work Among Hypnosis." *American Journal of Clinical Hypnosis* 24:33–40.

Weinstein, E. A. 1961. *Cultural Aspects of Delusion.* Glencoe, Ill.: Free Press.

Wilson, M. 1957. *Rituals of Kinship Among the Nyakyusa.* London: Oxford University Press.

Preamble: Bereaved persons should not be exploited; nor should they have to experience undue loss to their own self-esteem. These goals are most likely to be achieved when the bereaved have had information concerning the illness and treatment of the patient, when the patient has experienced death without indignity, and when communication surrounding the patient's dying has been marked by clarity, candor, and compassion.

Principle 9: Bereaved Persons Have Rights That Should Be Respected

9

The Rights of the Bereaved

ELIZABETH J. CLARK

Along with advanced medical technology have come the possibilities of prolonging life and of prolonging death—possibilities that have led to various ethical issues concerning patients' rights and the control of death.

The past two decades have witnessed the right-to-die movement, the hospice movement, brain-death legislation, and the advent of living wills. Since 1975, a number of right-to-die cases have been decided in the courts. These include the Quinlan case in New Jersey, the Saikewicz case in Massachusetts, and the Severns case in Delaware (Society for the Right to Die 1982). Opinions have generally upheld the right to have treatment terminated.

As early as 1973, the American Hospital Association approved a "Patient's Bill of Rights" (see for example, Gaylin 1973), which included the right to informed consent and the right to refuse treatment. In 1975, "The Dying Patient's Bill of Rights" was published in the *American Journal of Nursing*. Among other issues, this included the right to freedom from pain and the right to die in peace and dignity.

With few exceptions, the current legislation and the proposed bills of rights give scant attention to concern for the patient's family and their needs that occur because of the patient's death. What are, or what should be, the rights of the bereaved persons form the basis of this chapter.

Anticipatory Grief

For many bereaved persons, the problems of loss and grief do not begin at the time of death, but start during the period of anticipatory grief that follows notification of the patient's unfavorable prognosis (Kutscher 1970). Technology has extended death from an act to a process that can take weeks or months. This extended time interval has increased the period of anticipatory grief. Glaser and Strauss outlined the process of dying in their list of "critical junctures" that take place during the course of dying (1968:7):

1. The patient is defined as dying;
2. staff and family members make preparation for the patient's death;
3. the stage of "nothing more to do" is reached;
4. the final descent begins;
5. the last hours;
6. the death watch; and
7. death itself.

During the patient's final period of life, the family members have several rights.

Right #1. The family has a right to expect optimal and considerate care for their dying loved one.

The best care includes pain control and death without indignity. The family also has the right to expect the last wishes of loved ones to be carried out whenever possible—whether they are formally delineated (such as those in a living will) or informally requested. Additionally, the family has the right to compassionate communication and adequate information in preparation for their loved one's death. As Kutscher noted, "When grief has been prepared for by those who will survive, these bereaved may more readily find their way back to normal functioning" (1973: 44).

Sometimes there appears to be an inequity of care for terminally ill patients that is dependent upon the illness. Vachon et al. (1977) compared widows whose husbands had suffered from cancer with those who had been victims of cardiovascular disease, and found that the 73 cancer widows faced problems quite different from and more difficult than those faced by the 51 widows of heart patients. The former felt helpless, with no control over the treatment process. The latter felt they had played an active role in helping to provide their husbands with the right diet, alleviate their stress, and restrict their activities. Also, cancer widows expressed more anger toward the medical care system than did cardiac widows. The three major areas of concern for the cancer widows were quality of nursing care, accessibility of physicians, and accuracy of information. Neglect of cancer patients by nurses and difficulties in getting the patient admitted to a hospital during a crisis were frequently cited. Cardiac widows did not experience such problems. In fact, when the cardiac patients were dying, everything possible had generally been done to revive them.

Vachon attributed this to the social desirability of the cardiac patient. She stated (1977:153) that "cancer is still associated with evil, dirt, pain and death, whereas cardiovascular disease is seen as being more 'manly' and the aftermath of working too hard." In general, the women whose husbands had died of cancer seemed to perceive the final illness as much more stressful than those whose husbands had died of cardiovascular disease, and their problems during bereavement were greater.

Death upsets the smooth routine of a hospital. As Sudnow (1967) observed, death becomes routinized in a hospital setting. The patient has died; the medical and nursing personnel want to complete the related tasks and get back to caring for the rest of their patients. Family members are oftentimes hurried through the necessary procedures and the case is closed.

There are, however, several rights that the bereaved are entitled to at the time of death.

Right #2. The bereaved have a right to a compassionate pronouncement of the death and to respectful and professional care of the body of their loved one.

There is no easy way to tell someone that a loved one has died. It is equally true that no one can ever be completely prepared for the finality of the pronouncement of death. It takes time for the fact of death to become a reality, and the emotional reaction of loved ones is often initially buffered by shock. The words of the pronouncement live forever in the memories of many bereaved, so physicians and health care professionals should choose these words carefully and be as gentle as possible in the telling.

It is also extremely difficult for the family to make the necessary transition from "living" one moment to "dead" the next. The transition from loved one to body or corpse happens gradually and is often a product of the mourning ritual and the funeral practices. This enhances the need for and the right to respectful and professional care of the body of their loved one. To the family this is not an inanimate object, but someone they have loved and with whom they have shared a part of their life. Death does not end their caring. Often, primarily because of feelings of inadequacy, health professionals may appear callous or insensitive, and they may wish to hasten the necessary routine. This can have a detrimental effect if family members are prevented from beginning their mourning and expressing their sorrow at the time of death.

Right #3. The bereaved have a right to view the body and to grieve at the bedside immediately following the death, if this is their wish.

This right should be accorded whether the patient has been hospitalized for a long time or was brought in dead-on-arrival in the emergency room. Family members may wish time alone with their loved one to say a final and personal good-bye, or they may ask that a professional remain with them when they view the body. If at all possible, either request should be accommodated.

Right #4. The bereaved have a right to expect adequate and respectful professional care (both physical and emotional) for themselves at the time of their loved one's death.

There are many questions regarding medical treatment of family members at the time of death. Do they officially become new patients? Are they a type of secondary patient? If given any kind of medical attention, must a hospital chart or record be opened for them? Most hospitals have some standard routine or procedure, whether formal or informal.

It has been suggested by several studies that there is widespread use of drugs to alleviate the stress of bereavement both on a short-term and on an extended basis (Parkes 1972). Tranquilizers and sedatives are often dispensed at the time of death, ostensibly to calm the bereaved. Underlying this gesture however, may be the concern that the bereaved will become extremely upset and cause a scene at the hospital, thereby further disrupting hospital routine.

The mechanism of drug therapy in bereavement is unclear. It is not yet known if sedatives, tranquilizers, and antidepressive drugs minimize the pain of grief or simply postpone it, but medication for grief, once begun, may be continued indefinitely (Parkes 1972). The bereaved have a right not to accept or take any proffered medication, and have the right to make that choice without being subject to undue persuasion. It can be an impediment to the grief process and can further enhance the feelings of unreality that surround the survivors. Silverman (1973) found that many widows resented efforts to tranquilize or sedate them and felt that drugs would interfere with their ability to function as well as they could under the circumstances.

Established routine for emotional treatment of the bereaved is not as customary as for physical treatment. Emotional support should be provided for the bereaved at the time of death. This is often best done by a professional who is trained in grief counseling and who has adequate time to spend with the family members. Ideally, clergy and social workers should be available to perform this function. The inclusion of the hospital chaplain or social worker on the health care team is not only beneficial to the patient and family, but can also be supportive for the staff members who are touched by the death. In a practical sense, clergy and social workers can facilitate the necessary hospital procedures. These professionals can be available when the family is grieving at the bedside and can help them terminate that aspect of the mourning process in a timely fashion. They can also help to obtain necessary information regarding such questions as which funeral director should be notified. Another area, generally unrecognized, in which the clergy or social worker can be useful is in requesting consent for an autopsy.

Right #5. The bereaved have a right (except when the law indicates otherwise) not to consent to an autopsy without coercion regardless of how interesting or baffling the patient's disease.

Oftentimes it is overlooked, or at least not stated, that besides the medical, scientific reasons, information from an autopsy can be beneficial for the family members. It is not unusual several days or weeks after the death (when the shock has subsided somewhat) for the family to have questions regarding the exact cause of death, and unless an autopsy has been performed these questions may go unanswered. The presence of the hospital chaplain can help allay religious concerns regarding an autopsy, and a social worker who understands the process can gently and adequately explain that the loved one's body will be respectfully cared for and that an autopsy will not preclude a viewing with an open casket.

The clergy member or social worker can also act as a supporter if the family decides not to consent to an autopsy. People in crisis are often easily coerced into doing something they do not really wish to do. The bereaved have a right not to consent to an autopsy and deserve to be supported in their decision on this issue.

Too often the manner in which consent for an autopsy is requested is cold, awkward, and unfeeling. Reasons given for the request frequently include only those of the benefits to medical science or the benefits to those other patients who have a similar disease. A common objection from family members is that they do not want the body mutilated or that the loved one has already suffered too much. If the response is that it is now "just a body," consent will probably not be gained. As mentioned previously, the bereaved have generally not yet made that mental transition. Additionally, all too often the person requesting the autopsy is a resident or physician minimally familiar, or even unfamiliar, with this particular patient and family. The presence of a social worker or clergy member who knows the family and the situation can facilitate the process and can contribute to the emotional care of the bereaved at the time of death.

The rights listed so far are generally specific to the hospital situation. Obviously, this period is only the beginning of grief. The grief process continues for an extended time and there are several additional rights that need to be mentioned.

Extended Grief

Right #6. The bereaved have the right to an adequate explanation of the cause of their loved one's death and to answers regarding the illness, treatment procedures, treatment failures, and events surrounding the death.

Whether or not the bereaved have consented to an autopsy, they have the right to an explanation. Often this request for information is made several days or even weeks after the death. Generally, a family member will call the physician with a few specific questions. Close attention should be paid to this request. If possible, rather than explaining on the phone, a special appointment should be made for the bereaved to meet with the physician. This ensures adequate time for the discussion, and allows the physician to make certain that records are complete and all of the needed information is available. It also indicates to the family that the death of their loved one was a highly significant event, worthy of a little extra time and discussion. Equally important, a face-to-face discussion will afford the physician the opportunity to assess how the bereaved is handling the grief process, and can facilitate the provision of medical or psychological attention or referral when appropriate.

Parkes (1972: 174) stated:

> The family doctor, because he is likely to have cared for the dead person during his last illness and to have helped the relative to prepare for bereavement, is in a very advantageous position to give help after this event occurs. . . . Through his profession, he is acquainted with death, which should make it possible for the bereaved to talk with him about this taboo topic.

In this capacity, the physician helps to facilitate the grief process. Another professional who plays an important role, not only at the time of death but also during the extended grief period, is the funeral director, whose role has in recent decades been enlarged to include the function of grief counselor although this dual role has been criticized as having exploitative potential. Mitford's book, *The American Way of Death,* written in 1963 and updated in 1978, offers evidence regarding abuse of the bereaved by unethical funeral directors. The cost of a funeral is cited as a major factor. In 1963, Mitford found the average cost, nationwide, of a funeral (exclusive of burial plot) was about $750. In 1978, the cost had increased to $1650 and up.

Right #7. The bereaved have a right to choose the type of funeral service most consistent with their wishes and financial means and the right not to be coerced into practices they do not support.

Mortuary Law by Thomas Stueve, published in 1940 and revised numerous times, most recently in 1980, discusses in detail the rights of the bereaved with regard to funeral services. Specifically, "The party undertaking disposal rightfully has the power to exercise control over all matters relating to the funeral" (1980:34). This includes determining the mode of disposal, choosing the shroud and casket, if any, the use of flowers, the character of the service, the time and place of burial, whether it is to be a private or public service and the notification of relatives. Also, explicit permission must be obtained from the bereaved for embalming.

People choose a funeral director because they know him personally, he has served the family before or because he was recommended by friends as someone who will understand how they want things done (Silverman 1973). The bereaved generally need sympathetic guidance when making arrangements for disposal of the body and are unusually vulnerable to exploitation because of their emotional state. They have a right not to be coerced, or even subtly persuaded, into a funeral service or any related practices of which they are not supportive.

Right #8. The bereaved have the right not to be exploited for financial gain nor for educational or research purposes.

The bereaved are not only emotionally vulnerable in the hands of unethical professionals, but are also often the target of other exploitative groups and schemes. Newspapers frequently carry reports of houses being robbed while family members attend funeral services or of elderly widows being taken advantage of financially. Other examples are monument salespersons or real estate agents looking to capitalize on their bereavement. Family members may occasionally take advantage of a relative, usually one who is elderly, who has gained an inheritance through the death of a loved one.

There is one group that is not frequently mentioned that also may take advantage of the bereaved. This is the person, or persons, wishing to study the bereaved for educational or research purposes. With the current increased interest in death-related subjects, the process of grief and the coping mechanisms of the bereaved have come under scrutiny. Bereaved persons may be just as vulnerable to an invasion of privacy as they are to other schemes. They deserve sensitivity and should not be put in the position of defending their choice not to participate in a research project.

Also, the self-help movement has witnessed a proliferation of widow support groups. In an effort to provide help to the newly widowed, the same invasion of privacy issue may arise. Most reputable and experienced bereavement support programs are attuned to the acute needs of the bereaved, and both their referral process and the timing of their intervention are planned so as not to be intrusive. Both the family physician and the funeral director are in positions to make referrals to support programs or to help with evaluating participation in research programs.

Right #9. The bereaved have a right to observe religious and social mourning rituals according to their wishes and customs.

Mandelbaum (1959) noted that although the funeral ceremony is personal in focus, it is social in its consequences and the rites performed generally have important effects for the living. In a similar fashion, Jackson (1959) maintained that religious practices can facilitate the mourning process.

Realizing the finality of death and the permanent physical separation from the loved one is an extremely painful but necessary part of the mourning process. Funeral ritual and religious practices can be helpful in this aspect. Meaning must be given to death, and accustomed ritual can contribute to the meaning. The reality of the death is impressed on the bereaved by such practices as viewing the body, visitation by family and friends, the funeral service, and interment. Religious practices contribute to maintenance of reality in a similar way (Jackson 1959:231):

> Practically, the religious function within the community is to protect the bereft individual against destructive fantasy and illusion by surrounding the fact of physical death by a framework of reality that is accepted by both the grieving individual and the supporting community. This framework of reality is conceived to stimulate and make valid the expression of all the emotion that is a part of the process of mourning in a way that is acceptable to the community at the same time it satisfies the deep inner needs of the personality.

If ritual and religion can help alleviate the stress of grief and can facilitate the mourning process, deritualization should have the opposite effect. Kutscher noted (1973:51):

> The passing of certain cultural and ethnic rituals, such as portions (at least) of the formal funeral, sitting "shivah," and the wake, has probably been detrimental for the family as viewed sociologically and can hinder acceptance of the loss and the bereaved's ability to continue as a functioning human being.

This deritualization is closely related to the next right of the bereaved.

Right #10. The bereaved have a right to express their grief openly regardless of the cause of the loved one's death.

Along with deritualization have come restraints in the expression of sorrow. In earlier times, mourning was an acceptable practice. Modern society forbids survivors from showing too much emotion about death. Aries has written extensively on the denial of mourning in industrial societies. He stated (1967:16):

> Some form of mourning, whether spontaneous or obligatory, has

always been mandatory in human society. Only in the twentieth century has it been forbidden. The situation was reversed in a single generation. . . . It is no longer fitting to manifest one's sorrow or even give evidence of experiencing any.

Mourners no longer wear special clothes nor engage in any extended mourning behavior that would make other people uncomfortable. After the funeral, they are usually expected to return rapidly to their usual level of functioning and scant opportunity is afforded them to express their grief openly. There are several special circumstances of death that receive even less consideration and support from others. These include violent death, death from suicide, and fetal loss. Additionally, two groups, children and older widows, are not permitted adequate mourning.

Murder and suicide produce extreme reactions and discomfort among friends and acquaintances. Violent death is accompanied by unspeakable horror, and friends are afraid to mention it for fear it will remind the bereaved of the tragedy. Grief from violent death is usually accompanied by anger and hatred and can necessitate painful legal procedures, particularly if the death was a result of crime. Death from suicide is stigmatizing and results in anguish, guilt, and shame. Researchers have been struck by the severity of psychopathology found in survivor-victims of suicide (Cain 1972). Whitis (1972) noted that when a child commits suicide, there is increased potential for a highly pathogenic legacy for the bereaved family. Suicide is still considered a taboo topic in our society and because of social disapproval, discussion regarding a death from suicide remains limited, if not entirely prohibited (Shneidman 1970).

Failed pregnancy constitutes another special category of grief. Miscarriages are generally treated as incidents to be quickly forgotten. There is no standard mourning ritual. Recognition that a pregnancy loss is as much a form of bereavement as is any other death, and that it must be mourned is recent (Lasker and Borg 1981). Since opportunities to express emotions and grief in failed pregnancy situations are severely limited, unresolved grief may result.

Children and older widows are often not permitted adequate mourning, but for different reasons. With children, expression of grief is often limited in an attempt to protect them from hurt. As children grow, they are subject to a variety of losses. Some are developmental losses, some are object losses, and some include the loss of a loved one. Children need to have some intellectual understanding of death before they can react to it emotionally. Much has been written regarding the age level at which children understand death (Bowlby 1961; Furman 1964; Nagy 1948).

For the older widow, grief is seen not as serious or problematic, but as an expectable, normal part of the aging process. It is generally agreed that widows must go through the mourning process in order to relinquish the bonds to the spouse that will then permit the reestablishment of new relationships. Additionally, it is acknowledged that a major problem for widows occurs when they attempt to reintegrate themselves into society. It is conceivable that older widows would have diminished social support networks and could frequently lack the ability to replace past relationships with new ones, prohibiting the completion of the grief process. This is in agreement with Parkes (1964) who stated that widows in the older age groups show a different type of reaction to bereavement with less overt emotional disturbances than younger widows. Similarly, another study of grief reaction in later life (Stern et al. 1969) found that one of the most striking features in their 25 bereaved subjects aged 53 to 70 was a relative paucity of overt grief. Nevertheless, it does not necessarily follow that less overt grief means fewer difficulties. Perhaps their stoicism results from society's expectations and the limited opportunity available to them for the expression of sorrow.

Parkes has stated "There is an optimal 'level of grieving' which varies from one person to another. Some will cry and sob, others will betray their feelings in other ways. The important thing is for feelings to be permitted to emerge into consciousness" (1972:162).

Grief is a process of realization, of "making real" the fact of loss. It is painful and takes time. Mourning is essential to the successful completion of the grief process, and we do a disservice to the bereaved when we restrict their open expression of sorrow for any reason, including the type of death or because of arbitrary age categories and expectations.

The final three rights of the bereaved are closely related and have to do with characteristics of the grief process and suggested intervention.

Right #11. The bereaved have a right to expect health professionals to understand the process and characteristics of grief.

It is particularly important for those who work with the bereaved to know what is normal concerning the grief process. While it is not expected that all professionals will be grief specialists or experts in grief counseling, physicians, nurses, social workers, clergy, funeral directors, and others who have had contact with the bereaved throughout a loved one's terminal illness and death should be knowledgeable about the grief process. The practitioner who understands the characteristics of grief is in a position to help the bereaved adapt and cope more successfully with the grief process.

There are certain basic tenets of grief that should be emphasized:

1. Grief is a process, not a solitary event. Many who have observed the process of bereavement have described it in stages. Averill (1968) proposed three stages—shock, despair, and recovery. Parkes (1972) suggested four—numbness, pining, depression, and recovery. Both emphasize that the stages of grief are not invariable. Stages imply that time is an important consideration. It is generally agreed that it takes at least one year, and oftentimes two, for a reasonable recovery from grief.

2. Many factors contribute to the grief process. These include, among others, the personality of the bereaved, their relationship with the loved one who has died, and numerous antecedent events such as childhood experiences, concomitant problems, religion, cultural background, and mode of death (Parkes 1972). There are also subsequent determinants of grief such as availability or unavailability of social support, opportunity to express sorrow, and secondary stresses such as financial and family problems.

3. There is a syndrome of grief that is common to the normal grieving process. Lindemann (1944) first delineated such symptoms of acute grief as tightness in the throat, shortness of breath, a need to sigh, and lack of muscular power after interviewing persons who had lost family in the catastrophic Coconut Grove fire (see article 8).

Other symptoms of grief (Lindemann 1944; Parkes 1972) include sobbing and crying, restless and aimless hyperactivity, loss of appetite, preoccupation with thoughts of the dead person, searching behavior, loss of interest in persons, activities, and things, and depression, sadness, sorrow, relief, guilt, and anger.

4. Bereavement may be considered an illness. Kutscher has stressed this point (1970:283):

> Although it is recognized that the illness and death of a patient may precipitate emotional or physical disturbances in persons who have loved and cared for him, there is little acceptance of the concept that bereavement states per se may be considered an illness. The bereaved may be regarded as a patient with a definite complex of symptoms, often subclinical, which may become exacerbated, severe and even fatal. Despite this, the bereaved's illness, in general, is left untreated. His state is usually diagnosed from the medical and psychological points of view as a normal response to the circumstance of his situation—until overt signs and symptoms reach pathologic proportions.

Previous research has documented the effect of bereavement on health and even mortality. (See for example, Rowland 1977; Maddison and Viola 1968). With regard to increased mortality after bereavement, Young, Benjamin, and Wallis (1963) found there is a peak of mortality among widowers during the first year of bereavement. Studying 4486 widowers over the age of 54, they found an increase in the death rate of almost 40 percent during the first six months of bereavement. In Wales, Rees and Lutkins (1967) found that of 903 close relatives of people who had died 4.8 percent died within one year of bereavement whereas only 0.7 percent died in a matched nonbereaved comparison group. A frequent cause of death found in these studies was heart disease, which has led to the phrase "the broken heart syndrome" (coined by Parkes 1972). This does not mean that bereavement is the cause of death, but it does appear to be a contributing factor, perhaps exacerbating preexisting conditions.

The evidence regarding the seriousness of bereavement to one's health is too important to be ignored. Generally, in the case of serious illness, efforts are made toward prevention or early intervention. This does not appear to be the usual response to bereavement. Conversely, the bereaved are often abandoned directly after the death of their loved one. Grief is considered a "normal" syndrome and little intervention is provided by health care professionals. This may be a result of ignorance and lack of education regarding the grief process, or may be due to feelings of inadequacy on the part of health care providers. Nevertheless, research is continuing with the aim of enabling us to identify persons at high risk of poor bereavement outcome. Providing help for the bereaved has become a practical and necessary part of health care.

This help for the bereaved may be broken down into crisis intervention in acute grief and longer-range support or preventive intervention. Education and support are the two major types of help the bereaved need during both the acute and the extended grief process.

Contemporary crisis theory was developed by two psychiatrists, Erich Lindemann and Gerald Caplan (Lindemann 1944; Caplan 1956). They postulated that there are both adaptive and maladaptive ways of meeting life crisis. The definition of "crisis" that evolved from their work is (Klein and Lindemann 1961:284), "Acute, and often prolonged, disturbance to an individual or to a social network as the result of an emotionally hazardous situation."

A state of crisis is of course, of limited duration, with a defined beginning, middle, and end (Tyhurst 1957). In a crisis, habitual problem-solving mechanisms and activities fail to bring about the desired resolution of the problem, and the level of recovery from a state of crisis is variable.

The outcome of a crisis is determined less by previous personality factors and antecedent experiences in an individual's life than by the interplay of endogenous and exogenous forces occurring in the course of the crisis itself. While previous experiences have some influence, the dynamics of the crisis situation and the forces set in motion both in the individual and in the supporting environment are more critical determinants of the individual's ability to resolve a crisis than is the past (Linderberg 1972). Loss by death and the accompanying process of grief clearly fit the definition of a crisis situation for nearly all individuals.

The beginning of the crisis, the period of numbness directly following the death, leaves the bereaved confused and unbelieving—not knowing what to think or do. It is at this time that family and close friends usually draw together to support the bereaved. Parkes (1972) suggested that the bereaved, while in this dazed state, will need help with even simple decisions. Relatives will generally need to assist with funeral arrangements, notification of others, and everyday tasks. The professionals most frequently involved with the bereaved during this time are the clergy and the funeral director, who can be instrumental in providing support and in giving advice regarding funeral practices and religious ritual, and can also help the bereaved, the family, and their friends to understand the process of grief.

Right #12. The bereaved have a right to education regarding coping with the process of grief.

Specifically, the clergy and the funeral director can sanction the expression of emotion, telling family and friends that it is not necessarily bad if the bereaved becomes emotionally upset while talking with them, and that it is not only acceptable, but often desirable, to allow their own feelings of sadness to show. This reduces the sense of isolation that the bereaved may feel (Parkes 1972). Also, the bereaved should be assured that they are not going insane, and made to realize that preoccupation with the image of the dead loved one, intense sobbing, lack of interest in anything, and recurring waves of somatic distress are normal and natural. It is also important to emphasize that the period of acute grief is limited in time, and that recovery, while slow, will come.

After the period of numbness comes the period of adjustment, which of course varies among individuals. It is not a linear progression, with the bereaved getting better each day, but has its ups and downs and setbacks. Anniversary reactions at such times as birthdays, holidays, and other important events all take their toll. Particularly difficult is the anniversary of the death itself.

During the adjustment period, there are numerous practical aspects of bereavement that need attention.

Right #13. The bereaved have a right to professional and lay support including assistance regarding insurance, medical bills, and legal concerns.

Any death brings with it problems of settlement and decision. If the death was unexpected, and especially if no will was made, these problems multiply. The bereaved may be in a state of total confusion. A general suggestion is when possible to postpone making decisions. Getting the assistance of a qualified friend or the family lawyer or accountant also is valuable. The bereaved have a right to considerate understanding and timely assistance. Banks and insurance companies should make every effort to be accommodating. Ideally, they should have employees especially trained to work with persons who are trying to untangle the financial and legal problems that accompany a death.

A major problem in this period is the communication of advice and needed information to the bereaved. Funeral directors are particularly knowledgeable and helpful with the necessary paperwork and details that accompany death. They help in the preparation of forms and provide the essential data and assistance. Additionally, they can play an important role in linking the bereaved to other helpful people at a later point in the bereavement process. These mainly include the governmental agencies and institutions providing services that the bereaved may require. Also, the funeral director generally is aware of a broad spectrum of available community resources that can provide social support for the bereaved. The clergy can be another link in this support process. Along with the individual support they provide, they are aware of church groups and church-supported programs that can be of benefit to the bereaved, and they may be in a position to suggest pastoral counseling or professional intervention if deemed appropriate.

Most persons go through the adjustment period of bereavement without professional help, but that is not to say it would not be valuable if it were available and provided. Therapists with expertise in, and an understanding of, grief counseling could be a particular asset.

There are certain situations where professional help may be necessary. These include: "Absence of grief in a situation where it would have been expected, episodes of panic, lasting physical symptoms, excessive guilt feelings or excessive anger, or the persistence of intense grief beyond the normally expected period—these should be taken as signs that all is not going as it should" (Parkes 1972:165).

There also may be physical problems that need attention. Bereaved individuals should be encouraged not to neglect their personal health. Too often, caring for the dying patient has been a physical, as well as an emotional strain, so it would be wise for the bereaved to see the family physician for a checkup. In addition to medical care, if needed, this would provide the physician the opportunity to assess the bereaved's overall functioning and, if indicated, make a referral for professional counseling or make a timely suggestion regarding the availability of a reputable lay support group.

Bereavement support programs, self-help groups, and widow-to-widow programs fall in the category of preventive intervention. Assistance through a program specifically designed to meet the needs of the bereaved can be useful in preventing other difficulties. Additionally, people who themselves have experienced bereavement may be particularly well qualified to help a person cope with the grief process. Sharing the experience of loss with others can help ameliorate loneliness and can provide support, encouragement, and insight into how others cope with problems relating to bereavement.

The original "Widow-to-Widow" program began in Boston in 1967 under the direction of Dr. Phyllis Silverman. Since that time, numerous programs have developed around the country. Each takes its own special form depending upon the community, the sponsoring agency, and related factors, but each has the primary goal of providing assistance to the newly widowed (Silverman 1969).

The final period of grief, recovery, is equivalent to the end stage of the crisis. Nevertheless, there is no clear ending to grief. As stated earlier, we know that recovery from grief takes at least one year, often as long as two years, and that perhaps a person never completely recovers from the experience. The crisis theory frame of reference suggests that a person may return to a level of organization equivalent to that before the crisis or may remain at a lower level, or occasionally may reach a level of higher functioning (Hill 1965). These outcomes are applicable to the recovery from grief.

Recovery is a time of healing, of looking to the future and letting go of the past. It is a time of reintegration and establishment of new relationships. The supportive role of family and friends begins to change during this time because the bereaved is functioning more adequately. Parkes (1972:175) emphasized that this change is positive:

> If the early stage of bereavement is a time when family, friends, and others should rally round to relieve the newly bereaved person of some of his roles and obligations, the later stage is one when the bereaved person should be helped to establish his own autonomy. It may be important for a bereaved person to grieve. It is also important for him to stop grieving, to give up his withdrawal from life and to start building a new identity.

When the crisis of bereavement has ended, the person has returned to a state of productivity and well-being.

Conclusion

Wellman (1975) has defined a right as a sphere of decision that is or ought to be respected by other individuals and protected by society. This chapter has identified thirteen rights of the bereaved person that should be respected by others, particularly by health professionals, and that should be sanctioned by society. Essential to these rights is a thorough understanding of the grief continuum from anticipatory grief to the recovery stage. These rights accordingly require compassion, understanding, sensitivity, and patience.

References

American Journal of Nursing 1975. "The Dying Person's Bill of Rights." January: 99.

Aries, P. 1967. "Death Inside Out." *European Journal of Sociology* 8:169–195.

Averill, J. R. 1968. "Grief: Its Nature and Significance." *Psychological Bulletin* 70:721–748.

Bowlby, J. 1961. "Childhood Mourning and Its Implications for Psychiatry." *American Journal of Psychiatry* 118:481–498.

Cain, A., ed. 1972. *Survivors of Suicide.* Springfield, Ill: Charles C. Thomas.

Caplan, G. 1956. "An Approach to the Study of Family Mental Health." *U.S. Public Health Reports* 71:1025–1029.

Furman, R. 1964. "Death and the Young Child: Some Preliminary Considerations." *Psychoanalytic Study of the Child* 19:321.

Furman, R. 1970. "The Child's Reaction to Death in the Family." In B. Schoenberg, et al., eds. *Loss and Grief: Psychological Management in Medical Practice.* New York: Columbia University Press.

Gaylin, W. 1973. "The Patient's Bill of Rights." *Saturday Review of the Sciences* 1:22.

Glaser, B. and A. Strauss. 1968. *Time for Dying.* Chicago: Aldine.

Hill, R. 1965. "Generic Features of Families Under Stress." In H. Parad, ed., *Crisis Intervention: Selected Readings.* New York: Family Services Association of America.

Jackson, E. N. 1959. "Grief and Religion." In H. Feifel, ed. *The Meaning of Death.* New York: McGraw-Hill.

Klein, D. C. and E. Lindemann. 1961. "Preventive Intervention in Individuals and Family Crisis Situations." In G. Caplan, ed. *Prevention of Mental Disorders in Children: Initial Explorations,* New York: Basic Books.

Kutscher. A. H. 1970. "Practical Aspects of Bereavement." In B. Schoenberg et al., eds. *Loss and Grief: Psychological Management in Medical Practice.* New York: Columbia University Press.

Kutscher, A. H. 1973. "Anticipatory Grief, Death, and Bereavement: A Continuum." In E. Wyschogrod, ed. *The Phenomenon of Death,* New York: Harper and Row.

Lasker, J. and S. Borg. 1981. *When Pregnancy Fails.* Boston: Beacon Press.

Lindemann, E. 1944. "Symptomatology and Management of Acute Grief." *American Journal of Psychiatry* 101:141–148.

Linderberg, R. 1972. "The Need for Crisis Intervention in Hospitals." *Journal of American Hospital Association* 46:52–55.

Maddison, D. and A. Viola. 1968. "The Health of Widows in the Year Following Bereavement." *Journal of Psychosomatic Research* 12:297–306.

Mandelbaum, D. 1959. "Social Uses of Funeral Rites." In H. Feifel, ed. *The Meaning of Death.* New York: McGraw-Hill.

Mitford, J. 1978. *The American Way of Death.* New York: Fawcett Crest.

Nagy, M. 1948. "The Child's View of Death." *Journal of Genetic Psychology* 73:3–27.

Parkes, C. M. 1964. "Effects of Bereavement in Physical and Mental Health—A Study of the Medical Records of Widows." *British Medical Journal* 2:274–279.

Parkes, C. M. 1972. *Bereavement: Studies of Grief in Adult Life.* New York: International Universities Press.

Rees, W. and S. Lutkins. 1967. "Mortality and Bereavement." *British Medical Journal* 4:13–16.

Rowland, K. 1977. "Environmental Events Predicting Death for the Elderly." *Psychological Bulletin* 84:348–372.

Shneidman, E. 1970. "Suicide as a Taboo Topic." In E. Shneidman et al. eds. *Psychology of Suicide,* New York: Science House.

Silverman, P. 1969. "Services to the Widowed: First Stages in a Program of Preventive Intervention." *Mental Hygiene* 53:333–337.

Silverman, P. 1973. "The Funeral Director as Caregiver in the Early Stage of Bereavement." *The Director* May:1–4.

Society for the Right to Die. 1982. *1981 Handbook.* New York: The Society.

Stern, K., G. Williams, and M. Prados. 1969. "Grief Reactions in Later Life." In H. Ruitenbeck, ed. *Death: Interpretations.* New York: Dell.

Stueve, T. 1980. *Mortuary Law.* Cincinnati: The Cincinnati College of Mortuary Science.

Sudnow, D. 1967. *The Social Organization of Death.* Englewood Cliffs, N.J.: Prentice-Hall.

Tyhurst, J. 1957. "The Role of Transition States—Including Disasters—in Mental Illness." Symposium on Preventive and Social Psychiatry. Washington, D.C.: Walter Reed Institute of Research.

Vachon, M., K. Freedman, A. Formo, T. Rodgers, W.A.L. Lyall, and S. Freeman. 1977. "The Final Illness in Cancer: The Widow's Perspective." *Canadian Medical Association Journal* 117:1151–1154.

Wellman, C. 1975. *Morals and Ethics.* Glenview, Ill: Scott, Foresman.

Whitis, P. 1972. "The Legacy of A Child's Suicide." In A. Cain, ed. *Survivors of Suicide,* Springfield, Ill: Charles C. Thomas.

Young, M., B. Benjamin, and C. Wallis. 1963. "The Mortality of Widowers." *Lancet* 2:454–456.

Preamble: Bereaved persons bring special physical and psychological needs to the health-care professional; these needs should not be ignored. Among the effects of bereavement are disruptions of normal bodily and sensory reactions, loss of appetite, tearfulness, insomnia, feelings of numbness, fatigue, irritability, and diminished sexual interest—all these occur and support the contention that a grieving person is in a physically vulnerable state that may include a susceptibility to other illnesses.

Principle 10: Although a Normal Response, Bereavement Has Physiological and Psychological Manifestations That Qualify It Symptomatically as a Temporary Illness

10

Grief—Somatic Symptoms

MAHLON S. HALE

The psychiatric literature dealing with grief reactions and mourning has often focused primarily on the identification of psychological symptoms and their interpretation within either intrapsychic or interpersonal contexts. Strategies of intervention have been a secondary focus. Most forms of intervention have taken as a basic premise the need for grief and mourning to follow natural courses of psychological evolution and resolution, reflecting the generally accepted view that these processes (the grief work) are issues of object loss that must be accepted and worked through over a period of time. How long a time is required remains uncertain in spite of the epidemiologic and demographic studies done within the last fifteen years in an attempt to gain insight into what actually constitutes the natural course of "normal" or "uncomplicated" grief reactions. In any event, these latter, tertiary efforts have produced data yielding not just estimates of the approximate duration of grief reactions, but information on the resultant morbidity and mortality of these experiences, particularly among bereaved spouses and close relatives.

Curiously, much less attention has been paid to attendant physical symptoms of grief, although these seem to be the final common pathway leading to demonstrable somatic morbidity and even mortality. This chapter examines these somatic manifestations of grief and explores ways of integrating somatic symptoms into our identification, understanding, and treatment of grief reactions. To facilitate integration of these data for caregivers, a brief review of pertinent historical, epidemiological, and developmental information will be given.

The Role of Somatic Symptoms

Somatic symptoms during the grieving period often coexist with the more familiar psychological symptoms. Examples of these include pain, insomnia, appetite suppression, shaking, and hypochondriacal states. Their recognition—while potentially very helpful—can impede diagnosis and treatment of grief reactions because such physical complaints may be mistaken for harbingers of physical illness by medical clinicians and their coworkers and even as characteristics of non–grief-related psychopathology by psychologically-minded clinicians. Like psychological symptoms, somatic symptoms sometimes continue for months to years after the event of death has otherwise vanished from memory. But unlike their psychological counterparts they are less often recognized as stemming out of the failure to resolve a past loss or death.

There are various reasons for such misattributions, the most fundamental involving our tendency to dismiss the psychological meaning of symptoms when an apparent, and perhaps less anxiety-provoking, association can be made to direct physical etiologies. Another source of obfuscation can be the intensity of affective response that sometimes inundates individuals, families, and even larger social systems throughout a bereavement. Such intense psychological symptoms may lead caregivers to focus exclusively on the psychological manifestations, and inadvertently ignore meaningful somatic data. In other instances, caregivers may be unfamiliar with the variations in healthy, as well as maladaptive responses that occur in response to death and therefore simply may not process apparent data. Thus if the approach to grief reactions, no matter how well intentioned, is not unified, caregivers may well miss certain evidence or markers because they are contextually unfamiliar or seem attitudinally inappropriate.

Historical Perspective

If grief is not yet acknowledged as a disease with symptoms and sequelae like other illnesses, it is not for lack of efforts by students of its impact. The issue, initially raised by Engel (1961) over 25 years ago, of whether grief should be granted disease status so as to assure thorough, scientific study of its consequences and remedies, has been overtaken by the practical needs of many caregivers to understand better the dimensions of grief and to construct caregiving systems that realistically attempt to limit its course, or at least to prevent its prolongation beyond completion of the mourning process. This task has been complicated by varied interpretations of the meaning of grief phenomena and by the protean forms of grief reactions. The fact that this text addresses itself to treatment along with descriptive and epidemiologic issues surrounding grief does seem a sui generis argument for the acceptance of grief as a disease. Grief is, in addition, a state of dis-ease in which personal, familial, and social equilibria are disrupted. When grief reactions stray from natural courses, substantial psychological issues often arise both from the arrest of the mourning process and from the social consequences of the prolongation of grief reactions. These take the form of so-called morbid, prolonged, and even aberrant reactions.

A real consequence of the general psychological orientation many of us are inclined to employ is that while clinicians often have high indices of suspicion around psychological symptoms associated with grief reactions and those variants that imply a more pathologic course, these same caregivers may fail to interpret equally significant symptomatology when it is nonverbal or somatic. Inasmuch as the philosophical or psychological matrix one places on grief may determine one's therapeutic approach, several of the most common historical approaches will be discussed to give a foundation to the bridging we propose.

Whether one concentrates on psychological or somatic symptom clusters or attempts an integration of the two, most of us use a common organizing point to guide our attitudes and help our formulations about grief. The cornerstone of this orientation on grief and mourning remains the work of Freud (1957) and Abraham (1949), who formulated intrapsychic theories regarding object loss, with the eventual extension of unresolved mourning (the work of resolving grief) into melancholia. Modern psychiatry, while acknowledging the descriptive accuracy of these early commentaries, now tends to view the spectrum of grief reactions as an evolution from (a) grief at a traumatic loss through (b) a reactive depressive state in which an individual attempts to resolve the issue of object loss to (c) a more permanent, pathologic depressive state when object loss is not adequately resolved. In this last condition, some individuals fail to resolve their grief and internalize depressive affects into their character structure. This condition should more properly be called a trait than a state in that it remains a static component in individuals for whom losses of loved ones have occurred even years before.

A number of psychological theories have been proposed to account for those behaviors that are depressogenic and, by inference, pathogenic in etiology. Akiskal and McKinney (1975) have summarized these in a paper that develops an argument for a final common pathway for the development of such depressive behavior regardless of its etiology (psychological, biological, etc.). It is probable, though not provable, that similar mechanisms facilitate the perpetuation of somatic symptoms forward from the period of the acute grief reaction. Just as such individuals may have restructured their behaviors and cognitions around a loss, so may physical or somatic symptoms appear, change, even disappear and then reemerge during other periods of stress.

One of the more recent psychological theories, proposed by Bowlby (1969), has linked early life experiences around attachment or bonding to subsequent behaviors that emerge in anxiety-provoking situations and stress. Bowlby's approach, which depends heavily upon the effects of early attachments and losses, appears to be a reasonable matrix for integrating observations about psychological and somatic symptoms in bereaved individuals. Although psychological in origin, Bowlby's theory presents a second, organizing point that offers some needed escape from psychological theories and purely psychological symptoms. In presenting a developmental schema in which learning theory plays a role, he allows individuals who have difficulty in accepting intrapsychic theories considerable leeway for the substitution of symptoms and behaviors that have meanings analogous to the more familiar psychological symptoms (see below).

Epidemiology of Grief

The demographic effects of grief have been well studied by Rees and Lutkins (1967), Clayton et al. (1971) and others (Glick, Weiss, and Parkes 1974; Jacobs and Ostfeld 1977). In their epidemiological study of spouse- and relative-connected deaths in a small Welsh town, Rees and Lutkins found an increased death rate among survivors within six months after bereavement. Of particular interest was the significantly increased mortality of survivors whose spouses died either in a hospital or while working. In some respects this parallels Lindemann's findings of pathological reactions in individuals of relatives who died traumatically and away from their families (1944). It also confirms the findings of Holmes and Rahe (1967) that death of a spouse is viewed as the most stressful of life events. Such data give rise to several inferences regarding the context in which a death occurs and its impact upon survivors. Physical separation from an individual at the time of death appears to be a significant element in consequent morbidity and mortality among close relatives.

Although findings regarding morbidity are generally consistent, not all researchers have found undue mortality among survivors, at least when dealing with smaller groups. Clayton et al. have produced a number of studies examining the temporal dimensions of grief, but their conclusions differed in part from those of Rees and Lutkins around the issue of subsequent mortality. They found that 35 percent of a random sample of bereaved adult spouses experienced depression within thirteen months following the death of their spouse. They did not find, however, an increased incidence of mortality among survivors. Thus, clinicians are left with data that should increase their vigilance with survivors, but that fortunately does not assure an increase in premature mortality as a consequence of spousal death.

Possible Causes of Increased Morbidity from Grief

If increased morbidity and mortality are associated with grief reactions, it seems reasonable to seek to identify various potential causes of increased individual risk. Such causes fall into four areas: magnitude of the loss or stress; intensity of the grief reaction; personality type; and previous experiences with death or loss. Hinkle and Wolff (1957) found an association between the onset of illness and recent events that were perceived by patients as being distressing and demoralizing. There is an inference that a connection exists between the perception by survivors of the magnitude of loss and the subsequent consequences of that perception upon health. It appears that for some the intensity and abruptness of the death have considerable bearing on both short and long-term reactions. Just as distressing events may exacerbate latent chronic illnesses, so can catastrophic events such as deaths precipitate catastrophic responses. While one cannot be conclusory about the impact of such highly subjective variables, the subjective intensity each of us experiences in stressful situations appears to affect morbidity. Bennet (1970) studied those effects in Bristol, England following devastating floods in 1968. He found increases in physician referrals and hospital admissions that exceeded 50 percent in the six months following the floods. In addition, individuals whose homes were flooded suffered a 50 percent increase in deaths reported. While disasters are not bereavements per se, one cannot help but look at the parallels rather than the differences among these data.

Broader epidemiologic studies of death associated with some precedent stressful event are not concerned so much with individual mourning as with the concept of "premature mortality." In this context, psychological morbidity is suggested to be trait dependent—that is, stemming from a preexisting emotional disorder. Sims (1978) in a review of hypotheses that connect neurotic behaviors to early, unexpected death has listed the multiple causes associated with this increase in mortality among individuals believed to be neurotic. These include the last-straw hypothesis, predilection to death (Weisman and Hackett 1961), being scared to death, self-willed death, the blame of dying young and the giving up/given up complex (Schmale 1972). While some of these five hypotheses are discrete in their explanation of premature mortality, they share the presumption that certain stressors may predispose individuals to increased risks of morbidity and mortality. Grief reactions, particularly if not resolved by mourning so that they move from the status of state to trait, seem particularly susceptible. It is of interest that while Sims has questioned the validity of certain hypotheses on the grounds that these are common experiences, he has suggested that intensity and severity of neurotic behaviors carry an increasing risk. So again we are brought back to the severity of the threat that loss by death evokes.

Specific personality types and personality characteristics may also determine both grief responses and the potential for a pathological course to mourning (Bowlby 1980). These include individuals who have tended to make anxious or ambivalent relationships, which are a consequence, Bowlby has argued, of anxious or ambivalent attachment in childhood. Another group may be prone to impulsive and self-destructive acts and find that a death catapults them into rash and inappropriate activity. Lastly, some individuals who "assert" relative independence from close ties may be at risk of decompensation, although the data on such individuals, as Bowlby pointed out, are scant. The reasons for this are not hard to discern. On one hand, if such a stance is a trait that reflects counterdependency, it usually serves to mask deep needs that an individual conceals for fear they will not be met. These concerns cannot be avoided with the death of a loved one. Bowlby has suggested that such traits may indeed insulate them from the affective responses others experience at the death of a close friend or family member. On the other hand, since it is a characteristic of such individuals to function in relative isolation from close affective contact, their resourcefulness at a time of death may be limited. Such isolation eliminates the availability of a latent social network when real loss occurs.

The question of whether early parental death influences subsequent psychiatric illness has been studied by Birtchnell (1970). He has investigated the association between early parental death and major psychiatric illness in a group of 500 patients in a Scottish psychiatric facility. Fifty percent of these patients had a depressive disorder. In comparison with a control group of people who were not psychiatrically ill, these patients had experienced significantly more parental death before age ten, particularly losses of fathers and losses by daughters. The most striking difference, however, was in the number of losses these patients had experienced between the ages of 1 to 4. This included losses of either or both parents. The hypothesis that specific life events predispose to depressive disorders has recently been reviewed by Lloyd, with particular regard to depressive disorders (1980). In reviewing five such studies, including Birtchnell's, Lloyd cited consistent findings that adult depressives had experienced two to three times as many parental losses as controls. Such findings are congruent with studies showing an increased number of childhood bereavements in adult suicide attempters, again suggesting that clinicians must be particularly aware of the potential lethality of intense grief in predisposed or vulnerable individuals (Levi et al. 1966).

On the other hand, the literature of childhood bereavement—whether psychoanalytic or epidemiologic in origin—strongly suggests that the experience of bereavement for children, while accompanied by dysphoria, mild depression, and significant difficulty in school performance, is generally short-lived and typically does not extend into long-term psychopathology or social difficulties (Wolfenstein 1966; Van Eerdewegh et al. 1982).

One final area for review is the physiologic impact of grief and its relationship to increased morbidity and mortality. This literature appears to be still in its infancy, and reveals surprisingly little data on the physiology of grief. Engel has written on the roles of vasodepressor syncope and ventricular fibrillation in sudden death, and has theorized on the proximal cause of psychosocial stressors in triggering cardiac arrhythmias (1971; 1978). Jacobs and Douglas (1979) have reviewed other possible biological mechanisms, but except for neuroendocrine studies that point to corticosteroid alterations (Bartrop et al. 1977) and some tentative work examining alternations in immune systems, such as depressed T-cell function following bereavement (Bartrop et al. 1977), this work has not led to increased understanding of underlying mechanisms. It seems that the issue that must be dealt with biologically is not how it is that separation anxiety appears as a "state" phenomenon in bereavement, but how for some individuals it becomes a "trait" that acts as an autonomous driver. Sweeney and Mass (1979) have begun to study this by comparing biological parameters with state anxiety in depressed patients.

Theoretical Considerations

An individual's ability to tolerate object loss remains the fulcrum upon which the intensity and duration of grief reactions pivot. How particular individuals respond to specific losses then depends upon multiple personal factors reflective not just of development, but of past experiences with death, character structure, and the presence of available support systems. So far as understanding the underlying mechanism that prompts some persons into highly specific modes of grieving, Bowlby's (1969) hypothesis that adult manifestations of separation anxiety are to a substantial degree ramifications of early attachment behavior offers the best grounding for an integrated approach to grief. He has offered a core formulation of early behavioral experience that to a substantial degree influences the responses of adults to separations and losses (1973).

Attachment theory has as its premises that an individual (initially a child) will remain close to an important and accessible person during certain periods of individuation; that emotional ties will be promoted between an individual and this significant person; and that there will be an arousal of anxiety and protest upon the separation or loss of this attachment. Since this conceptual framework has been derived from work with children, Bowlby's argument can be taken within a developmental sequence that has almost a dialectical quality. How one learns to make and maintain attachments, and whether one also learns to deal with disattachment, have universal application throughout a variety of subsequent adult experiences. Not surprisingly, Bowlby rapidly extended this framework into an examination of childhood and adult psychopathology, stating that a variety of anxiety states—and traits—are to a substantial degree the consequence of early anxious attachment or tenuous emotional bonds with significant individuals.

While Bowlby associates later psychopathological states, particularly separation anxiety and phobias, with these early problems involving attachments, our focus will be on the underlying principle that early attachments with their attendant anxiety may be reevoked in adult life when individuals perceive certain separations and losses as equivalent in magnitude to these early experiences. At the least, such experience predisposes an individual to react to separations and losses in certain ways. Some might be historically adaptive, but others may be quite pathological and nonproductive within the current context. Thus, the recapitulation of separation anxiety replicates other developmental and life experiences and often brings with it intense affective responses that susceptible bereaved individuals and their families have much difficulty in resolving. The Bowlby model encourages us to look at a wide variety of behaviors following upon loss and to evaluate any unusual symptom or symptom cluster for its possible connection with separation anxiety. It might be argued that the model does not fit extended or aberrant reactions, but this misses the point that the model, while established out of normality, is intended to clarify the etiology of psychopathological states.

Some readers may not wish either to work without a model or to find themselves discomfited by the model of separation anxiety. They will no doubt be even less accepting of Bowlby's last and most recent use of information processing schema to explain the various maneuvers individuals use to cope with or defend against loss (1980). Yet I believe that this recent attempt at systematic conceptualization, whether dependent on psychodynamic perspectives or the analysis of systems, is a most useful framework for understanding how it is that individuals' responses to certain experiences in early life may preprogram them to process certain stressful events in specific ways. In some respects Bowlby has looked for explanations of behaviors that may be described psychodynamically, but for which psychodynamics do not reveal causation. Whether or not one wishes to grant a universal applicability to Bowlby's theory, one cannot help but be struck by the model of the grief reaction in which the issues of disattachment, separation, and loss appear to generate affects and behaviors that are the adult parallels to childhood experiences.

From Bowlby's work, Graves (1978) has offered a thoughtful clinical commentary. For clinical purposes, he distinguishes between grief—the sequence of abnormal psychological, affective, and cognitive states that follow upon loss—and mourning, the psychological process that incorporates the view that lengthy psychological restitution is required. The hypothesis that the grief reaction is a defensive/protective maneuver preparatory for working through the mourning process gives clinicians a two-tiered working model to apply to many clinical situations, particularly those where the grief process does not meet our own expectations in terms of time and resolution. Thus, subsidence from the initial dismay and protest that often herald grief reactions should not be taken as any more than a relative indicator that the process of grief work has been entered into. The timing for its resolution, however, is not predictable.

Somatic Manifestations

Although we all tend to think in terms of psychological reactions to the news of death, our immediate responses are as much somatic as psychological. Little work has been done to define these aspects of grief in spite of Engel's challenge. Lindemann's clinical descriptions of sudden and pathological grief, taken from both wartime experiences and the post-traumatic states following the Coconut Grove fire, remain the most graphic. Other writers have tended to focus on statistical data—i.e., the increase of spousal morbidity, increased resort to physicians, and increased reporting of illnesses—rather than on individual symptoms. Nonetheless, there are often somatic responses that run, initially at least, parallel to emotions.

Because my primary locus is within a general hospital, my perspective and experience inevitably reflect syndromes I and my staff witness through requests for psychiatric consultation, rather than grief reactions that might be seen by a pastoral counselor, a social worker, or a supporting agency such as a hospice. We sense that the responses we witness are more intense than many other grief reactions, but this is probably a distortion. It is more likely that the experience of grief does run, like other life experiences, on a continuum, dependent not just on locale and the wishes of individuals and families that may direct them to that locale, but on an array of psychosocial factors over which none of us has control. Our basic premise, however, is that our experience parallels rather than differs from other treatment settings. Yet because we function within an acute care facility, where medical and surgical courses sometimes turn very rapidly, it is likely, though perhaps not verifiable, that the somatic manifestations we witness, while perhaps not as dramatic as those reported by Lindemann, are still quite representative. In some respects our consequent treatment may differ from options exercised in other settings; that is, we may function more along a stimulus/response paradigm than other psychologically oriented systems. But we believe this has more to do with specific resources and the point of time in the grief reaction and its attendant mourning process when intervention is made than on philosophical factors.

Responses at the Time of Death

With the shock of announcement there is a freeze of emotions and thinking that is typically translated into "this cannot be." In addition there is often a freeze of activity. It is as though the combined trauma and perplexity of the information combine to give a sense of psychological and physical inertia. These sometimes seem to act as transient insulation from a reality that may not be indefinitely denied, but from which, in the context of the immediacy of learning of death, a bereaved person needs to be partially protected. Some individuals experience intense periodic waves of somatic anxiety, including a tightness in their throat and a feeling of nausea—a "pit" in their stomach. Typically this immediate reaction rapidly gives way to affective symptoms that are often intense and dramatic. Parkes has pointed out that panic attacks are common early in bereavement among widows (1972). I have not witnessed these in men, but those in women have a dysphoric quality such as one sees in secondary and atypical depressions. Such responses reflect the intense bonding or attachment that has been broken. These responses are not unique to sudden death; they may appear as reactions to deaths after prolonged illnesses in spite of what seem to have been expressions of anticipatory grief.

Many individuals experience a fluctuation in both feelings and thinking, with peaks of intense emotion followed by flattened periods during which the bereaved's attention switches back to practical issues of coping. Perhaps because many of us are cued into this kind of response, we may tend to take for granted equally dramatic evidence of somatic distress. Again, physical activity parallels verbal behavior. Individuals may appear blocked on the point of loss. Behaviors may seem to lose their purpose or goal directedness. The bereaved tend to "busy" themselves, and when they do try to rest, they complain instead of restlessness. When well-meaning friends or professionals attempt to intervene, they are frequently met with puzzlement, as though the bereaved are inattentive. Suggestions that a bereaved person take a certain course of action may result in expressions of lack of interest, half-hearted attempts at following through, and even expressions of hostility.

Intermediate Symptoms

Clayton, Desmarais, and Winokur (1968) prospectively studied the relatives of 50 hospitalized patients who had died in order to determine parameters for normal bereavement as compared with the pathologic states described by Lindemann. These relatives were interviewed twice, the first time between two and 26 days following the death of the patient and the second time within four months after the first interview. Depression, sleep disturbance, and crying were found to characterize more than half of the interviewees, with loss of interest, loss of concentration, and anorexia less commonly reported. In the followup interview, they found that 80 percent of the bereaved had improved and dated their recovery period from six to ten weeks following the death. From these data Clayton and her coworkers suggested that normal bereavement was a time-limited experience that might serve as a model for a reactive depression. Interestingly, few of the relatives interviewed sought psychiatric assistance. Such symptoms may typify many intermediate reactions, and present two difficulties for clinicians. The first is that in presupposing that this is simply a reactive state, they do not inquire, as Clayton and her coworkers did elsewhere, about increased intake of sleeping medications or alcohol (1972). The second is that denial takes many forms during the intermediate process. I have offered treatment to such individuals during the same time period after having become convinced that grief work was not truly in process. Several of these individuals seemed to be adopting a stiff upper lip attitude, which would break under the most moderate questioning. One wonders then about the meaning of stoical façades during this period, and whether grief is not easily found hidden behind them. These symptoms are more hidden than free-floating anxiety or panic attacks, and if they are less apparent, one might incorrectly infer that some homeostasis is returning at a time when the grieved individual is using other, deleterious supports.

Moreover, for a certain population the experience of grief

does not appear so time-limited. Parkes (1970a and b) conducted multiple interviews with a group of 22 widows over a thirteen-month period following their spouses' deaths. In all of these cases there had been evidence of impending death; ten deaths, for example, were attributable to cancer, and nineteen of the wives had been informed of the seriousness of their husbands' illnesses. While these widows experienced bereavement in somewhat different phases, after thirteen months only three of them were able to view the future optimistically and to reminisce about the past with pleasure. According to Parkes, almost every area of psychological and social functioning was impaired, although intense affective outbursts were the exception. Parkes concluded that earlier estimates of grief reactions as lasting only a few weeks substantially underestimated the full impact of bereavement. It is of further interest that Parkes was able to confirm a phasic quality of bereavement, but with some overlapping of symptoms. Since it appears certain that grief reactions are manifested in different forms over extended periods, it seems reasonable to attempt to delineate the various phases in order to understand better how both cognition and affective responses are altered. The initial phases are "numbness," "protest," and "disorganization," labels that reflect the eventual erosion of cognitive or intellectual capability along with the initial inability of those who are bereaved to accept and process the reality of their loss and the intense affective response of protest or despair. "Yearning" and "protest" typify the second phase, with psychological and somatic restlessness characterizing the protesting behavior. Finally comes "disorganization." The period is indeterminate in length, and Parkes has found two-thirds of one sample to be in this phase after one year.

The identification of specific phases, even with acknowledgment that they may overlap, compensates for the clinical reality that each bereavement is different. It helps explain further how different somatic symptoms might also be expected at different periods of bereavement. Without some knowledge of a substantial personal data base, it is easy to see how some symptoms and behaviors could be misconstrued as not belonging to the overall process.

Extended Reactions

It is difficult to define the period of extended grief reactions, but we might tentatively mark this period from the time, several months after bereavement when, according to Parkes, the panic attacks begin to lessen and the individual returns to his original social matrix and begins to function purposefully within it. This view leaves room for the possibility that the grief period may be open-ended. Depression may coexist with otherwise reconstituted functioning. Individuals may begin to reorganize themselves, but demonstrate by various symptoms, including somatization, the continuance of grief. There are four fairly specific kinds of extended reactions: longer term depressive reactions, hypochondriacal states, panic attacks, and specific somatization, particularly pain. To revert to Akiskal and McKinney's (1975) final common pathway, it is apparent that some bereaved individuals not only manifest prolonged grief, but also develop the traditional host of neurovegetative signs characteristic of unipolar biological depression. These include sleeplessness (particularly early morning awakening) and loss of appetite, libido, weight, concentration, and memory, as well as unprovoked crying. Psychiatrists are well aware that with older individuals depression is frequently manifested by physical symptoms and preoccupation with bodily functions. This parallels observations that the vehicle for expression of psychotic episodes in middle age is frequently some threat to bodily integrity. Hypochondriacal states border upon depressive episodes. They are thought by some to be variants of depression and respond to specific pharmacotherapies used in biological depressions (Klein, Zitrin, and Woerner 1978). In these states the preoccupation with bodily function may achieve the level of obsessive and morbid rumination. Patients often show concerns about malignancy—particularly of the head or gut—after other family members have died from these diseases. I have seen a number of younger patients in a headache clinic who questioned whether they had a brain tumor. Many of these were depressed and all of them had experienced the death of either a close relative or friend as a result of a primary tumor or metastatic disease.

Even years after manifest grief has waned, some individuals find themselves experiencing panic attacks, perhaps while driving. I have found this in several middle-aged women, who not only iterated the usual history of fear of impending doom, but also associated their panic with the experience of the death of a parent. Lastly, the symptom of pain is a universal pathway for the demonstration of continued grief. Particularly among the elderly, the pain of a spouse's death is reflected in intense physical as well as psychological discomfort. This often extends over long periods. Parkes has listed a variety of other disorders that may be triggered by death (1970). These are generally moderate illnesses with some immunological component. It is probably safer to say, since the connection between stress and such illnesses is not clearcut, that it should not be surprising that these illnesses should be exacerbated by severe stress for which the individual has no optimal resolution.

Delayed Grief

The absence of telltale signs of grief and mourning is a complicating factor that should key caregivers to the possibility of a delayed grief reaction and a potential need for psychiatric intervention. The variety of possible manifestations of grief continuously reinforces the observations that feelings (affects) and thoughts (cognitions) of and about dead persons seem to have a life of their own. These sometimes appear to take over normal functioning. Caregivers, involved in using their own coping maneuvers to protect themselves while working with the bereaved, sometimes find that survivors have limited defensive options, which inhibits their ability to progress through the phases of grief.

The threat provoked by a loss may destabilize individuals who were previously thought competent to deal with any adversity. It may promote in others a paradoxical stoicism because of personal traits that proscribe the release of intense feelings regardless of the severity of the psychic trauma. Even the absence of demonstrable psychological symptoms with bereavement—as may occur in the case of a welcomed death after a prolonged, debilitating illness—does not exclude the possibility that grief will belatedly be manifested by symptoms indicating that the process is underway. When prolonged illness has caused survivors to mourn before the actual loss, anticipatory grief may explain the absence of typical symptoms. This is apparent, for example, in situations where survivors are able to discuss their relief that a painful illness has come to an end. But clinicians must also beware of atypical grief syndromes in which customary mourning and grief behaviors are either suppressed or repressed, sometimes to the point that a survivor will behave as though nothing has occurred. Though some individuals simply do not grieve at all, there is a presumption that almost all of us deal in some way with disengagement. When caregivers avoid what looks like an aberrant reaction, and familiar symptoms are not apparent, intervention may be delayed. Even those individuals whose personality structure appears to be permeated with fatalism are simply using denial in their constant restraint of optimism to protect themselves from disappointment.

Grief that takes an unusually long time to manifest itself is often accompanied by unusually intense grieving when symptoms finally occur. Coping maneuvers such as avoidance and denial that seem pathological in their intensity often occur in these individuals beyond the time that one might otherwise expect (Parkes 1965). Such aberrations inevitably raise concerns for more prolonged and pathological reactions and, again, somatic symptoms are a common arena for the portrayal of atypical delayed reactions. In my experience, the very fact of delay in the manifestation of some appropriate reaction seems to predispose survivors to unusual somatic symptoms, which may ensue months to years later. Since many such individuals never seem to verbalize their sense of loss, but demonstrate it in other behaviors, particularly somatization, the question arises of whether there are indeed individuals who are "alexythymic," as Sifneos has argued (1967). In other words, beyond the dynamic reasons for delayed reactions, there may be individuals who are simply not equipped to deal verbally with loss and whose avenues of release are primarily somatic. A familiar subsequent symptom is pain, "expressed" in terms of physical rather than psychological complaints. In some instances, there may be some symbolic meaning to the site, such as the head or the heart, but more commonly the pain seems to be an exacerbation of a preexisting illness, no matter how indolent. It is an open question whether such individuals actually have intensified perceptions of their own body stimuli, whether the symptom reflects withdrawal and self-preoccupation, or whether in fact the stress of the loss does predispose these individuals to exacerbations of continuing illnesses.

Morbid Grief

Morbid or pathological grief occurs when the natural processes of mourning are inhibited to such a degree that major elements of the mourning process remain uncompleted and even intrude upon premorbid personality traits. We are dealing here with an incomplete process of loss from an attachment and a resultant heightening of the discordant behaviors seen during the more acute bereavement period. While cultural factors may obviously play a role, i.e., for some the period of grief, and the characteristics of the reaction may be predetermined by the cultural setting, unresolved grief usually involves some continuous overidentification with a dead person. This pattern is supported by an intensity of affect that does not resolve with the passage of time, and eventually psychopathology develops that incorporates either chronic anxiety reminiscent of separation events or depressive behaviors. Somatic symptoms frequently play a role in these morbid patterns, with survivors either adopting symptoms seen in the deceased's last illness or suffering a reappearance of symptoms they had experienced in a previous illness.

Etiologies of Extended Reactions

The psychological principles that predispose survivors to this repetition of earlier separations are probably common to all extended grief reactions. They reflect the inability of the bereaved to use the mourning process. Barry (1973) has divided the dynamics into external and internal factors. The former, he suggests, are circumstances outside of the bereaved's control that accentuate practical coping activities to the possible exclusion of dealing with unpleasant affects and that hence facilitate the extended use of denial; the latter refer to an intrapsychic structure based on past experiences that inhibit the bereaved from experiencing painful affects and typically involve either the isolation of feelings or their repression. A more extreme example of this behavior would be the absence of grief. As Barry (1973) has rightly pointed out, this is a logical extension of the adage "grown men don't cry," but this cultural pseudo-sanction may unfortunately cut mourners off from access to affects that are appropriate to the circumstances, although very painful. There are infrequent statistics on the incidence of either of these phenomenona.

Specific Delayed Reactions

The "anniversary reaction" is the most striking example of this prolonged and unresolved experience (Musaph 1973). Psychological and medical complaints, particularly those that emerge near the anniversary of either the death of a significant other or the onset of the deceased person's terminal illness, are probably underreported if only because historical data are not sought. It is frequently helpful to ask patients who have puzzling physical complaints not only the family history of major illnesses, but also the specific chronology of these illnesses. On the other hand, the phenomenon of age correspondence, associating the age of onset of emotional disorder with the age of the deceased significant other at death, which was once thought to be fairly common, has been found by Birtchnell (1970) to be relatively rare, and he offers other explanations for the onset of this psychiatric disorder. Lieberman (1978) has identified three other distinct patterns that are associated with morbid grief: phobic avoidance of certain anxiety-provoking situations, the absence of expected grief but ventilation of angry affects toward other individuals (including therapists), and a prolonged grief experience sometimes accompanied by a physical illness and recurrent nightmares of the deceased.

Lieberman has correctly pointed out that diagnostic specificity leads to discrete treatments for these syndromes, including forced mourning in the case of phobic avoidance, but has not commented on the potential utility of psychotropic medications such as monoamine oxidase inhibitors (Parnate and Nardil) or imipramine for the treatment of phobic anxiety (Marks 1970).

In addition to these variant experiences, two further conditions must be viewed with great concern. The first is the emergence within the mourning period of suicidal ideation and even suicide attempts by individuals unable to deal with intense grief. Such ideas and acts are not limited to patients with psychiatric illnesses. They occur in individuals who have been closely bound to or dependent on the deceased person. They may also develop in survivors whose character pathology, as Bowlby suggested, lends itself to impulsive actions as a means of resolving unacceptable levels of anxiety. The development of such ideation, even without a gesture, should be taken as a psychiatric emergency, as such individuals often act quickly without transmitting their level of distress to family members or others who are close to them. Second, a more chronic, but also debilitating sequela is a rigid reaction to the death of loved ones in which their belongings and rooms are preserved as though the decedent were still alive. This phenomenon is referred to as mummification, a doubly appropriate term since it accurately describes the deliberate freezing of the external environment and concomitant internal state in which emotions are fixed at the level of denial.

Such conditions are extraordinarily difficult to change either by psychotherapy or pharmacotherapy. The intrusive, almost delusional quality of such conditions often substantially impairs the function of the survivor or survivors for many years. The author has treated one such patient, a 55-year-old unmarried woman who kept intact her mother's bedroom, pictures, and clothes for twelve years after her death. In this case, a psychotic core appeared to have evolved, with the patient seeing and speaking to her dead mother. Memories of what she reported to have been her mother's deathbed agony and pain were particularly vivid, with no diminution of affect when the patient spontaneously reported these events. The physicians who attended her mother reported, however, that the predominant agony was with the daughter and another sister over their impending loss rather than with the mother, who experienced minimal discomfort.

Mistaken Diagnosis of Grief

Although the focus of this material is on symptoms that are grief-related, misattributions will inevitably be made. These may be the result of conscious patient behaviors as well as misdiagnoses. Psychiatrists are familiar with three conditions in which there is a risk that causal linkages may be prematurely made between a psychopathologic condition and a significant precedent loss. The first condition is a depressive episode in which a linkage is made to a past loss. In our society it is the rule rather than the exception that depressed individuals make repeated references to events such as separations from individuals and losses of loved ones during periods of depression when feeling states are particularly intense. This is, however, a culturally determined phenomenon. In other societies, feelings of guilt, with their attendant cognitive ruminations, do not necessarily rest at the core of depression. Similar issues are sometimes raised by individuals who have suffered a psychotic reaction and who, in its aftermath, attempt to rationalize irrational and uncontrollable experiences by association with past life crises. Losses and separations may indeed act as stressors, but they are not the only trigger points for individuals who also possess other vulnerabilities. It therefore remains an issue of diagnostic acumen to determine the degree to which any particular loss influences the development of a psychopathological condition different from grief.

Such conclusions should not go so far as to ignore the role such stressors might play epidemiologically with regard to premature morbidity and mortality, but they should be used to point to the possibility that other illnesses, while exacerbated by grief reactions and the mourning process, are not necessarily their result (Klerman and Izen 1977).

A second, frequently confused condition is that of grief-related facsimile illness. Zisook and De Vaul (1977) have reported a collection of cases in which the bereaved spouse, parent, or child had symptoms characteristic of a deceased relative. The longest period that elapsed between a death and the manifestation of this facsimile syndrome was seven years. I have also treated one such patient, a widow of 57, who complained of pains in the back of her head and spontaneous tearfulness seven years after her husband's terminal intracranial hemorrhage. In all these cases the symptoms appear to be provoked by an arrest of the acute grief process and its subsequent nonresolution. Zisook and De Vaul sought to mobilize the arrested process by psychotherapy and commented on the hysterical quality of their patients' complaints. I too felt that my patient was experiencing a conversion, but thought that the symptoms represented a "masked depression" and successfully treated her with tricyclic medication and supportive therapy.

The third condition is feigned bereavement, in which the association of the illness to grief appears to be a deliberate misattribution (Snowdon, Solomon, and Druce 1978). This unusual syndrome has been found predominantly in male patients who have gained psychiatric admission for depression, self-destructive behavior, and reported bereavement. Clinical clues include aberrations in the reaction, such as delayed grief, overly dramatic behavior, or the description of the deceased as a young person. These patients are often uncovered by staff members who find inconsistencies in repeated history-taking and are confirmed by developments following such a discovery. These symptoms serve a conscious purpose. The patients seem, by report, to be similar to patients with Munchausen's syndrome (Asher 1951), except that the illnesses seem predominantly psychiatric, at least as reported. Treatment and management of these patients is probably as problematic as for

Munchausen's patients, for whom refusal of treatment appears part of the illness.

Hallucinations and Misperceptions

Labeling as "unusual" symptoms that a substantial percentage of any cohort possesses may seem to indicate that the observer's bias or unfamiliarity rather than the patient's experience defines the illness. Nonetheless, "awareness" of the presence of a dead person is both widely experienced and a very unusual symptom. These are not preternatural experiences—and few patients actually raise that question—but even when transient they are very real. My surmise is that these percepts or experiences are triggered by situations that either repeat experiences a survivor has shared with the dead person or occur under conditions that provoke anxiety and the wish or need to be cared for. Visual hallucinations of dead persons seem to be an extension of these experiences. Rees (1971) studied hallucinatory experiences of dead spouses by their bereaved spouses in the Welsh population where he has performed his other epidemiologic studies. Illusory feelings of the dead spouse's presence were the most commonly reported experiences (39 percent), but both auditory and visual hallucinations were reported by approximately 14 percent of spouses. In all, 47 percent of the population experienced some form of hallucination, some of which lasted for many years. While I have tended to view these experiences as depressogenic in character, I have had some success in treating such persons with low doses of phenothiazines or haloperidol.

Treatment of Grief

Although we commonly infer that grief is a time-limited experience, review of the literature suggests that we accept a wide range of grief reactions, some of which last for weeks and some for years. Therefore, consideration of duration alone seems to me an inadequate standard by which to gauge the reasonableness of intervention, and that it would be wiser to start with the premise that almost every grief reaction deserves some form of intervention. Unfortunately, as McCawley (1976) has pointed out, bereaved individuals do not ordinarily turn to professional help, which in part reflects the turning away from the outside world that accompanies many grief reactions. Physicians, in particular, often have long-term relationships with families and are therefore in a somewhat better position to intervene than other caregiving professionals who may await referral. Usually the initial physician's intervention is couched in humanistic terms (Jacobs and Ostfeld 1975; Schmidt and Messner 1975; De Vaul, Zisook, and Faschingbauer 1979). Hackett (1974) suggests that the key service lies in helping an individual acknowledge the loss and deal with the inevitable life changes. In writing of the role of pediatricians, Lorenzen and Smith (1981) were mindful of parental needs to "see and hold their child after death," and emphasized the need to talk to the father—to assure that he does not isolate his feeling—and to deal with siblings to avoid feelings of abandonment. Their strategy, however, seems more designed to monitor than to treat, and they did not clarify how long a period might elapse before they would make a psychiatric referral—perhaps because the time intervals at which individuals reconstitute seem heavily dependent upon such things as their past experience, and probably their susceptibility to unipolar depression. If one gives credence to the hypothesis that every major loss reevokes separation anxiety, then it seems sensible for the purposes of secondary prevention to offer the temporary presence of a "significant" individual while survivors attempt to master the experience of loss. This, by inference, is what Lindemann sought to accomplish in his cryptic reference to providing 8 to 10 visits for bereaved spouses over four to six weeks. If we establish that at one level this very basic mode of intervention is a productive strategy regardless of situation, we may then draw a continuum from straightforward interventions, which may be carried out with equal efficiency with bereaved individuals and families, to more complex interventions, which require multiple levels of caregivers and psychological as well as pharmacological measures.

The most direct of these is a crisis-intervention model, evolving like other crisis efforts, from the work of Caplan (1970). This does not have to be done on a one-on-one basis even though that is a familiar model for most nonpsychiatric physicians. Constantino (1981) has reported significant differences in the degree of depression and some change in resocialization among a small group of widows receiving group counseling versus untreated controls. Vachon et al. (1980) have studied the effectiveness of peer counseling in a crisis mode, thereby using the personal experiences of survivors in a therapeutic setting. This group found that although the counseled group of widows proceeded along the same adaptive pathway as the uncounseled group, its progress was accelerated. Members of the counseled group also tended to resocialize more effectively when treated in group therapy by widows who had some mental health training. Williams and Polak (1979), however, have questioned the effectiveness of crisis intervention and asked whether the morbidity associated with bereavement is effected over the long term.

I believe that both very pronounced and prolonged grief reactions deserve at least a psychiatric consultation. There is clearly a point when bereaved persons begin to flounder. Psychiatric consultation can be more rapidly administered when a patient is still afloat and has not exhausted all personal resources and family supports. Whether psychiatric help beyond the consultation should be offered depends upon individual situations. My own clinical experience has been that a number of individuals benefit by regular weekly therapy for six months to a year. It is probably the case with such patients that the therapist takes on the role of a transient object as well as a guide and a listener during the mourning process. It is equally true, however, that some individuals back away from more than brief intervention. Like others, I question the real and lasting effectiveness of brief contacts. If the question of resistance in dealing with a death is in the therapist's mind, one must ask if it can really be far away for a patient who seems to avoid continuation of treatment. Raphael (1975) has sought to deal with these issues in the psychotherapeutic treatment of pathological grief. His method includes a direct approach toward opening areas inhibited by grief.

However, this is systematic only in its direct attack on morbid defenses and offers clinicians no particular timetable. Mawson et al. (1981) have reported successful treatment of a small group of patients with morbid grief as compared with a small control group. They used the method of "guided mourning" developed from Marks' (a co-author) work with phobic patients, which entailed forced consideration of painful memories and feelings. They found the method helpful for patients who had avoided or delayed grief, but less useful in patients who verbalized feelings of guilt.

The issue of longer psychotherapeutic intervention is more complex. In spite of the epidemiologic studies suggesting that the course of grief work may last approximately one year, the experience of long-term therapeutic relationships tells us that the themes of loss of close relatives are constant in many patients, even when they are not clinically depressed. This does not mean that issues of separation and loss must necessarily form the major content of the therapy, so much as that the effort of working through these issues is a natural one that individuals sensitive to the losses of close relatives will tend to rework as part of their attempts to master their own destinies. This is an undeniable movement to health and really cannot be labeled as pathological. As familiar as this is to psychiatric clinicians, the reemergence of these themes may disturb other clinicians when patients allude to past losses. I have found that their touching upon these issues is usually a way of rechecking. It does not necessarily mean either that a pathological state is about to emerge or that the grief work was not done.

Psychotropic Medications

Although it might be tempting to employ major psychotropic medications with individuals undergoing grief reactions, clinical experience indicates that these are unwarranted unless such reactions are so intense as to be debilitating, or so prolonged that it appears that the bereaved will not reconstitute without additional intervention.

The usual psychological picture in the former case is substantial affective disorganization. This picture so dominates the presentation that clinicians may ignore the equally serious problem of cognitive disorganization that impairs the bereaved's functioning in broader interpersonal activities, thereby reducing the effectiveness of any social network or support system that might otherwise aid the bereaved. Intense despair coupled with inability to make good use of support systems may therefore indicate that intervention with psychotropic medications does have a place in therapy of grief.

Such concerns become paramount with older patients when psychiatrists are trying to distinguish between depressive states and demented conditions. With the elderly, this issue may be confused by the development of a depressive condition manifested primarily by cognitive deficits to which I have alluded and that is mistakenly inferred to be an organic brain syndrome. While such a presentation may be confused with dementia, logic suggests that it is more properly pseudodementia, in which the cognitive deficits associated with both depression and dementia are more evident than affective aspects. In these cases, a strong argument can be made for more aggressive intervention that includes a trial or trials on antidepressant medications.

The use of psychoactive medications in pronounced grief states by nonpsychiatric clinicians, however, must carry the same admonitions that psychiatric clinicians consider when prescribing medications to depressed patients, especially those with suicidal potential. It is fortunate that many of the medications suggested later in this section for use in intense, acute grief reactions have extremely high lethal dosages. This is not the case with the tricyclic antidepressants or the monoamine oxidase inhibitors. These medications do have a role in the treatment of prolonged reactions, but carry with them some risk in terms of potential morbidity and lethality and should be prescribed within a careful framework that includes assessment of potential self-harm and a guarantee of very regular doctor-patient contact. Additionally, there is a need to appreciate the sensitivity of the elderly to such medications, their side effects, and the potential for drug-drug interactions. Aware that a number of individuals seen in these situations may be elderly, I offer the following pharmacological suggestions.

First, with regard to the period immediately following death, attention might be paid to difficulty in falling asleep and nighttime awakenings. While a strong argument may be made for allowing a bereaved individual or family to experience grief as a trigger to initiate mourning, insomnia simply impairs everyday function by rendering an individual less competent to cope. It thereby impairs the work of grief as well. Two benzodiazepines, flurezepam (Dalmane) and termazepam (Restoril) are extraordinarily effective as hypnotic agents. At least over the short and intermediate terms they appear to have no addictive potential. Of the two, termazepam has the shorter half-life (the time that it takes half of the administered dose to be eliminated from the body) and is reported not to interfere with REM sleep. In the elderly, the half-lives of both are extended; for flurezepam, the half-life may reach 100 hours. Nonetheless, over the short term these are effective hypnotic agents. The standard adult night-time dose for each is 30 mg, but I have found that the so-called geriatric dose of 15 mg is also quite effective in all populations. The morning-after effects of these medications are minimal and do not impair normal function. Unlike chloral hydrate, their lethal dosages are quite high, and they do not cause central nervous system (CNS) depression the way barbiturates do in the elderly. In any event, this latter class of drugs should never be used since its abuse potential and lethality are quite high. An alternative medication for induction of sleep over the short term is diphenhydramine hydrochloride (Benadryl), 25 mg hs; many individuals tolerate this medication quite well.

When daytime agitation becomes a problem, small amounts of benzodiazepines may be used though again, with the elderly, clinicians must beware of several complicating factors. So-called paradoxical effects of these medications, which probably represent cortical disinhibition, have been reported in elderly patients. Certain benzodiazepines undergo hepatic metabolism that may be either slowed by metabolic problems or aging or complicated by other medications. Oxazepam (Serax) has a short half-life (eight hours) and is not demethylated, making it a useful medication in these cases, unless patients have had good experiences with other agents in that class. Alprazolam (Xanax) is a newer benzodiazepine, which, it has been suggested, has little addictive potential. Again, some consideration should be given to using lower doses initially with these patients so that tranquilization is not accomplished at the expense of sedation. If agitation is particularly severe and some of the more unusual psychologic elements, e.g., hallucinations, appear, very low-dose major tranquilizers are often quite helpful. Clinicians may steer away from these medications for fear of dyskinesias, without realizing that they are often used in transiently agitated individuals in general hospitals. Particularly with the elderly, the author has found that perphenazine (Trilafon), acetophenazine (Tindal) and haloperidol (Haldol) have been effective in reducing anxiety and providing for some cognitive and affective restitution. Given orally, the doses for these medications range from 1–4 mg per day for perphenazine, 10–20 mg per day for acetophenazine, and 0.5 to 4 mg per day for haloperidol in divided dosages. Given in somewhat larger dosages in the evening, these medications may also serve as hypnotics because of their sedative effects.

It is important to recognize that the major tranquilizers carry with them a number of potentially unpleasant side effects. I tend to avoid agents like chlorpromazine and thioridizine because of their sedative and hypotensive side effects. In low doses, these other medications infrequently produce parkinsonian side effects. Acetophenazine in particular seems to be the safest, but is sold in doses that make it less convenient than the other two. The point at which clinicians must determine that they are dealing with a depressive episode rather than a grief reaction is extremely difficult to define.

In summary, clinical psychopharmacology has a very definite role along the continuum of grief reactions. Use of these agents, however, may become rather complex. The need for frequent contact with patients on these medications again suggests that psychiatric advice could be useful. Use of these agents must be based on clinical estimates of the intensity, direction, and even appropriateness of a grief reaction. We might hope that a movement to integrate somatic symptomatology into clinical judgment throughout the course of these reactions would not just sharpen diagnostic skills. The thrust of this integration should be the more appropriate intervention and treatment of these conditions by caregivers in many fields in order to minimize morbidity and mortality.

References

Abraham, K. 1949. "A Short Study of the Development of the Libido; Viewed in the Light of Mental Disorders." *Selected Papers on Psycho-Analysis*. London: Hogarth Press.

Akiskal, H. S. and W. T. McKinney, Jr. 1975. "Overview of Recent Research in Depression: Integration of Ten Conceptual Models into a Comprehensive Clinical Frame." *Archives of General Psychiatry* 32:285–306.

Amkraut, A. and E. F. Solomon. 1975. "From the Symbolic Stimulus to the Pathophysiological Response: Immune Mechanisms." *International Journal of Psychiatric Medicine* 5:541–563.

Asher, R. 1951. "Munchausen's Syndrome." *Lancet* 260:339–341.

Barry, M. J. 1973. "The Prolonged Grief Reaction." *Mayo Clinic Proceedings* 48:325–335.

Bartrop, R. W., E. Luckhorst, L. Lazarus, et al. 1977. "Depressed Lymphocyte Function After Bereavement." *Lancet* 1:834–836.

Bennet, G. 1970. "Bristol Floods 1968. Controlled Survey of Effects on Health of Local Community Disaster." *British Medical Journal* 3:454–458.

Birtchnell, J. 1970. "Early Parent Death and Mental Illness." *British Journal of Psychiatry* 116:281–288.

Bowlby, J. 1969. *Attachment and Loss: Attachment*. New York: Basic Books.

Bowlby, J. 1973. *Attachment and Loss: Separation*. New York: Basic Books.

Bowlby, J. 1980. *Attachment and Loss: Loss*. New York: Basic Books.

Caplan, G. 1970. *The Theory and Practice of Mental Health Consultation*. New York: Basic Books.

Clayton, P., L. Desmarais, and G. Winokur. 1968. "A Study of Normal Bereavement." *American Journal of Psychiatry* 125:168–178.

Clayton, P. J., J. A. Halikas, and W. L. Maurice. 1971. "The Bereavement of Widowhood." *Diseases of the Nervous System* 32:597–604.

Clayton, P. J., J. A. Halikas, and W. L. Maurice. 1972. "The Depression of Widowhood." *British Journal of Psychiatry* 120:71–78.

Constantino, R. 1981. "Bereavement Crisis Intervention for Widows in Grief and Mourning." *Nursing Research* 30:351–353.

DeVaul, R. A., S. Zisook, and T. R. Faschingbauer. 1979. "Clinical Aspects of Grief and Bereavement." *Primary Care* 6:391–401.

Engel, G. 1961. "Is Grief a Disease?: A Challenge for Medical Research." *Psychosomatic Medicine* 23:18–22.

Engel, G. 1971. "Sudden and Rapid Death During Psychological Stress." *Annals of Internal Medicine* 74:771–782.

Engel, G. 1978. "Psychologic Stress, Vasodepressor (Vasovagal) Syncope, and Sudden Death." *Annals of Internal Medicine* 89:403–412.

Freud, S. 1957. "Mourning and Melancholia" (1917). Standard Edition, 14:243–258, Hogarth Press, London.

Glick, I., R. S. Weiss, and C. M. Parkes. 1974. *The First Year of Bereavement.* New York: Wiley.

Graves, J. 1978. "Differentiating Grief, Mourning and Bereavement." *American Journal of Psychiatry* 135:874–875.

Hackett, T. P. 1974. "Recognizing and Treating Abnormal Grief." *Hospital Physician* 1:49.

Hinkle, L. E., and H. G. Wolff. 1957. "The Nature of Man's Adaption to His Total Environment and the Relation of This to Illness." *Archives of Internal Medicine* 99:442–460.

Holmes, T. H., and R. G. Rahe. 1967. "The Social Readjustment Rate Scale." *Journal of Psychosomatic Research* 11:213–219.

Jacobs, S. and L. Douglas. 1979. "Grief: A Mediating Process Between Loss and Illness." *Comprehensive Psychiatry* 20:165–174.

Jacobs S. and A. Ostfeld. 1975. "The Clinical Management of Grief." *Journal of American Geriatric Society* 28:331–335.

Jacobs, S. C. and A. Ostfeld. 1977. "An Epidemiological Review of the Mortality of Bereavement." *Psychosomatic Medicine* 39:344–357.

Klein, D., C. M. Zitrin, and M. Woerner. 1978. "Antidepressants, Anxiety, Panic, and Phobia." In M. A. Lipton, A. DiMascio and K. F. Killam, eds., *Psychopharmacology: A Generation of Progress,* New York: Raven Press.

Klerman, G. L. and J. E. Izen. 1977. "The Effects of Health on Bereavement and General Well Being." *Advances in Psychosomatic Medicine* 9:63–100.

Levi, L. D., C. H. Fales, M. Stein, et al. 1966. "Separation and Attempted Suicide." *Archives of General Psychiatry* 15:158–164.

Lieberman, S. 1978. "Nineteen Cases of Morbid Grief." *British Journal of Psychiatry* 132:159–163.

Lindemann, E. 1944. "The Symptomatology and Management of Acute Grief." *American Journal of Psychiatry* 101:141–148.

Lloyd, C. 1980. "Life Events and Depressive Disorder Reviewed." *Archives of General Psychiatry* 37:529–535.

Lorenzen, M. and L. Smith. 1981. "The Role of the Physician in the Grief Process." *Clinical Pediatrics* 20:466–470.

Marks, I. 1970. "Agoraphobic Syndrome (Phobic Anxiety State)." *Archives of General Psychiatry* 28:538–553.

Mawson, D., I. M. Marks, L.. Ramm, and R. S. Stern. 1981. "Guided Mourning for Morbid Grief: A Controlled Study." *British Journal of Psychiatry* 138:185–193.

McCawley, A. 1976. "Grief and the Primary Physician." *Connecticut Medicine* 40:115–122.

Musaph, H. 1973. "Anniversary Disease." *Psychotherapy and Psychosomatics* 22:325–333.

Parkes, C. M. 1965. "Bereavement and Mental Illness. Part 2: A Classification of Bereavement Reactions." *British Journal of Medical Psychology* 38:13–26.

Parkes, C. M. 1970a. "The First Year of Bereavement: A Longitudinal Study of the

Reaction of London Widows to the Death of Their Husbands." *Psychiatry* 33:444–466.

Parkes, C. M. 1970b. "The Psychosomatic Effects of Bereavement." *Modern Trends in Psychosomatic Medicine*. London: Butterworth.

Parkes, C. M. 1972. *Bereavement: Studies of Grief In Adult Life*. New York: International Universities Press.

Raphael, B. 1975. "The Management of Pathological Grief." *Australian and New Zealand Journal of Psychiatry* 9:173–180.

Rees, W. D. 1971. "The Hallucinations of Widowhood." *British Medical Journal* 4:37–41.

Rees, W. D. and S. G. Lutkins. 1967. "Mortality of Bereavement." *British Medical Journal* 4:13–16.

Schmale, A. H. 1972. "Giving Up as a Final Common Pathway to Changes in Health." *Advances in Psychosomatic Medicine* 8:20–40.

Schmidt, D. D. and E. Messner. 1975. "The Management of Ordinary Grief." *Journal of Family Practice* 2:259–262.

Sifneos, P. E. 1967. "Clinical Observations on Some Patients Suffering from a Variety of Psychosomatic Diseases." *Proceedings of 7th European Conference on Psychosomatic Research*. Basel: Karger.

Sims, A. 1978. "Hypotheses Linking Neuroses with Premature Mortality." *Psychological Medicine* 8:255–263.

Snowdon, J., R. Solomon, and H. Druce. 1978. "Feigned Bereavement: Twelve Cases." *British Journal of Psychiatry* 133:15–19.

Sweeney, D. R. and J. W. Maas. 1979. "Stress and Noradrenergic Function in Depression." In *The Psychobiology of the Depressive Disorders*, pp. 161–176. New York: Academic Press.

Vachon, M. L. S., W. A. L. Lyall, J. Rogers, et al. 1980. "A Controlled Study of Self-Help Intervention for Widows." *American Journal of Psychiatry* 137:1380–1384.

Van Eerdewegh, M. M., M. D. Bieri, R. H. Parrilla, and P. J. Clayton. 1982. "The Bereaved Child." *British Journal of Psychiatry* 140:23–29.

Weisman, A. and T. Hackett. 1961. "Predilection to Death: Death and Dying as a Psychiatric Problem." *Psychosomatic Medicine* 23:232–256.

Williams, W. V. and P. R. Polak. 1979. "Follow-up Research in Primary Prevention: A Model of Adjustment in Acute Grief." *Journal of Clinical Psychology* 35:35–45.

Wolfenstein, M. 1966. "How is Mourning Possible?" *Psychoanalytic Study of the Child* 21:93–123.

Zisook, S. and R. DeVaul. 1977. "Grief-Related Facsimile Illness." *International Journal of Psychiatry in Medicine* 7(4):329–336.

Preamble: The course of bereavement is usually predictable. In time, the bereaved characteristically return to a state of productivity and well-being, even if they are not totally unaffected by the nature and the extent of their loss. When, in addition to expected depression, the reaction includes undue loss of self-esteem, feelings of self-condemnation, suicidal thoughts, or grief that is inappropriate to the occasion, special professional assistance may be necessary.

Principle 11: Especially Severe Reactions to Bereavement May Require Special Professional Care

11

Severe Reactions to Bereavement and Special Professional Care

VAMIK D. VOLKAN

It has been demonstrated (Bowlby 1961; Bowlby and Parkes 1970; Engel 1962; Pollock 1961) that the course of mourning has predictable sequential phases through which anyone who has lost a loved one can be expected to pass. It can be divided into two stages.

The Course of Mourning

A. THE INITIAL STAGE

The beginning of mourning, a stage lasting from a few weeks to a few months, begins with numbness and shock and denial of the death. It is quickly followed by the splitting of ego functions in respect to the perception of the death. The bereaved perceives that death has occurred, but behaves pretty much as if it had not happened. Certain images of the deceased are evoked, along with an exaggerated inner relatedness to that person. Painful emotions are also accompanied by weeping with frustration over the absence of the loved one (Pollock 1961).

This stage concludes with anger toward the deceased, which indicates the ego's attempt to accept the loss, along with all of its psychological implications. This narcissistic response to separation initiates integration under the reality principle of the initially split ego functions pertaining to the death. The different constellations involved may appear serially or simultaneously, and may disappear only to reappear. Finally, however, it is anger—sometimes displaced onto others—that marks the conclusion of the initial stage.

B. THE WORK OF MOURNING

This second stage, which usually takes from one to two years but may go on much longer, involves a slow-motion review of the mourner's relationship to the one mourned. There is also a struggle between keeping or rejecting a close tie with the representation of the deceased—a painful awareness that no longer will the deceased be able to justify the mourner—and regressive disorganization. Ultimately this is followed by a new inner organization better able to test reality for confirmation that the death, with all its psychological implications, has indeed taken place.

It can be anticipated that the mourner will identify during and at the end of mourning with selected aspects of the one mourned. Such aspects are depersonified and changed into functions; the mourner will assume some functions of the departed. When the work of mourning is successful, the mourner's ego can be expected to manifest enrichment, because of the internalization of such new functions. Mourning thus ends with a new inner adaptation to the external loss. The psychological process of mourning can be compared with the organic process involved in the healing of a wound or the mending of a broken bone—the return to health of an organism that has suffered some damaging blow (Engel 1961; Bowlby 1961; Volkan 1981). But just as a wound can become infected, so can the process of mourning run into complications, some of which may respond well enough to such social support as that provided by family, friends, and, perhaps, religious resources. Some may, however, be serious enough to require attention from a professional trained in dealing with complicated psychological problems.

Elements Affecting the Course of Mourning

Certain general elements affect the way a mourner deals with death and determine the kind of pattern to be expected in the initial response and in the work of mourning.

A. ANTICIPATORY GRIEF

The mourning process may be initiated by an anticipated death, or even a fantasied one. Anticipatory grief (Lindemann 1944) is based on a belief, realistic or not, that death impends. This belief gradually accustoms the mourner to imminent loss. It may lead to positive results because it sufficiently prepares the person so that when actual death occurs, the initial response to it and the work of mourning require less energy than would otherwise be the case. The mourner has been vaccinated, so to speak, so when he is finally exposed to the "illness" itself he experiences it in attenuated form.

Anticipatory grief can also have negative results, especially when the death that has been anticipated does not, in fact, occur. For example, a bride fantasied that her husband would not return from his assignment to the war zone, and when he did return uninjured she perceived him as a "ghost"—someone quite other than the man she had married—and soon divorced him (Volkan 1981).

B. SUDDEN EXPOSURE TO A DEATH

This is, of course, an experience contrary to that undergone when death has been anticipated. The sudden and altogether unexpected death of someone important (Volkan 1970) in one's life evokes a response quite different from that evoked by the demise of someone whose age and physical condition have suggested for some time that he had a frail hold on life. When the mourner is unprepared for the death, its occurrence may trigger something like traumatic neurosis, and the trauma will be responded to according to the maturity of the mourner's psychic organization.

C. UNFINISHED BUSINESS

The amount and nature of "psychological business" between the two parties that was left "unfinished" by the death will have its effect, according to how the mourner had depended on the deceased for his own psychological equilibrium and the hope of advancing his own psychological growth. If the one who died is anyone whom the mourner had idealized, enhancing his own self-esteem by connection with the "superior" other, the death will bring marked consequences; if the mourner "kills" his idealized dead, his own psychological equilibrium will suffer. With such a strong psychological need to keep the dead person's image "alive," the process of mourning becomes complicated, just as it does when the bereavement impedes the mourner's efforts to grow psychologically. An example is provided by the case of a young man who lost an elderly man who represented for him the oedipal father. When he died, the young man was involved in a reactivated oedipal struggle in which he was seeking to identify with him in order to grow psychologically.

Unfinished psychological business with an important other is usually accompanied by ambivalence, conscious or not. Thus need for the other person is side by side with hate toward him, and ambivalence about "keeping" his representation or "letting it go" produces conflict.

D. LOSS

The degree to which reactions to past loss are reactivated (Klein 1940) will help determine whether the death of someone important in one's life will reawaken the trauma. Loss is considered here in sufficiently general terms to include the surrender of dependence on others as one individuates, forms a new identity, and move through the life cycle. When one's response to past loss, caused either by real separation or by psychological detachment in the course of development, has been stormy but repressed, the death of an important other may trigger its unconscious return and complicate the mourning process.

E. VIOLENT DEATH

On the basis of my prior research, I believe that mourning is often complicated when the death was a violent one—a suicide, perhaps, or an accident involving mutilation. This is because the mourner's natural anger toward the dead, a response to being rejected (left behind) and thus damaged narcissistically, must take recognition of the violence into account. In this situation the mourner feels more than the usual guilt, thus becoming unable to pass smoothly through the mourning process.

F. CHANGED CIRCUMSTANCES

Changes in the real world brought about by the death of someone close must be taken into account. A death may bring not only its own emotional trauma but wrenching changes in the mourner's circumstances. For example, the unexpected death of the family head sometimes presents the family with a serious reduction in its living standard.

All of these elements are considered here in connection with the mourning reactions of adults. There remains considerable controversy in the literature as to when children become capable of mourning in the adult sense. The child's mental apparatus must be sufficiently mature to permit him to maintain internally a representation of the other—to develop object constancy—before he can come close to grieving as adults do (A. Freud 1960). Still, children use the adults in their environment for their own psychic functions and as resources for the mastery of anxiety. For example, a mother performs functions necessary for the child's psychological well-being, and her loss cannot be mourned properly unless there is a good enough substitute for her. Otherwise, the child will take into adulthood a search for persons to perform the functions of his lost mother. Passage through adolescence—the period in which the youth surrenders the images of the parents of his childhood and experiences a mourning model as part of this developmental milestone—is a necessary precondition for "normal" adult mourning (Wolfenstein 1966).

The professional faced with a patient whose mourning is severely complicated will do well to keep all the above elements in mind, and to assess their role in keeping the mourning process from resolution.

Complication in the Initial Stage

A. THE SIGNS AND SYMPTOMS EXPECTABLE IN THE INITIAL STAGE OF RESPONSE TO DEATH MAY BE EXAGGERATED.

This does not necessarily mean that the mourner will be unable to avoid complications in the initial stage of dealing with the death if he has help from family members, his religious beliefs, and adequate inner strength; only time can tell whether the exaggerated responses will persist. For example, a woman who sobs with narcissistic hurt, "How could my husband leave me! I want him back!" may abandon this dramatic response within a few weeks and settle down into a quiet course of mourning that will ultimately be resolved without intervention. Nevertheless, the continued exaggeration of *two* special responses is alarming and usually leads to the need for professional attention. These two most symptomatic behavior patterns are denial and anger.

i. Denial of the Death. Although it is "normal" for one bereaved to deny the death initially, exaggerated and dominant denial lasting for more than a few days will be considered "pathological" because it is so clearly at odds with reality. The family of the denier, or his religious advisor, may be able to help him face reality, but if their efforts fail, psychiatric help may be sought, although the psychiatrist is seldom faced with a patient able to maintain total denial into chronicity. I have seen only two patients who have exhibited denial of death long enough to be brought in for psychiatric treatment. One was a man who had been summoned to a hospital to identify the body of a brother killed in a car accident, but who had not attended the funeral, continuing to believe that his brother's death was nothing but a dream.

ii. Anger. It is usual for the mourner to be angry at a doctor, a relative, the funeral director, or someone else during the initial phase of his grief. Even when there is an objective cause for such anger, this emotion absorbs the "normal" anger one expects, and that is unconsciously directed toward the deceased, toward whom there may even be some open, direct anger. When such anger is greatly exaggerated because of some associated negative reaction, however, the mourner is likely to be brought to psychiatric attention. This will almost certainly be the case if the mourner arms himself with a gun and threatens to kill strangers with it, although such behavior, however alarming, may be simply a storm that will subside, allowing the patient to resume an orderly course of mourning. In a situation described elsewhere (Volkan 1970), I discussed the case of a man who had threatened to kill others with a gun as a response to his grandfather's death. After being treated during brief confinement in a protective hospital environment, he resumed a "normal" sort of mourning, and a five-year followup showed that his complications and his bizarre behavior never returned.

B. WHEN SIGNS AND SYMPTOMS EXPECTABLE IN THE INITIAL STAGE ARE ABSENT OR MINIMAL

Denial of a death is not the same response as accepting it with apparent equanimity. Sometimes a patient who does not deny that the death so important to him has occurred simply fails to show shock or to weep; he is neither angry nor preoccupied with the image of the dead. It was Deutsch (1937) who demonstrated that this negative response may point to the presence of complications and indicates that, sooner or later, in one form or another, a complicated reaction will become evident.

One young man who failed to manifest the usual signs and symptoms of the initial response to a death was enabled by professional help to express his grief ten years later. He had been in his late teens when, as he sat with his mother and sister in their home one evening, someone came to the door and told them that his father had been killed in a mine accident. Stoically, he then became "the man of the house" himself. In his late twenties he entered the neurological ward of a hospital because he had trouble standing up, especially in the early evening. The first attack of this disability had come on the ninth anniversary of his father's death, and he had suffered from it for a year. An insurance policy that had been supporting the family was terminated when the youngest child turned 18, nine years after her father's death. This put a heavy financial burden on the patient, who had been able to establish himself as a professional man without having to support his mother and sister. He then developed the symptoms that yielded him the secondary gain of disqualifying him as the family wage-earner. It took psychotherapy to induce in him the responses characteristic of the initial response to death, whereupon he went into a forward-moving process of mourning.

C. WHEN SIGNS AND SYMPTOMS OF THE INITIAL STAGE FAIL TO DISAPPEAR AFTER A FEW MONTHS

A "protracted course" (Wahl 1970) indicates the presence of complications. One sometimes sees a person who was bereaved five or even ten years earlier who bursts into tears at any reminder of the lost one and manifests intense pain, although appearing "normal" in every other way. When such signs and symptoms occur often enough to disturb daily adjustment and reduce productivity, it is evident that the complication has become chronic, although such chronicity in a pure form is rare. It is even more usual for the persistent initial reactions to be condensed with the complications of the work of mourning.

D. WHEN SIGNS AND SYMPTOMS OF THE INITIAL STAGE GIVE WAY TO UNUSUAL NEW SYMPTOMS

In speaking of "unusual new symptoms," I refer to recognizable psychological or psychosomatic illnesses, either of which needs professional treatment. The reasons such illnesses appear in this context differ from one person to another and must thus be formulated in psychodynamic terms, with appropriate treatment plans being similarly individualized.

An example is provided by a young physician with a hysterical personality organization who continually competed anxiously with other men, especially those older than himself, and who often seduced other men's women in an attempt at oedipal victory. His "victories" were illusory ones, however, and he repeated this behavior over and over. One evening, called to the home of an ailing uncle, he seduced his uncle's wife, a woman considerably younger than her husband, having intercourse with her in a room not far from the sickroom. After going to sleep that night in his own apartment he was awakened by the news that his uncle had just died. On the following day he manifested a severe obsessive-compulsive neurosis, entertaining obsessional thoughts about having a fungal infection of the penis and spending hours washing it. He prescribed medication for himself to use on the skin that was supposedly infected. He saw several dermatologists about his problem, but they all agreed that he had no infection, so he sought psychiatric help. The psychiatric formulation was that guilt over "killing" the father figure and taking his woman had led him to regress, and that the "infection" of his penis was punishment. Washing it away was his attempt to repent and wash away his incestuous feelings for his mother and his murderous feelings for his father. Other condensed psychological constellations could also be discerned in this patient.

The following vignette exemplifies initial grief reactions giving way to psychosomatic response. A teenager's father was dying slowly of multiple sclerosis while his son, caring for his physical needs, began some preparatory mourning. The boy was highly ambivalent toward the dying man, who at times had been very harsh. As the boy carried his father's wasting body to the bathroom he began to think of flushing him down the toilet even as he acted more and more faithfully as his slave. When at last the man died, his son began to grieve in the usual way. He was Jewish and conformed to the relevant Jewish customs, but before the ritual was completed his mother insisted that he be sent to a relative who lived in the country in order to escape from a grieving household and to rest. He caught a small snake in the country, killed it, and put it in a bottle of acid, watching it being slowly eaten away. His later psychotherapy indicated that this was an act of "killing" his father, an effort made prematurely to complete the initial stage of grieving that had been interrupted, with the snake representing the dead man. The boy himself at the same time developed severe dermatitis, which was associated with his disruptive identification with the snake's rotting skin.

Complications in the Work of Mourning

In the long run complications in the work of mourning result either in reactive depression or established pathological mourning (Volkan 1981). Similarities and dissimilarities of mourning and "melancholia" (the term reactive depression in this connection is used interchangeably with melancholia) have been noted since the work of Abraham (1911; 1916; 1924) and Freud (1917), but the concept of established pathological mourning, which more directly reflects fixation in the work of mourning, is a relatively original contribution (Volkan 1974; 1981).

Furthermore, complications in the initial response to death may condense in either reactive depression or established pathological mourning if they become chronic. Although one sometimes sees other unusual clinical pictures associated with complications in the work of mourning, they are psychodynamically akin to the two cited here.

A. WHEN COMPLICATIONS IN THE WORK OF MOURNING RESULT IN REACTIVE DEPRESSION

Freud (1917) indicated that mourning is a typical and expectable reaction to the loss of someone loved, whereas "melancholia" may be a more selectively determined response to such an event. The phenomenology of the latter state involves profoundly painful dejection, loss of interest in the outside world, loss of the ability to love, and inhibition of any activity not concerned with thoughts of the lost one. These also occur in mourning, but mourning is distinguished from reactive depression by the marked lowering of self-regard characteristic of the latter state. One hears from the depressed individual statements full of self-reproach and self-revelations that culminate "in a delusional expectation of punishment" (Freud 1917:244).

As noted, as a result of the work of mourning, the mourner identifies with selected aspects of the one he mourns, which he depersonifies and turns into functions. This process leaves the mourner's ego enriched. In depression provoked by a death, however, internalization results in a "total" sort of identification, and hated and dreaded traits of the deceased are internalized along with the loved and admired ones. The ambivalence with which the dead had been regarded then becomes an internal conflict; the love for the deceased promotes "keeping" him within the self, while hate toward him promotes his "destruction" (Fenichel 1945). The mourner's self-system thus becomes a battleground; aggression preserved in oneself through identification makes for guilt and self-reproach.

Suicide in reactive depression: One possible outcome of the complication of the work of mourning that goes into depressive reaction is the "melancholic" suicide. The mourner, having become himself the battleground between the thrust to keep the dead person's representation, with which he has identified, and the thrust to destroy it, is likely to attempt self-destruction. People in this state obviously require professional care.

B. WHEN COMPLICATIONS IN THE WORK OF MOURNING RESULT IN ESTABLISHED PATHOLOGICAL MOURNING

The individual in established pathological mourning, like the one depressed after a death, has been faced with some complications in the work of mourning. Unlike the depressed individual, however, he has not developed a disruptive total identification with the dead person's representation, but keeps it as an unassimilated *introject,* which is a special kind of object representation not entirely absorbed into the self-representation nor altogether identified with it (Volkan 1976). It is functional in strongly influencing the self-representation, but it leads to no structural change and does not influence ego organization as identification does. The mourner describes his introject as an "inner presence" living inside himself where contact with it can be maintained (Schafer 1968). The ambivalent relationship of the past continues in the mourner's involvement with his introject; he is torn between a strong yearning for the restored presence of the one he mourns, and an equally deep dread that he might indeed confront him. The presence of the introject provides the illusion that he can choose, and in this way it reduces his anxiety.

An interest in reincarnation and impulses to search for the lost one on earth sometimes give evidence of such ambivalent yearning. A glimpse of some stranger who resembles the dead person often leads the individual in established pathological mourning to anxious pursuit and scrutiny to either establish or rule out the possibility that the one he mourns continues to live. The compulsive reading of obituary notices, rather common in this state, not only betrays anxiety about one's own death but also demonstrates a hope of denying the death that has occurred by finding no current mention of it. The person in established pathological mourning continues using the present tense in speaking of the one he lost: "My father likes to walk"—"My mother has blue eyes," etc. The daily life of such people seems focused on death, their conversation on graveyards and tombs; they refer to people who are about to die or who have just died, and one gets the impression that the dead person and other figures representing him by displacement populate the mourner's mind.

i. Dreams. People with established pathological mourning have typical dreams, which often continue for years, the manifest content of which can be classified under three headings: (a) "frozen" dreams, (b) dreams of a life-and-death struggle, and (c) dreams of death as an illusion. Such dreams provide important diagnostic clues.

a. Frozen dreams. This term is often spontaneously used by patients themselves to describe dreams composed of one tableau after another, with no action. One patient likened his dreams to a slide series, and another compared his to slices of bread slipping out of their wrapping (Volkan 1981). "Frozen" also indicates "lifeless." Associations to such dreams reflect fixation in the work of mourning, a defensive situation in which the patient tries to deny his aggression toward the dead person while at the same time finding a way to bring him back to life; the conflict between the wish to do so and the dread of success is handled by "freezing" the conflict and averting resolution.

b. Dreams of a life-and-death struggle. In this kind of dream, the dreamer sees the dead person as living but engaged in a life-and-death struggle, perhaps on the point of drowning, for example. The dreamer tries to save him, but usually awakens with anxiety before succeeding. Such a dream leaves the mourner again in the indeterminate position of being faced with "killing" or "saving" the one he mourns.

c. Dreams of death as an illusion. The dreamer dreams of seeing the one he mourns dead, but exhibiting such paradoxical signs of life as sweating, twitching, and so forth, so that doubt about his being truly dead persists.

ii. Linking objects and phenomena. Another diagnostic clue to established pathological mourning is the presence of linking objects and phenomena (Volkan 1972; 1981). The individual in this state not only maintains internal contact with the representation of the one he mourns through the introject, but maintains also the illusion of external contact by means of a linking object, something he uses in a magical way to be, in metapsychological terms, a locus for meeting with the representation of the dead individual. Its employment facilitates the illusion that the mourner has full control of the choice between "killing" or "not killing" the one he mourns, and thus need never resolve the dilemma of his grief. The relationship between a linking object, the fetish, and a reactivated transitional object has been described elsewhere (Volkan 1972; 1981; Winnicott 1953).

A linking object may be (1) a personal possession of the deceased (perhaps something he wore, like a watch); (2) a gift from the deceased; (3) something the deceased had used to extend his senses or bodily functions (such as a camera—an extension of sight); (4) some realistic representation of the deceased, (a photograph); or (5) something that was at hand when the mourner first learned of the death or saw the dead body.

Linking phenomena are fantasies, sensations, or behavior patterns that perpetuate the possibility of contact between the mourner and the one mourned without reference to any tangible object. Religious belief in the hereafter may be an example of this, although in any culture that fosters this belief only an exaggerated application of it should be considered suggestive of pathology. Something with sensory impact, like a song, could be a linking phenomenon. One patient who had attended her father's funeral in the rain used the song "Raindrops Are Falling on My Head" as a linking phenomenon; even after many years it would induce eerie feelings in her, helping to freeze her mourning process in the illusion that through this song she had the choice of being in contact with her father or burying him. Linking objects and linking phenomena can be advantageously used in "re-grief" therapy, as will be shown.

iii. Suicide in established pathological mourning. The risk of suicide is not so great in established pathological mourning as in reactive depression, since the individual in the former condition is protected from the impulse to self-destruction by a stable linking object or stable introject. He has not identified in the manner of the depressed person, but maintains the illusion of contact with a representation of the dead that is not included in his self-representation but remains exterior to it. When he is aggressive toward the introject or the linking object, his aggression is then not addressed toward the self. Moreover—and more importantly—the illusion he is maintaining manages his feelings of guilt since through it he can, if he chooses, "bring the dead back."

In the rather rare circumstance of a person in established pathological mourning attempting suicide, his effort is not of the "melancholic" type, but one that reflects his wish for magical reunion with the representation of the dead. The anniversary reaction of persons in established pathological mourning may initiate such a strong desire to merge with the representation of the dead (which exists independently of the self-representation) that suicide seems a compelling prospect.

C. WHEN COMPLICATIONS IN THE WORK OF MOURNING LEAD TO UNUSUAL NEW SYMPTOMS

We have noted that the signs and symptoms of the initial stage of mourning may give way to unusual psychological or psychosomatic manifestations. Some complications in the work of mourning (the second stage) may also initiate unusual symptoms, the appearance of which is influenced by the individual's personality organization, the nature of his object relations, the severity of the structural conflicts reactivated by the death, the points of fixation, the tendency to (re)somatization, and so forth. Accordingly, the treatment of such conditions, especially when they become chronic, may be time-consuming and require highly developed professional skills such as the ability to conduct psychoanalysis proper or psychoanalytic therapy.

Even a brief review of the psychiatric and psychoanalytic literature (Brown and Epps 1966; Cobb, Bauer and Whiting 1939; Crisp and Priest 1972; Evans and Liggett 1971; Greene and Miller 1958; Hill 1972; Lehrman 1956; Lidz 1949; McDermott and Cobb

1939; Parkes 1964a; 1964b; Parkes and Brown 1972; Peck 1939; Schmale 1958; Volkan 1965) shows widespread awareness of the number of psychiatric and psychosomatic illnesses associated with, triggered by, or condensed with complications in the work of mourning. This phenomenon has, as a matter of fact, long been known to poets and novelists—or at least used by them for dramatic effect—as when a fictional person losing a lover to death sinks into a physical decline because of grief. Reference to creative artists underlines the possibility that some complications in the work of mourning have positive rather than negative outcomes, since such writers as Hamilton (1969; 1973; 1975; 1979) believe that the creativity of many artists is the end result of their inability to pass smoothly through the mourning process themselves. It is also suggested that complications in mourning can lead certain persons into political leadership (Pollock 1975) or archeological activity (Niederland 1965), and so on.

I wish to emphasize here my finding (Volkan 1981) that some complications of the work of mourning, when condensed with complications stemming from the initial stage of response to death, can lead to a clinical picture like that of psychosis. I stress the importance of giving close attention to death-related events and their psychological consequences when making a diagnosis, since the condition brought on by complications in the mourning process is *not* a true psychosis, in spite of the resemblance, but one that can be treated successfully in even *brief* psychotherapy.

Described elsewhere (Volkan, Cillufo, and Sarvay 1975) is the successful "re-griefing" of a man who had the delusion that his wife was trying to poison him. Here I report another case, that of a woman in her fifties who seemed psychotic but who was put back on the course of "normal" mourning by the briefest of psychotherapeutic experiences, one that offered nothing beyond one significant clarification/interpretation. This technique is reminiscent of the one that Socarides (1954) used when he applied psychoanalytic explanations and interpretations to a patient's symptoms and history.

My patient had had two married sons, the younger of whom had been killed piloting his own airplane. The son's wife, in the plane with him, escaped without a scratch. My patient could not dismiss the notion that her son's wife had been responsible for the accident, which was officially attributed to pilot error. My patient often spoke of "foul play" in connection with the accident and saw her daughter-in-law as somehow a danger to herself; she had delusions about her daughter-in-law's having poisoned her husband. She spent a year, and much of her energy, trying to understand the nature of the foul play in which she believed so firmly. She even went so far as to employ a detective to investigate her daughter-in-law and to review the autopsy findings and official report connected with the plane crash. Unable to sleep because of her suspicions, she seemed greatly disturbed. Her husband, a mild and loving man, comforted her with assurances that the daughter-in-law would not have gone with her husband on any flight she knew would crash, and that there was no reason to suspect the survivor of any malign intent, because everything pointed to hers having been a happy marriage.

My patient had so persisted in adhering to her conviction of foul play in the absence of any justification for it, however, that she had been diagnosed as paranoid before I saw her. During our diagnostic interview the patient freely discussed her theory of foul play. When I probed for background information, I realized that her son's death had reactivated some past concerns about another death. She was one of six siblings, some older and some younger than she, and the only girl. Her childhood had been spent in a home oriented to boys, but parental kindness made it tolerable. When she was 13, one of her brothers died suddenly from a ruptured appendix, and the mother's reaction to this loss was extreme. It seemed that the mother had been deeply involved in established pathological mourning, withdrawing from the family and centering all her thoughts on her dead son. The patient had felt victimized by foul play when it was assumed that as a girl she was responsible for looking after the family, including her grieving mother. Her own needs were disregarded, and her mother did not even attend her high school graduation. Her reaction formation led her to become a "do-gooder," working throughout her early twenties to make money and to help a brother who needed surgery for a brain tumor. Then she met and married an undemanding man by whom she had two sons. Her altruistic devotion persisted; anger over her mother's withdrawal was repressed until the mother died, three years before the plane crash.

The mother was still suffering from established pathological mourning at the time of her death. On her deathbed she summoned her children and their families and told them about her "secret objects"—linking objects she had kept over the years to bind her to her dead son. She wanted her remaining children to treasure them after she died. Obliged to humor her, my patient had felt angry, reviewing the death-related "foul play" that had kept her bound for so long, and the way that her mother had seemed "uncaring" and had deprived her of the maternal warmth that was her birthright. She subsequently repressed this anger again.

Her recital of all this led my patient to say how "uncaring" her son's wife had seemed during his funeral. This perception stimulated thoughts of foul play and the displacement onto the daughter-in-law of the image of the mother whose complicated grief had made life so difficult. The one basic understanding given the patient during this interview was that the treatment she thought she was getting from her daughter-in-law reflected the earlier experience with her mother. It was, in fact, established that the bereaved wife had been sedated by her physician before the funeral and this accounted for her apparent composure.

A week later my patient said that on the way home from this interview she had decided to visit her daughter-in-law. As it turned out, the visit was in the service of testing reality, and the two women stayed up all night talking and weeping together about their common loss. My patient then saw the younger woman as a deeply caring widow, one no longer contaminated with the mother's image; this revelation put her mourning process on the right track, so to speak.

I saw this patient eight times in the next six months to check on the progress of her work of mourning, which was now showing the expected manifestations. Although I neither encouraged her to report childhood conflicts nor explored defensive-adaptive aspects of her personality, she spontaneously reported a childhood memory that I felt needed limited attention in the service of tying it up with the theme of foul play. My patient, while in early latency, had been teased by her brothers and had seized a toy airplane belonging to the brother who was soon to die, throwing it from the stairs to crash on the floor below. This memory and the accompanying feelings of guilt had stayed in her mind for years. She even thought of the possibility that she had encouraged her dead son to become a pilot in response to her unconscious guilt over crushing her younger brother's toy aircraft. We dealt with this notion without pushing her to reveal any symbolic meaning connected with planes or any psychosexual fantasies. She remains symptom free in respect to her "paranoid condition," and on the second anniversary of her son's death her whole family, including her son's widow, gathered in a public park to unveil a picnic shelter dedicated to the dead pilot's memory. This memorialization marked the end of her work of mourning, and she no longer needed my services.

Treatment

Since the mourning process is nature's exercise in loss and restitution, it seldom needs special professional attention unless it becomes complicated. Indeed, uncomplicated grief is not often handled by a psychiatrist. Clayton et al. (1968) showed that 98 percent of those who suffer from bereavement sought no psychiatric assistance, and of that 98 percent, 81 percent began to improve from six to ten weeks after the death; 4 percent did not improve.

I believe that "improvement" is hard to assess statistically without a searching study of the inner adaptation to death made by the individuals in question. Also, some people who initially displayed little or no reaction may appear healthy enough to be included among those who mourn without difficulty, whereas we know that the state of some of these may very well sooner or later reflect complications of the initial stage. Thus, when the absence of initial reaction is striking, professional help should be sought, if only because such a move is good preventive medicine. The professional should then search for psychological reasons for the negative response and help the mutely bereaved to initiate mourning. If short-term therapy is not beneficial, at least it gives the patient the option to seek more intensive therapy, and encourages him to think of professional help should he have future need of it.

Generally, the use of drugs to suppress the symptoms and signs of the initial stage of grief is contraindicated. In fact, one should support rather than suppress the initial responses; this is an economic move since it prevents the need for further grieving at some later time, when it is likely to be less socially acceptable. The development of a variety of religious rituals to deal with death and the emotions it generates is no accident; we should advise the mourner to indulge in them fully, for he will find them beneficial.

The grief-stricken person is distant from others and, at times, hostile. His hostility may be projected onto the professional caregiver, who, being familiar with this symptom, is able to absorb the patient's hostility without returning it. Whenever the anger is highly exaggerated, however, it should be taken seriously, although I still prefer to refrain from the use of drugs if possible in such cases. The professional should set limits—perhaps insisting that the patient be hospitalized. After the patient is placed in the protective environment of a hospital, the therapist can respond to his anger by assuming a role in which he can bear his patient's narcissistic hurt. He must reject the use of drastic measures in response to the patient's behavior patterns and allow him to experience pain, anger, and other emotions, empathically helping him to heal his "wound," always remembering that he is responding to a process of nature. Some mourners may even be relieved by little more than an educational and therapeutic effort to assure them that anger is an expectable initial reaction to the death of someone close.

I would like to state once again that the appearance of severe signs and symptoms in the initial stage does *not* necessarily mean that the patient will have complications in the second stage—that of the work of mourning. An individual is prone to reactive depression as a complication of the work of mourning if he is fixated at the oral stage, in which self-esteem depends on external supplies (Fenichel 1945), since, with the loss of such supplies, self-esteem is reduced. Thus the treatment of the depressed requires work on characterological makeup to forestall a depressive reaction when future important losses occur. The psychotherapy recommended for the depressed patient is a long-term, intensive, insight-oriented treatment dealing with the underlying matrix of the individual. The "re-grief" therapy that may be suitable for some patients with reactive depression caused by a death, and that may put a complicated mourning process back onto its "normal" track—one that works toward an appropriate resolution and the restoration of the mourner's ability to reinvest his libido and take up his life once again—is described below.

The individual who develops an established pathological mourning may also benefit greatly from long-term insight psychotherapy. The short-term therapy called re-grief therapy was originally developed in response to the need to care for patients hospitalized for a short time for established pathological mourning and reactive depression occasioned by a death (Volkan 1971; 1981; Volkan, Cillufo, and Sarvay 1975; Volkan and Josephthal 1979; Volkan and Showalter 1968). I will briefly outline its technique; a detailed explanation of this procedure, with case examples, appears in the references cited. In the case of psychosomatic involvements it is essential to combine medical or surgical assessment and treatment plans with the psychological therapy.

Re-grief Therapy

The patients chosen for this therapy had met with complications in the course of mourning that resulted in either established pathological mourning or reactive depression. It should be noted that these two states may coexist, or that some symptoms indicative of complications in the initial stage may appear in both. Although the clinical picture may be mixed, one identifies established pathological mourning more clearly in the patient who uses a linking object and is preoccupied with longing for—yet dreads—the return of the one he mourns, although he may also have some degree of disruptive identification with him.

Since the patient taken into re-grief therapy has a strong and persistent hope of seeing the one he mourns alive again, but still has a desire to "kill" him in order to complete his mourning, he places a high value on being in psychological contact with the deceased's representation, which he may perceive as an introject. Those able to externalize the representation onto their linking objects may not report an introject, but in any event the patient is clearly trying to relate ambivalently to an unassimilated representation of the one he lost.

During the initial phase of re-grief therapy the therapist helps the patient to grasp the distinction between what is his and what belongs to the dead person's representation. In first conceptualizing re-grief therapy, we considered using rather mechanical means, which we called demarcation exercises (Volkan and Showalter 1968). For example, one patient was preoccupied with a letter written by his father just before he died, in which he had expressed criticism of his son. The therapist saw that his patient's feelings of guilt kept him from being upset by this criticism, and that he was, in fact, presenting it as though he had made the statement himself. The mechanical way of the demarcation exercise was to encourage the patient's recognition that the criticism appeared in his father's handwriting, not his, so that his secondary-process thinking was directed toward acknowledging that two entirely different people were involved. I no longer use such methods, since I have discovered that the detailed and empathic uncovering of the patient's history can serve the same purpose.

The therapist is well advised not to question the patient directly when taking his history, but to develop nondirective exchange. In this the therapist can help the patient to begin differentiating his own thoughts, attitudes, and feelings from those influenced by his introject. The patient in established pathological mourning can be counted on to broach the subject of death and his lost one himself. A focus on the history and the associations pertaining to the relationship between the patient and the one he mourns enables the therapist to help the patient see what he has taken in and thus what he feels about the introject or representation of the other, and which of its aspects bother him so much that he wants to reject them.

One must realize that although the patient himself may use the kind of physical terminology we have used in referring to an introject, what is actually involved is an affective-dynamic *process*. The therapist treating patients of the kind under discussion should be sufficiently experienced to refrain from anything that is no more than intellectual gymnastics. The manifest content of the patient's dreams helps to show how his mourning process became arrested, and how it happens that he feels that he has within himself a special representation of the one he mourns; it can, in short, help him to understand his fixation. The therapist who shares too quickly his formulation of the reasons for his patient's fixation, however, may find that he has slowed the affective-cognitive process involved in the activation of a forward-moving mourning process. In the "demarcation," which may take several weeks, the therapist does not encourage an outpouring of great emotion but helps his patient prepare for it. If the patient feels frustration at being unable to accommodate to the flood of emotion he feels building up within him, the therapist may say, "What is your hurry? We are still trying to learn about the circumstances of the death and the reasons why you can't grieve. When the time comes you may allow yourself to grieve."

Meanwhile the therapist has expanded the formulation that will later guide his clarifications and interpretations; he has learned more about the reasons for his patient's arrest and inability to grieve. He encourages his patient to go over his reminiscences of the deceased, the circumstances of the final illness or the accident, the conditions in which he had news of the death, his reactions to seeing the body, the particulars of the funeral, and so on. Again, direct questioning of the patient is far less productive than encouraging him to offer such topics himself and permitting the display of appropriate feelings as he does so.

The ambivalence felt toward the dead person is clarified. Instead of commenting that such ambivalence is normal, the wise therapist conveys the appropriate message through therapeutic neutrality and empathy. He promotes the patient's curiosity about this ambivalence and his insight that this ambivalence is what is largely responsible for his being torn between wanting to "save" the deceased or "killing" him once and for all. As soon as the patient can rather readily alternate between negative and positive aspects of the ambivalence, he is apt to become angry. His anger may be diffused and directed toward others, but it authenticates the reality of the death much as though the patient had gone back to the initial stage of his dilemma. With his understanding of the patient's need to keep the dead "alive," the therapist then slowly clarifies the relationship between the two and interprets it, along with the reasons for anger's being so expectable. Abreaction—"emotional reliving" (Bibring 1954)—concerning certain past experiences connected with the deceased or his death may occur at this point if everything is going well. Such abreactions reflect the (re)visiting of the initial response to death and the (re)commencement of the work of mourning. The patient has begun to re-grieve. It can be assumed that certain impulses such as death wishes are now surfacing. The patient's readiness to have these impulses interpreted and to reduce his guilt feelings can be assessed.

The patient with established pathological mourning typically uses the mechanism of splitting his ego functions just as he started doing in his initial reaction to the death. The therapist calls his attention to this by helping him to focus at an appropriate time on how he became aware that the dead person was in fact no longer alive. This focus will obtain good results if it is made at an emotionally suitable time, and not as an intellectual exercise. The patient may show real surprise and blurt out something like: "I thought he was not breathing anymore. But I didn't really look!" The therapist has helped him to revisit the point where splitting began and to reevaluate reality.

Our patients often report that there were problems at the funeral and that they did not actually see the coffin lowered into the grave. When the therapist asks at an appropriate time, "How do you know that he is buried?" the patient is likely to surprise himself by realizing that one part of his awareness never did hold that the burial had been accomplished. He is then likely to feel anger at those who stood in the way of his participating in the funeral ritual. It has been made clear to him that although he felt, and even knew, that death had occurred, he had paradoxically continued to behave as though nothing had happened.

The most important part of this phase of confrontation, clarification, and interpretation of death-related impulses, fantasies, and wishes, and of the defenses the patient has been using against them, is the focus on the linking object. Because it has physical existence, with properties that reach the senses, it has greater "magic" than the introject. Once the patient grasps how he has been using his linking object to maintain absolutely controlled contact with the image of the dead person, as well as to postpone mourning and keep it frozen, he will use it to activate his mourning. It is suggested that he bring the linking object to a therapy session, where he will usually avoid it at first. The therapist then asks permission to keep it, and points out that its magic exists only in the patient's perception of it. When it is finally introduced into a therapy session, it is placed between patient and therapist long enough for the former to feel its "spell." He may then be asked to touch it and to report what comes into his mind. I am even now astonished at what intense emotion is congealed in it, and warn others about this. This emotion serves to unlock the psychological processes that until then were contained in the linking object itself. Emotional storms so triggered may continue for weeks; at first diffuse, they become differentiated, and therapist and patient can then together identify such emotions as anger, guilt, sadness, etc. The linking object then loses its power at last, whether or not the patient chooses to dispose of it.

Clarifications and interpretations concerned with death and the deceased, and the sharper focus on these subjects made possible by the use of the linking object, lead to the final phase of the treatment—disorganization. This is then followed by organization and the appearance of sadness. A sort of graft of secondary-process thinking then is required to help heal the wound that this experience has torn open. Patients who have never visited the grave of the one they mourn do so now, as if to say goodbye, and those who have been unable to arrange for the tombstone make arrangements to have one put in place. The mourner can feel sad but no longer need feel guilty. Many patients at this point spontaneously plan some memorial ritual, and many consult priests, ministers, or rabbis for religious consolation as they begin accepting the death.

With suitable patients near the end of their therapy, I have been able to use the *manifest* content of the serial dreams to indicate where they were in their re-grieving. These patients seem to feel that their introject has departed, leaving them in peace. They feel free, even excited, at the lifting of their burden, and begin to look for new objects for their love. My experience has been that the re-grieving that so liberates the patient can be completed within two to four months with three or four sessions a week.

I believe that the elucidation of some of the important meanings of the patient's loss will benefit him little if emotions and ideation are not blended. Throughout the treatment, patients experience a variety of emotions as they gain insight into their inability to let the dead person die. This insight is arrived at by the clarifications and interpretations given, the therapy being designed to reactivate the mourning process. It should be noted that the patient's resistance to acknowledging his fixation in the work of mourning is interpreted on such levels that the interpretations do not necessarily effect resolution of the infantile conflicts underlying the fixation. One must assume that the patient may indeed further repress these conflicts even as he loosens whatever condensations into the conflicts he has made on a higher level. The use of the linking object brings about special emotional storms that are not curative unless interpretation engages the close scrutiny of the patient's observing ego. Thus the link to the representation of the dead, externalized into the linking object, is brought into the realm of the patient's inner experience.

In spite of the use of a special device—the linking object—in re-grief therapy, the transference relationship becomes the vehicle whereby insight into ambivalence and the conflict between longing and dread may be gained and resolution accomplished. Through his activity the therapist offers himself as a new object—a healer—for the patient's consideration, aiming, as in psychoanalytic therapy, to develop a therapeutic alliance without encouraging an *infantile* transference neurosis. Rado (1956) used the term *interceptive interpretations,* which I have modified for my purpose in describing my interception of the development of infantile transference neurosis by premature interpretation of the transference phenomena whenever I think it could lead to a ripened infantile transference neurosis. For example, one interferes with *full* displacement of the dead person's representation onto the therapist, so the patient is kept aware of being faced with complications in his mourning of the original lost one. However, the patient's reactions to parallel situations of loss involving the therapist—separations at weekends, for example—are interpreted in due time. Such interpretation makes it possible to work through past conflicts with the dead person in a focal way. (Also, the fresh grief caused by separation from the therapist when therapy is terminated can be put to appropriate use.) Transference reactions are inevitable, but infantile transference neurosis is not. Selected reference to and interpretation of the transference reactions may be therapeutic by providing close and intimate contact within the therapeutic setting as the patient's conflicts are understood. Thus, although re-grief therapy is brief and lasts for months rather than years, it is intense, intimate, and certainly not superficial.

References

Abraham, K. 1911. "Notes on the Psycho-Analytical Investigation and Treatment of Manic-Depressive Insanity and Allied Conditions." In D. Bryan and A. Strachey, eds. *Selected Papers,* pp. 137–156. New York: Basic Books, 1960.

——1916. "The First Pregenital Stage of the Libido." D. Bryan and A. Strachey, eds., *Selected Papers,* pp. 248–279. New York: Basic Books, 1960.

——1924. "A Short Study of the Development of the Libido, Viewed in the Light of Mental Disorders." In *Selected Papers,* pp. 418–501. London: Hogarth Press, 1927.

Bibring, E. 1954. "Psychoanalysis and the Dynamic Psychotherapies." *Journal of the American Psychoanalytic Association* 2:745–770.

Bowlby, J. 1961. "Process of Mourning." *International Journal of Psycho-analysis* 42:317–340.

Bowlby, J. and C. M. Parkes. 1970. "Separation and Loss Within the Family." In E. J. Anthony and C. Koupernik, eds. *The Child in His Family,* 1:197–216. New York: Wiley Interscience.

Brown, F. and P. Epps. 1966. "Childhood Bereavement and Subsequent Crime." *British Journal of Psychiatry* 112:1043–1048.

Clayton, P., L. Desmarais, and G. Winokur. 1968. "A Study of Normal Bereavement." *American Journal of Psychiatry* 125:168–178.

Cobb, S., W. Bauer, and I. Whiting. 1939. "Environmental Factors in Rheumatoid Arthritis." *Journal of the American Medical Association* 113:668–670.

Crisp, A. J. and R. G. Priest. 1972. "Psychoneurotic Status During the Year Following Bereavement." *Journal of Psychosomatic Research* 16:351–355.

Deutsch, H. 1937. "Absence of Grief." *Psychoanalytic Quarterly* 6:12–23.

Engel, G. L. 1961. "Is Grief a Disease? A Challenge for Medical Research." *Psychosomatic Medicine* 23:18–22.

——1962. *Psychological Development in Health and Disease.* Philadelphia: W. B. Saunders.

Evans, P. and J. Liggett. 1971. "Loss and Bereavement as Factors in Agoraphobia: Implications for Therapy." *British Journal of Medical Psychology* 44:149–154.

Fenichel, O. 1945. *The Psychoanalytic Theory of Neurosis.* New York: Norton.

Freud, A. 1960. "Discussion of Dr. John Bowlby's Paper." *The Psychoanalytic Study of the Child* 15:53–62. New York: International Universities Press.

Freud, S. 1917. "Mourning and Melancholia." *Standard Edition,* 1957, 14:237–258.

Greene, W. A. and G. Miller. 1958. "Psychological Factors and Reticuloendothelial Disease." *Psychosomatic Medicine* 24:124–144.

Hamilton, J. W. 1969. "Object Loss, Dreaming and Creativity, the Poetry of John Keats." *The Psychoanalytic Study of the Child* 24:488–531. New York: International Universities Press.

——1973. "Jensen's *Gradiva:* A Further Interpretation." *American Imago* 30:380–412.

——1975. "The Significance of Depersonalization in the Life and Writings of Joseph Conrad." *Psychoanalytic Quarterly* 44:612–630.

——1979. "Joseph Conrad: His Development as an Artist, 1889–1910." *Psychoanalytic Study Society* 8:277–329.

Hill, O. W. 1972. "Child Bereavement and Adult Psychiatric Disturbance." *Journal of Psychosomatic Research* 16:357–360.

Klein, M. 1940. "Mourning and its Relation to Manic-depressive States." *International Journal of Psycho-analysis* 21:125–153.

Lehrman, S. R. 1956. "Reactions to Untimely Death." *Psychiatric Quarterly* 30:565–579.

Lidz, I. 1949. "Emotional Factors in the Etiology of Hyperthyroidism." *Psychosomatic Medicine* 11:2–9.

Lindemann, E. 1944. "Symptomatology and Management of Acute Grief." *American Journal of Psychiatry* 101:141–148.

McDermott, N.T. and S. Cobb. 1939. "A Psychiatric Survey of Fifty Cases of Bronchial Asthma." *Psychosomatic Medicine* 1:203–245.

Niederland, W.G. 1965. "An Analytic Inquiry into the Life and Work of Heinrich Schliemann." In M. Schur, ed. *Drives, Affects, Behavior,* vol. 2. New York: International Universities Press.

Parkes, C.M. 1964a. "The Effects of Bereavement on Physical and Mental Health: A Study of the Case Records of Widows." *British Medical Journal* 2:274–279.

Parkes, C.M. 1964b. "Recent Bereavement as a Cause of Mental Illness." *British Journal of Psychiatry* 110:198–204.

Parkes, C.M. and R.J. Brown. 1972. "Health After Bereavement. A Controlled Study of Young Boston Widows and Widowers." *Psychosomatic Medicine* 34:449–461.

Peck, M.W. 1939. "Notes on Identification in a Case of Depressive Reaction to the Death of a Love Object." *Psychoanalytic Quarterly* 8:1–18.

Pollock, G.H. 1961. "Mouring and Adaptation." *International Journal of Psychoanalysis* 42:341–361.

——1975. "On Mourning, Immortality and Utopia." *Journal of the American Psychoanalytic Association* 23:334–362.

Rado, S. 1956. "Adaptational Development of Psychoanalytic Therapy." In S. Rado and G.E. Daniels, eds. *Changing Concepts of Psychoanalytic Medicine,* pp. 89–100. New York: Grune and Stratton.

Schafer, R. 1968. *Aspects of Internalization.* New York: International Universities Press.

Schmale, A.H. 1958. "Relationship of Separation and Depression to Disease, I. A Report on a Hospitalized Medical Population." *Psychosomatic Medicine* 20:259–277.

Socarides, C.W. 1954. "On the Usefulness of Extremely Brief Psychoanalytic Contact." *Psychoanalytic Review* 41:340–346.

Volkan, V.D. 1965. "The Observation of the 'Little Man' Phenomenon in a Case of Anorexia Nervosa." *British Journal of Medical Psychology* 38:299–311.

——1970. "Typical Findings in Pathological Grief." *Psychiatric Quarterly* 44:231–250.

——1971. "A Study of a Patient's Re-grief Work Through Dreams, Psychological Tests, and Psychoanalysis." *Psychiatric Quarterly* 45:255–273.

——1972. "The Linking Objects of Pathological Mourners." *Archives of General Psychiatry* 27:215–221.

——1974. "Death, Divorce and the Physician." In D.W. Abse, L.M. Nash and L.M. Louden, eds. *Marital and Sexual Counseling in Medical Practice,* pp. 446–462. New York: Harper & Row.

——1976. *Primitive Internalized Object Relations: A Clinical Study of Schizophrenic, Borderline, and Narcissistic Patients,* New York: International Universities Press.

——1981. *Linking Objects and Linking Phenomena,* New York: International Universities Press.

Volkan, V.C., A.F. Cillufo, and T.L. Sarvay. 1975. "Re-grief Therapy and the Function of the Linking Objects as a Key to Stimulate Emotionality." In P.T. Olsen, ed. *Emotional Flooding,* pp. 179–224. New York: Human Sciences Press.

Volkan, V.D. and D. Josephthal. 1979. "The Treatment of Established Pathological Mourners." In T.B. Karasu and L. Bellak, eds. *Specialized Techniques and Psychotherapy,* New York: Jason Aronson.

Volkan, V.D. and C.R. Showalter. 1968. "Known Object Loss, Disturbance in Reality Testing, and 'Re-grief Work' as a Method of Brief Psychotherapy." *Psychiatry Quarterly* 42:358–374.

Wahl, C.W. 1970. "The Differential Diagnosis of Normal and Neurotic Grief Following Bereavement." *Psychosomatics* 11:104–106.

Winnicott, D.W. 1953. "Transitional Objects and Transitional Phenomena." *International Journal of Psycho-analysis* 34:89–97.

Wolfenstein, M. 1966. "How Is Mourning Possible?" *The Psychoanalytic Study of the Child* 21:93–123, New York: International Universities Press.

Preamble: The overwhelming context of Thanatology resides primarily in approaching what should be the ideal routine doctor-patient-family care relationships, such care forming the indispensable base upon which the core of care specific to Thanatology can and will easily be extended.

Principle 12: The Essence of Good Thanatologic Care Is Good Patient Care

12

Clinical Care of Dying Patients

HAROLD B. HALEY
and ALEXANDER P. REMENCHIK

Seeing acutely ill patients, making intellectually interesting diagnoses, and carrying out active treatment with medications, personal involvement, or procedures that result in "cure" are the obviously rewarding parts of medicine. Yet some patients do not fit into this kind of caregiving design. They have chronic problems, which must be endured, with the best possible care directed toward the treatment of individual episodes but without permanent relief. Many times physicians develop much satisfaction from the interpersonal relationship with such patients and from helping the patients live with serious problems.

Introduction

The care of terminally ill patients, however, may have many different effects on the physician. Such care may be very frustrating because of the physician's inability to halt the process and because of the associated stresses in interpersonal relationships between the physician and the patient, the patient's family, or other caregivers. Illness and dying probe at physicians' own self-images and beliefs and fears concerning their own mortality. Nevertheless, the care of dying patients may also be very rewarding. Two of the rewards of the practice of medicine are the development of skills and the recognition that these skills actually do help people. The care of the dying may stretch every ability that the physician has. The use of these abilities can make the last stages of a person's life better than they would have been otherwise, and on occasion can lead to a meaningful relationship between patient and physician.

While this article will focus on physicians and their roles as models for caregivers, the care of dying patients requires the active participation of many different individuals, all concerned with their patients and with bringing skills and abilities to them. We will make reference to team care and relationships among various individuals who care for the dying and will offer case illustrations to highlight some of the problems to be resolved in treating critically ill patients.

There is much public and media interest in various aspects of the clinical care of dying patients. With the general increase in government centralization and legalistic solutions to problems, the courts have been called on for resolution of many situations. Certain of them have been controversial, and one legal opinion often results in another one when a different case appears. Although public interest is drawn to general topics such as "dying with dignity," the development of hospices, communication with patients and families, and so forth, there are specific issues to be analyzed, discussed, and resolved.

Our exploration of providing good care for dying patients will include an examination of the principles of good patient care in general, the specific issues arising from public concern, and various aspects of clinical care that are either unique to or much more significantly applicable to dying patients. We will look at similarities and differences between care of dying patients and others. Particularly, we will examine several specific problems in detail.

I. Objectives of Care of Dying Patients

1. Specific goals that meet the needs of an individual patient must be established and understood by the patient, physician, other caregivers, and family.

2. Palliation and not cure for whatever clinical problem is present must be established as the principal objective of patient care, in recognition of the fact that we are beyond the point of being able to cure and that our efforts are to be placed in other directions.

3. The goals relating to the currently popular phrase "quality of life" should be defined and addressed in the regimen of caregiving. The first factor in assuring quality of life is relief of suffering (particularly that induced by the two most overwhelming and common clinical symptoms, dyspnea and pain). Other aspects too relate to quality of life. Normalization of living and function is most important and often can be best achieved if the patient can be cared for at home rather than in an institution. Aspects of normal living may include obtaining nourishment from the foods one likes cooked the way one likes, living with one's own furniture, having easy access to the television set, having one's own bathroom, enjoying the presence of pets, etc. If any kind of activity, however limited, is possible, it greatly improves the situation. Even for those patients who cannot be treated at home, normalization of function is an important objective.

4. Recognition must be given to the major role of physicians and others caring for a patient as providers of strength and support. A seriously and dangerously ill patient has many differend kinds of weaknesses. The strength to survive, to be obtained from others, is most helpful. Beyond strength, we all can give support.

5. Small, understandable, achievable, short-term goals are worthy of developing when caring for terminally ill patients, among them an increase in patient's function (sitting up, feeding themselves, going to the bathroom), the relief of secondary symptoms (sleeplessness, itching, etc.), or patients' renewal of relationships or communication with friends or family members. Often these goals are different from those developed for an acute medical or surgical patient.

II. Good Thanatological Care as Good Patient Care

The following individual items are not an inclusive list of attitudes, approaches, and processes of good patient care, but they are ones that appear to be closely related to the themes of this presentation.

1. *The patient is the primary interest and responsibility of the physician.* Doctors exist for patients. There are many pressures that work against this principle, some of which involve the physician. Pressures on a busy physician limit the time that can be spent with a patient. One colleague has commented that "the biggest problems in patient care would be resolved if doctors spent 10 more minutes with their patients." Financial conflicts of interest occur between physicians and patients, especially with increasing government and third-party payor roles. Conflicts occur in belief systems. Physicians often come from different socioeconomic backgrounds than do some of their patients, which may greatly limit communication and understanding between patients and physicians unless such differences are recognized, examined, and dealt with.

A specific issue is that the physician's responsibility is to the patient, not to the family. Families are extremely important and in many circumstances the patient will receive much better care if patient, family, and physician are all in communication and consensus. This does not hold in every situation, however, for if the patient does not wish it, the physician has no right to involve the family.

In today's society, third-party influences sharply attack the physician's responsibility to the patient. Third-party payors, government guidelines for medical practice, and increasing pressure for cost control mean that there are pressures on the physician to limit the quality of care to be given. In the near future, we will probably see many public, legal, and ethical conflicts around the third-party limitations on patient care. If the physician can serve only one master, that master must be the patient.

2. *The physician has the responsibility to make recommendations that are in the best interest of the patient.* The concept of best interest needs to be constantly balanced against the concepts of autonomy. There are many circumstances in which physicians

must substitute their judgment for the patient's on the basis of the patient's inadequacy of experience, background, education, or current status. In philosophical ethics this relates to beneficence or "soft" paternalism.

3. *Competent patients have the right to make their own decisions.* Much of society is strongly taking a position that medical decisions should be shared ones. Certainly in many cases this is true. Physicians have learned that when patients share in decisions they cooperate much more in their care, with better results for everyone. It is a general clinical experience, however, that many patients—particularly very sick ones—whose right to make a decision leads them to the conclusion that they want the doctor to make the medical decisions. There are various reasons for this.

General symptoms, weakness, and fatigue make many sick people decide to leave much of the responsibility to the physician. In some instances this arises from fear of the illness and possible death and from wanting to do anything they can to overcome these, including pleasing those who help them. They want to please the physician, hoping that the physician will help them more.

4. *The physician must work in comfort in the balance just described.* The patient's best interest and the patient's autonomy must be in harmony with the physician's dedication to the best care that can be given to the patient.

5. *Families and significant others have roles that the physician must analyze and to which the physician must be appropriately sensitive.* With the wide variation in living styles today there are many ramifications of this issue. Recently in a tumor conference a patient with advanced malignancy and serious problems was discussed. A family friend met with the staff. It became clear that the friend was an intelligent person with appropriate personal interest in the patient and an individual with whom we should be working even though no actual family relationship existed. Another recent case was a 26-year-old man admitted with an extensive sarcoma of his back. During the first months in the hospital, when he was treated with active radiation and chemotherapy, he had been getting devoted care from a young lady he had been living with for several years. With limited funds, she traveled across a major city daily by public

transportation. She was of tremendous support to him. When he finally was put on the "seriously ill" list, a clerk going through the records saw the name of a wife and telephoned her. What the clerk did not know was that the patient had left his wife some years before and that there had been no contact between them. On getting the message, the wife in Pennsylvania became very disturbed and immediately flew to Texas. We now had the abandoned wife and the present girlfriend on the scene. In such a case, with whom does the physician work?

6. *What is "family?"* The literature tends to suggest that the family is a single-minded, monolithic organization. In practice this frequently is not true. Conflict, antagonism, different opinions, and different objectives are all common. How much does the closeness of the kinship affect the situation? Is a parent, a spouse, or a child "closer"? What roles do the general closeness and the different relationships of family members to the patient play in decisions and attitudes? We are all familiar with the family in which some consensus has developed, only to have it disrupted by the arrival of an individual from a distant state who hasn't seen the patient in five years. Obviously, many of these situations relate to guilt feelings in that person for past neglect of the patient, but there are other possible explanations. When there is a difference of opinion, to whom does the caregiver listen? Is a four-to-one vote in the family better than a three-to-two or a two-to-three vote? These are difficult issues, especially in our litiginous times.

7. *Good patient care is care that the physician feels right about giving: scientifically, ethically, and personally.* There are various demands on this principle. Patients may ask for care that the physician in good conscience cannot give. In 1984 an article in a national journal gave a history of a cancer patient who had demanded treatment with an experimental combination chemotherapy protocol that the physician was qualified to give but felt was an incorrect treatment for her. Surprisingly, the authors of the article felt that the physician was wrong and should have given the desired care. But physicians should *not* be asked to give care that is against their considered judgment of what is best for a particular patient at a particular time.

8. *Good patient care requires constant balance.* Consideration must be given to potential harms, benefits, costs, risks, and effects on the patient. The physician must make the choice that appears best at the time, and all must live with the outcome.

III. Special Aspects of Caring for Dying Patients

A. CLINICAL ISSUES OF FREQUENT AND SIGNIFICANT CONSIDERATION IN THE CARE OF DYING PATIENTS.

1. *Relief of pain, dyspnea, and other symptoms are prime concerns.* One of the greatest fears of many people is a long, difficult death with inadequate relief of pain. With today's pharmacological, neurological, neurosurgical, psychological, and interpersonal methods, most pain can be relieved. However, prices must be paid for this relief in the form of side effects. Patients may lose their appetites or be somewhat obtunded. Careful attention to detail can maximize the relief of pain: Literature studies show that half of terminal cancer patients have little or no pain.

With terminally ill patients, many situations require management that might appear unorthodox with healthy patients. A patient with terminal lung cancer may have been a heavy smoker. If this patient still wants to smoke, it should be allowed because the damage has already been done. The use of alcohol can be a needed satisfaction for the patient. In the care of an elderly family member, one of the authors had as a responsibility being sure that the supply of Drambuie never ran out. If comfort and relief are provided and no actual immediate harm occurs, then the patient's desires should be met.

2. *Palliative procedures can be important.* When a patient is dying, it is easy to forget that there are individual pathological states that can be relieved. In a dying patient an abscess should still be drained, bleeding should be stopped, and obstructions should be relieved. All of these procedures will relieve symptoms and add to the quality of life without extending it.

3. *The side effects of medication must receive consideration.*

Patients frequently die of a combination of diseases, each requiring many different medications. Side effects may be additive or multiplied. Whenever possible, drugs should be dropped, shifted, or decreased to minimize their actions and side effects. Obviously, long-term effects are of no concern in these cases.

B. ASPECTS OF THE DOCTOR-PATIENT RELATIONSHIP THAT ARE PARTICULARLY RELEVANT TO DYING PATIENTS:

1. *Offering presence.* When a patient is cranky, slightly confused, possibly hostile, or has an offensive odor, it is easy to find excuses not to visit. It is tempting not to awaken such patients when they are sleeping. However, the visibility of the physician to patient, family, and other caregivers gives coherence to the total treatment program and can be of tremendous support.

2. *Considering Alternatives.* If one medication doesn't work, something else should be tried. If the x-ray didn't show anything, we need to see what something else reveals. We can never reach the point at which there is no alternative. While the patient has no alternative, the physician still has some.

3. *Providing a future.* We live in a future-oriented society. What are we going to do this afternoon, tomorrow, next year, next century? The dying patient suddenly does not have a future. The physician can provide some. Saying to the patient that one will be late tomorrow but that a visit will be paid at some point says to the patient, "I am concerned with you and I will be with you." It is also saying that your relationship has a future even if that future is only tomorrow.

4. *A visit to some patients should include sitting down.* Even if only for a brief period, such contact carries a message that many patients hear.

5. *Respecting intimacy.* Possibly the most important part of taking a pulse is the touching. The degree of intimacy desired by patients varies. An arm around the shoulder is welcomed by some, but not by all. If we know our patients well enough, perhaps we can know what is appropriate in given situations.

6. *Understanding and uses of communication.* Some doctors communicate a lot; others, for various reasons, think it is wise

not to. The patient's side of communication deserves some individualization of thought also. What does it mean when the patient doesn't or won't communicate? Dying patients may consider themselves to be isolated, or may desire it. They may be withdrawing into themselves and preparing themselves to die. Breaking down such a mechanism is not necessarily good. It behooves physicians to let their patients know that they are willing to communicate, but not to insist upon it unthinkingly. There also may be a class or social difference (officer-enlistee, ethnic, racial) between doctors and patients that patients may not want to breech.

7. *Communicating insights.* The care of dying patients requires doctors, nurses, social workers, and chaplains, as well as people who clean the room or change the patient's bedding. These people must be in communication with each other and should be communicating the same messages to the patient. In many cases, any one of these staff members may be the one with whom the patient communicates. This person should then provide insights to the others.

8. *Maintaining continuity of care.* Whenever possible patients should see the same physician. One of the greatest criticisms of care given in clinics is that patients see different doctors every time they visit. The dying patient needs to develop a relationship with the same people during this time of stress. The medical-supportive care can determine how the patient dies.

C. SPECIAL PROBLEMS

1. *The intensive care unit.* The quality of care and its effects on patients in intensive care units has had extensive publicity. Suffice it to say here that individual personhood continues to be the essence of living even there. The patient dying in such a setting deserves and needs all the considerations present elsewhere.

2. *Roles of residents.* Some hospitals are "resident hospitals." There, the residents are the physicians who see the patient, make most of the decisions, and have the most involvement—presumbly all under supervision of the attending physicians, who often are not known to the patient. In teaching hospitals with primarily

private patients, the private physician may be the person with whom the patient identifies, yet the resident still is involved with the patient. What is the proper role of residents? They may be at any level of training, so that their levels of medical sophistication and professional maturation affect how they interact with patients. All the issues of impotency, guilt, personal mortality, and ignorance of a resident's role affect the relationship with the dying patient. Residents and attending physicians have experiences and relationships with a given patient that require working through.

IV. Death, Dying and Bereavement

A. THE PATIENT AND THE PHYSICIAN

1. *Is there a God? Is there an after-life?* What importance does the patient give to these questions? Are these guiding influences in how the patient is living, and therefore dying? What influence do these concepts have on the communication needed or desired by the patient? Personal beliefs or formal religion can be a most important foundation in care of the dying. Hospital chaplains, the patient's clergyman, family, other patients, doctors, and nurses are all involved in this role of religion.

2. *Experience.* Although physicians are individuals exposed to different kinds of clinical problems, most experienced physicians develop ways of working with dying patients. This relates to identifying the kind of person, the fatal illness, probable prognosis, what works, and what doesn't.

3. *Emotional situations.* With patients, families, and other caregivers, many negative emotional situations develop. Hostility, anxiety, fear, and panic are one group. One of the important clinical roles is maintaining equanimity and equilibrium. Hostility needs to be understood but not returned. Is the hostility due to fear, guilt, or stress, or is it just an unpleasant, ever-present habit pattern?

4. *Grieving.* The grieving process varies in individual situations. Patients may grieve for their own loss. Families may do sig-

nificant advance grieving. In some cases most of the grieving may have occurred before the patient's death, with a relatively rapid recovery afterward. Grieving is an area in which physician discussions with family members can do much good.

B. SOME CONTROVERSIAL ISSUES:

1. *Determination of the degree of aggressiveness of therapy.* How active or passive should the doctor's interventions be? Can anything be done to slow the basic disease process? How actively should complications be treated? The issue of letting the patient die in peace is a simple concept, but the decisions involved are not. There are many clinical situations in which the prognosis is not completely clear. The patient is probably going to die soon but it is possible that another medication or another operation might help.

2. *Do Not Resuscitate orders* (DNR): DNR says that the hospital has a planned protocol and procedure by which patients can express their desires that extraordinary means not be used to keep them alive in an unresolvable situation. The manner of a patient's death can involve four different situations that must be considered in developing a DNR protocol: (a) The person in good health who thinks about the future can complete a "living will" and anticipate its being respected, as is now possible under the statutes of many states. This is a directive to people as to what one's preferences are. (b) Patients with an ultimately fatal disease (metastatic cancer, advanced chronic obstructive pulmonary disease, Alzheimer's disease, advanced cirrhosis) but who are not actively deteriorated and for whom no individual time prognosis is possible cannot be candidates for DNR. (c) DNR orders are for patients who are seriously ill and who will probably die from their present illness in the reasonably near future. Time and opportunity for planning and communication exists. The death may occur in either home or hospital, but the DNR issue is not important for the patient at home. It is very important in the hospital and has some significance in the nursing home. (d) For patients in the emergency room or who have had major trauma, major cardiovascular event, or something from which death will come within a very short time, there is no planning

component. Every effort is made to preserve life if possible. Again, in the acute phase this is not a DNR issue. If a patient is incompetent, the family, physician, or court-appointed guardian may, of course, have roles to play.

A difficult question is: Can a patient in an intensive care unit have a valid DNR order? In the minds of those who run them, intensive care units are to provide maximum resources to salvage a salvageable patient. If the patient is not salvageable and has a valid DNR order, then the question can be raised as to whether such a patient should be using the expensive resources of an ICU.

Even with a valid DNR order, the patient still deserves extensive supportive therapy. Questions about the use of antibiotics and additional nutrition other than intravenous fluids have to be considered for the individual patient's circumstances. Pain control is always appropriate.

3. *Death in old age or youth.* Most discussions about the care of dying patients are limited to consideration of older patients or those who are expected to die from a long disease. Consideration must be given also to the tragedies of the sudden death of younger persons: the automobile accident, the overwhelming infection, the heart attack or stroke, the sports injury, the death in childbirth. These have a special anguish. Part of this relates to the idea that while death is expected in the old, it shouldn't happen to the young. When it does happen to the young, it says to each of us "That could be me." So much unlived life seems a waste. This raises such issues as the purpose of life, the existence of God, and if there is one, how God could allow such a thing to happen. In the sudden event there is no time for the psychological adjustment that occurs in a chronic situation. This means that everything happens to excess. There can be more sadness, more grieving, more hostility, and more depression in those who are near the situation.

4. *Incompetence of the patient.* When patients are not able to make their own decisions, it may mean that their minds are not functioning at a level that allows decision-making because of organic illness or heavy medication. Mental illness or coma due to trauma are causes of incompetence also. Incompetence can be temporary in a patient who is mentally obtunded from high fever or is

on too much medication. When any of these situations change, however, competency may be restored.

There are different kinds of competency. An individual may not be sharp enough at the moment to be making major financial decisions but may know whether or not he wants to consent to an operation or another procedure related to his illness. Questions of competency usually do not arise unless the patient or family disagrees with the physician's recommendations for care.

When the patient is incompetent, the question of who is qualified to make the decisions arises. There is a strong impression in the literature and popular custom that the family can make the decisions in the best interest of the patient. The legal basis of this is not well-established. The family may not have the understanding to do so. The family may be divided. How does the decision get made? When physician and family can come to the same decision, the situation is usually simple. When this does not occur, other possibilities exist. In a small number of unusual cases, physicians or hospitals or others have gone to court asking for appointment of a guardian. The guardian could be a family member or an outside third party. This kind of problem is dealt with in both legal and medical ethics. What is not discussed is when the physician, meeting family opposition, concludes that because the patient is dying it isn't worth the difficulty of trying to convince an arbiter that a particular treatment is indicated.

5. *Allocation of resources*. This is a euphemistic term. On academic levels the term "distributive justice" can be heard. What is being talked about is the rationing of medical care. With the tremendous pressures on cost containment in health care, rationing is going to increase. Physicians are going to be under greater pressure to shorten hospital stays and to eliminate expensive methods of care. These external pressures are going to affect the quality of care given to dying patients.

6. *Conflicts of rights and principles*. These conflicts are the bases of many problems. One such conflict was hinted at in the section immediately preceding; that is, the right in principle of the patient to receive the best available care versus the principle that government can control cost of care and thereby limit its availabil-

ity. Many other examples can be given. A dying patient with intractable pain may present such issues. Certainly, we each have a right to have our pain relieved. When medications to relieve pain have to be given in such large doses that they cause mental obtunding, anorexia, immobility, and other possibly negative states, conflicts develop among caregivers. There are nurses who don't want to give as much analgesic medication as is needed to relieve pain if it too significantly alters the patient's awareness. The resolution of these conflicts is certainly part of the art of caring for dying patients.

7. *Sudden Death.* The patient who dies suddenly or relatively soon after admission to a hospital may die in a situation for which family and caregivers have not been able to prepare. This becomes a time of conflict, hostility, and fear in which the physician has to try to develop the responses in people that facilitate their recovery from the situation.

8. *Meaning of Multiple Diseases:* Different diseases have different mystiques to the physician, the patient, the family, and others. Cancer, heart disease, infectious diseases, and mental diseases have different meanings. Questions of contagion, guilt, and heredity influence the care of the patient. The understanding of what a disease means to the patient and to the family may affect the way in which the physician handles the particular situation.

V. Medical Education and Thanatology

How does the doctor learn care of dying patients? We all grow up in a family, a country, a culture with conflicting viewpoints. We develop explicitly or implicitly our own beliefs concerning our own and other people's deaths. Newspapers, television, books, and other sources bring various theories, concepts, and ideas that get weighted by and built into the individual's own system. Formal education in death and dying is rare prior to medical (or nursing) school, or pastoral training. There are occasional college elective courses that a few individuals may take, but very few people receive organized education in this area.

Some years ago one of the authors received questionnaire responses from 500 medical students in seven medical schools. Three questions had been asked. The first one was, "How much education in care of dying patients did you receive?" From the answers they were offered, a significant number said "the right amount" and a significant number said "not enough." To the question "What was the result of the teaching you had?", one out of six answered, "It left me more confused." When asked how such teaching should be done, 90 percent of the respondents picked one of two answers: "from experience with clinical patients" and "observation of how faculty physicians care for their patients." Faculty physicians thus have the responsibility to develop a philosophy and methods for caring for dying patients, in recognition that students and residents are learning from them.

As physicians who have practiced thirty years, we are aware that our own concepts and practices have changed over time, as our own thinking has developed. Primarily we have learned from experience how patients and their families and other caregivers respond in the different situations we have encountered. We have learned from those around us; we have learned from some readings and meetings. It continues to be a very subjective area. One has problems knowing that a patient for whom one is responsible is going to die. What do we do to maximize the quality of living for that patient? Some guilt feelings arise periodically and usually can be rationalized away. We have had situations in which we developed comfortable relationships with dying patients that endured to the very end. We have also been in situations that were uncomfortable from start to finish.

Our current recommendation is that there should be formal, organized teaching of the principles of thanatology in medical schools. Medical students should learn that this is an area in which they can expect to participate actively over much of their careers. It is an area in which there are problems. To resolve these problems in the best interest of both patient and physician, doctors need to have identified their own concepts of death and to decide how they are going to work with dying patients. They should be introduced to the available literature and should know where to seek guidance. What can be done through formal education is limited. Nevertheless, formal education can introduce students to the recognition that they will learn primarily from their own experiences and from their observation of others who function as positive role models.

Approach to the role models can be difficult. With the wide range in physicians' personalities, education, cultural background, and responses to their own situations, no uniformity can be expected. Professional societies, professional literature, and medical school conferences can foster some insight and awareness of these problems.

VI. The Dying Patient's Location and Its Effects on the Physician

Physicians must frequently care for dying patients in hospitals, the patient's homes, nursing homes, hospices, and at the site of sudden fatal events. Each site has its own effect on care given by the physician:

A. THE HOSPITAL

The patient is in the hospital because of the perception of the need for resources, people, and care that are not available in other areas. For the patient, the hospital can be a place of anxiety, fear, and expenditure of money. On the other hand, the patient and family, for any combination of reasons, may perceive that the hospital is the only place they can accept care. This may be a valid perception. On the other hand, patients sometimes feel this way when they actually could be cared for elsewhere.

1. *There are many problems in the hospital.* It is a very expensive place to be in. The institutional component of the hospital is frustrating to everybody. Family tensions tend to be increased within the hospital setting.

2. *The hospital is the work place for the doctor to care for sick patients.* The hospital is usually located with some consideration of convenience to other aspects of the doctor's life, primarily

his home and office. The hospital is the place where the doctor is used to working, is familiar with its mechanisms and procedures, and is able to function with time-saving efficiency. This makes frequent visits to the patient easy.

3. *Care in the hospital is usually covered to a significant degree by a third-party payer.* Currently, this considerable expense is forcing patients to leave before they want to, and sometimes before their doctors want them to go.

4. *In the hospital the physician has many roles.* The physician must respond to other physicians, to nurses, to committees, and to various kinds of administrative pressures, such as to lengthen or shorten the stay of patients under different circumstances. Basically the hospital is a pressure place.

5. *Consultants, equipment, and expensive resources.* Among these are intensive care units, laboratories, and much technology. Most important is the immediate availability of a strong support team.

6. *Who is responsible for the patient?* The referring doctor frequently calls in specialist consultants. What is the role of the referring physician in these cases? Many times the referring or primary care physician is the one whom the patient knows and has confidence in, yet others are now directing therapy. The financial aspects of this arrangement come up periodically. The primary physician, even though not in charge, sometimes feels that he must charge a fee every time he sees the patient in the hospital. One hears complaints from patients, "I got a bill from the doctor who came in and shook my hand every day and that is all he did; why was I charged?" It seems that situations could be developed in which an old patient could be visited on a friendly basis rather than a commercial one.

B. THE HOME

1. *Why is the dying patient at home?* In most cases it is because that is where the patient (and family) wants to be. The family is a major support system in many circumstances. Most important is that it is not like an institutional environment. When

third parties are not paying the bills, giving care is far less expensive.

The home is a familiar place, with familiar belongings and resources that the patient is accustomed to using at his own discretion. Probably the most important resource though is the familiar people. For many, the quality of living is higher at home. One aspect of this is that the patient has more control of his activities than he would in the hospital. Comfort is important, including having one's own bed, bathroom, television set, and other belongings. In most people's minds the food is better there. To some individuals the availability of their pets is important, as are the advantages of privacy and the opportunity for physical intimacy.

To an intelligent patient, the ability to control one's own medication is an important bonus, but this may also be an area of confusion or error.

There are other problems with home care. Family members may end up being overburdened. The family may not wish to assume the responsibility of home care or may be afraid to do so. Good preparation and the consent of the family are needed. Without these, suspicions or hostility may be aroused. For patients who are going to be ill for an extended time, occasional readmission to hospital as a respite mechanism for the family is of value. Some nursing homes have planned respite programs that are very useful.

More patients would go home for terminal care if they were sure of the availability of help from physicians, nurses, and others, particularly if they were certain of readmission to the hospital as needed.

2. *The physician has to give home care to understand all of the above problems and to be able to adjust them to the care of a patient.* For the physician, home care is less convenient, more time-consuming, and may not be so comfortable as his ordinary "workshop." For care of seriously ill patients the physician needs a support team in the home. Combinations of visiting nurses, social workers, outpatient hospice teams, etc., allow good care to be given at home in a way that physicians cannot do on their own.

It is important to state that the home environment can be an attractive place to care for patients. The patient and family in their own environment may be more cooperative and more understanding of their situation, which may provide a basis for a better relationship with the physician. Little rituals develop. I have been in a situation in which as the doctor enters the house he is handed a Coca-Cola, because the family has learned the doctor's preferences. The communication may be better in the home and there may be less tension than in the hospital environment. The preparation for death and anticipatory grieving by patient and family can be more "normal" than in an institutional environment and may include the doctor in a more personal role.

Overall, the physician will probably see the patient less frequently, have greater inconveniences and make less money, but for some patients it will provide better care and thereby be a very satisfying type of care for the physician to provide.

C. The Nursing Home

1. *Some patients dread or dislike the possibility of going to a nursing home.* It has various connotations of isolation, dying, and neglect. Many adjust and actually like it; probably more just survive. There are patients with essentially no family for whom people in the nursing home become family. Quality of care varies in nursing homes. Small-town homes may provide better care, because of the availability of highly qualified people on a part-time basis (a married registered nurse, perhaps, who would like to work only two or three days a week). Often the nursing home personnel live in the same area and know some of the patients or their families. This makes for highly personalized care.

2. *Distance.* The location of doctor's office, patient's home, and the available nursing homes may introduce major logistical problems. For example, the doctor may make the legally required once-a-month visit but otherwise not see the patient unless there is urgent medical need. In this circumstance the physician is not playing much of a role in the care of this patient. Most nursing homes

have a medical director or comparable physician who will take referrals from the patient's physician and become the nursing home doctor for that patient. When a physician has a larger number of patients in a nursing home, he is more likely to go there frequently and to be able to continue an interpersonal relationship with the patient. This is of particular importance with the dying patient, where responding to subtle changes in the needs of patient and family can add much to the quality of their living.

Overall, the physician-patient interaction is often less satisfactory in the nursing home than in the hospital or in the patient's home. The hospice concept and practice are gradually growing in acceptance and use. Both the outpatient hospice, in which an organized team gives regular support to the patients in their homes, and the inpatient hospice, a free-standing institution or part of a larger institution, are developing their roles in American medicine.

D. OTHER SITES

A stroke, sudden heart event, or serious accident provides a situation in which there is heavy emphasis on direct and immediate physical care. There is no time or opportunity for interpersonal activities. Police, ambulances, and other people cause confusion and pressure. Patients may die in such environments in a relatively short time. In those circumstances the physician's only role is to offer good medical care and the relief of symptoms.

VII. Patients' and Families' Unrealistic Expectations

This problem can lead to inappropriate diagnostic and therapeutic interventions. If a good relationship is established by the physician with the patient and the family, these expectations can be dealt with. Circumstances and external forces, however, can and do preclude rational resolution of these expectations. Not the least of reasons for the lack of resolution may be the activities of physicians who are primarily investigators and teachers and who undertake diagnostic and therapeutic interventions that seem to be of no help to the present patient but that may lead to future improvements.

Unrealistic expectations occur when patients do not accept the clinical situation or build fantasies requiring the physician's participation. Nevertheless, as is illustrated in the following two cases, many more problems occur with family members than with the patient. Sometimes this is because communication between patient and family is poor; in other cases, the patient may not be able to communicate well.

In May 1982, M. H., a 70-year-old white woman, was admitted to the intensive care unit via the emergency room, because of severe chest pain that had not been relieved by nitroglycerine. She had experienced a myocardial infarction with malignant cardiac arrhythmia one month before. She had been hospitalized elsewhere but was released the week before. That day, while having lunch, she experienced chest pain associated with dyspnea and nausea. Because of the severity of the pain she was brought to the closest emergency room.

Initial examination revealed atrial fibrillation with a rapid ventricular response. Appropriate therapy established a normal sinus rhythm. She was relatively stable until the morning after admission, when she developed marked bradycardia with hypotension. Initial therapy stabilized her clinically, but shortly thereafter her condition deteriorated and a permanent AV sequential pacemaker was implanted. Her hospital course was uneventful, and she was discharged on the tenth day.

Except for progressive deterioration characterized by the development of congestive heart failure, which responded to conventional treatment, her clinical course was uneventful until August of 1984, when she experienced an episode of syncope. Evaluation revealed that the pacemaker was functioning normally. An echocardiogram showed a dilated left ventricle, thin akinetic septum, markedly decreased left ventricular function by percent fractional shortening and apical dyskinesia with mural thrombus.

During the course of this patient's treatment, her clinical status and grave prognosis had been explained to her husband in great detail, but he apparently did not understand. Not until the episode of syncope was there some appreciation of the fact that the patient was in imminent danger of sudden death. The patient was oriented, depressed, and knew her condition, even though the family did not want her to be specifically told. At this time the family requested that she be evaluated for a heart transplant. After considerable discussion it became clear to the family that their request was unrealistic. Subsequent to evaluation and treatment of the syncopal episode the patient continued to be symptomatic and died in October.

In this instance, the physician spent much time explaining the disease process, prognosis, and the general situation to the family, but these explanations really were not heard. Frequently the ear only hears what the brain is willing to accept and digest. The physician has a major responsibility to continue on repeated occasions to make communication as open, clear, and understandable as is possible. It must be recognized, however, that at times patients or families will not understand. This is bad enough when the one-sided communication is related to the real situation. It is made worse when unrealistic expectations enter in. Through newspapers, television, and other outside sources, this family developed the idea that the patient was a candidate for heart transplant. The experimental nature of such procedures, the expense, and the prognosis for this patient were all factors that made her a poor candidate for a transplant. This was very difficult for her family to accept and they kept pushing the idea even though it was inappropriate.

Another communication problem arises if a patient has been under the care of one physician but experiences a medical emergency when he is in a different location and therefore must be cared for by a different physician. This is not infrequent. Certainly in the Sun Belt seriously ill patients show up from the North every winter and new doctors have to take over their treatment with or without adequate information about their previous medical problems or medical care. This can be a problem in terms of the medications that a patient might be taking.

VIII. Compliance and Non-Compliance

A. B., a 76-year-old white man, was first seen in the office in March 1982. He had a history of chronic obstructive pulmonary disease, congestive heart failure, and recurrent bronchitis. He had been treated by many physicians and had never been able to establish a permanent relationship with any one of them. Following a review of his clinical status and a discussion of his previous therapy, a regimen was outlined for him. Hospitalization was advised. The patient refused. That evening he deteriorated rapidly and was brought to the emergency room and admitted to intensive care for treatment. He was treated with diuretics, lanoxin, bronchodilators, IPPB, and bedrest. On this regimen he improved clinically. He had considerable edema and this resolved. He became less dyspneic. Considerable effort was made to ensure his understanding of the therapeutic regimen. His subsequent course was that of progressive deterioration. An appropriate interpersonal relationship was established by the physician's willingness to accommodate to numerous complaints about the nature of the treatments and to change medications judiciously when the program distressed the patient psychologically. His last hospital admission was in February 1983, because of increasing dyspnea and orthopnea. His arterial blood gases deteriorated with P_a CO^2 rising into the 80s and 90s. Despite this high level he was alert and responsive. The critical situation was discussed with his son who, in turn, reviewed the patient's status with the patient. At that time the patient decided that he did not wish to be placed on a ventilator. In accordance with his request he was not ventilated and died on the 14th hospital day, having sustained cardiac and respiratory arrest.

The case of A. B. is important because it illustrates that flexibility on the part of the physician in association with education of patient and family can lead to significant comfort and to acceptance of the fact that continuing existence requires a respirator or other machine. The background for rational decisions is thus established.

Care of noncompliant patients appears to be an increasing

problem for physicians. When a young doctor first encounters patients who refuse treatment, his initial reaction is to tell them to go elsewhere. One learns that this is no solution. The physician, in many cases, must continue active treatment even when the patient refuses what the physician knows or believes is the best treatment. A competent patient has final control of what decisions are made and what is to be done. In most cases, the physician, over time, can work with this.

E. P., a 57-year-old white woman, was apparently well until September 1981, when she developed a headache and unstable gait. Evaluation led to the diagnosis of a brain tumor. A craniotomy was performed in another hospital and an astrocytoma was partially removed. The surgery was followed by radiation therapy. Chemotherapy was advised but the patient and her husband refused it. They elected to visit a clinic in Nevada where she had diet, vitamin, and DMSO therapy. She first presented to APR in December 1981 because her primary physician had become upset with her and her husband because they had refused chemotherapy. At that time she was alert and oriented in all respects. The physical examination was essentially within normal limits. She and her husband discussed at length why they had refused chemotherapy. Her surgery and radiation had taken place in a large cancer hospital and they had had an opportunity to observe patients who were receiving chemotherapy. They were both upset with the clinical status of these patients and had decided they wanted no part of it. It was quite clear that they wanted support of their decision and access to medical care when she began to deteriorate. Their request was accepted. The patient's condition was fairly stable until January 1982. She went to bed complaining of malaise. The next morning she could not be aroused. She was brought to the emergency room by ambulance and immediately admitted to intensive care. Physical examination revealed that she was responsive to painful stimulation only. A diagnosis of intracerebral hemorrhage was made. The patient deteriorated very rapidly after admission and expired approximately 17 hours later.

The case of E. P. is of interest because the primary physician was a long-standing friend of the patient and her husband, and they were disturbed when he failed to accept what they believed was a rational decision. This patient and her husband clearly had a strong, mutually supportive relationship. They made a decision about the quality of life that was acceptable to them. There was no rejection of the physician. Rather, they wanted and needed the physician's support for their decision and future care. This was not a difficult situation because the couple communicated well with each other and with their doctor. Had there been high likelihood of significant objective benefit from chemotherapy, a more serious effort could have been made to have them accept it.

IX. Dyspnea

Dyspnea (difficult or labored breathing) is one of the two most burdensome common causes of suffering. It can be an overwhelming symptom in pulmonary, neurological, and cardiac disease, in cancer and infection, or as part of general weakness. In chronically ill people, dyspnea can be a constant source of discomfort, frustration, weakness, and fear. In the acutely ill, all of these are magnified. The sensation of smothering can engender or magnify the fear of death. Labored breathing is terribly fatiguing. The relief of dyspnea is a great clinical challenge to the physician.

P. W. was a 90-year-old white woman admitted to the hospital in July 1984 after experiencing an episode of syncope. A permanent pacemaker had been implanted shortly before because of hemodynamically significant bradycardia. She had had numerous episodes of dysrhythmia that required cardioversion prior to the implantation of the pacemaker. Findings during this admission were atrial filbrillation with intermittent rapid ventricular response. Because her atrial fibrillation was paroxysmal, an attempt was made to cardiovert her pharmacologically. After medication, however, she developed severe gastrointestinal complaints and the medication was discontinued. She had numerous multisystemic complaints after any medication was prescribed to her. During this hospitalization she stated several times that it was time for her to die. She was finally stabilized and discharged to be seen in the office of her family physician. She continued to deteriorate. Her congestive heart failure progressed and she was continuously dyspneic and orthopneic. She was unresponsive to all treatment regimens. She had numerous subsequent hospitalizations, all for treatment of dyspnea, orthopnea, and dysrhythmia. During hospitalization in October 1984 she was extremely withdrawn and depressed. At that time she was seen in consultation by a psychiatrist who prescribed antidepressive medication. She responded to the treatment of her depression. In November 1984 she developed gangrene in her toes, caused by the low flow state associated with her congestive heart failure. In late November she was readmitted to the hospital *in extremis* and expired quietly on the next day.

Dyspnea was the overwhelming issue in this patient's life. Recurring episodes required the attending physician's persistent attention to medical, psychological, and family problems. Relief of dyspnea and depression were objectives tolerably but not completely achieved much of the time.

T. K., a 60-year-old white man, was first admitted to the hospital by his family in November 1977 for evaluation of progressive dyspnea of approximately five years duration. He was a smoker with a 45-year history of smoking a pack a day. He had worked for a can manufacturing company and attributed his respiratory distress to fumes in the working environment. Physical examination revealed increased AP diameter of the chest, hyporesonance to percussion of the chest, and distant breath sounds with numerous wheezes. Pulmonary function tests were compatible with a diagnosis of moderately severe combined obstructive restrictive ventilatory defect. Treatment with bronchodilators and low-flow oxygen yielded symptomatic improvement. During the next six years he was seen frequently both in and out of the hospital, primarily for complaints of severe dyspnea. Continuing care was provided by his family physician, but when his dyspnea was intolerable he was referred for management. The dyspnea was usually not responsive to conventional bronchodilator therapy. Most of his episodes of dyspnea required intravenous and then oral administration of steroids. During this time he developed a squamous cell carcinoma of his earlobe and transitional cell carcinoma of the urinary bladder. His subsequent course was complicated by complaints and complications relevant to radiation and chemotherapy of his transitional cell carcinoma. By May 1983 his condition had deteriorated to such an extent that he required nursing home care. His clinical status was very poor and he died shortly after transfer to the nursing home.

These two cases illustrate how disturbing the complaint of dyspnea can be to patients. Whereas T. K.'s symptoms were of fairly long duration and were very distressing to him, they were out of proportion to the degree of incapacitation suggested by the ventilatory functions test. P. W.'s complaints were also most distressing and were frustrating for those of us who provided care for her. The severity of her congestive heart failure is illustrated by the fact that she developed gangrene of her toes (a phenomenon we had not seen since our entrance to the practice of medicine more than 30 years ago).

X. Overtreatment

R. T. was a 55-year-old man who was admitted to intensive care via the emergency room in April 1983. He had a history of Eisenmenger's complex and had suddenly fallen into a coma while at work. At age 19 he had developed a brain abcess that was treated by burr hole drainage with complete recovery and without any evident neurological deficit. The patient was cyanotic, comatose, and responsive only to painful stimuli. A CT scan of the brain showed right mesencephalic hemorhage extending toward the pons and right thalamus. Blood was present within the ventricular system and obstructive hydrocephalus of the third and right lateral ventricals was present. An old infarct was present within the right parietal lobe adjacent to the right sylvan fissure. There were changes suggestive of chronic ischemic demyelination within the white matter adjacent to the anterior portion of the right lateral ventricle. The EEG showed moderate diffuse slow wave abnormality indicating generalized cerebral dysfunction. An ECG showed sinus tachycardia with sequential premature ventricular contractions, right atrial hypertrophy, left ventricular hyperthrophy with strain, and a septal fibrosis pattern. An echocardiogram showed aortic root dilatation with left atrial dilatation, left ventricular dilatation, right ventricular dilatation, flat septal motion, and left ventricular hypertrophy with poor wall motion.

He was seen in consultation by a neurologist and psychiatrist. Consensus among the physicians was that the patient had sustained a large hemorrhagic infarct on the right and that the prognosis was grim. On the sixth hospital day the patient's wife requested that he be transferred to another hospital. She had discussed the patient's condition with his employer, who told her that a friend of his with a cerebral hemorrhage had recovered spectacularly after the hemorrhage was evacuated. In accordance with the wife's request the patient was transferred to another hospital. He underwent craniotomy and died shortly thereafter.

Both the wife and the patient's employer were unrealistic in their expectations. Furthermore, the neurosurgeon who accepted the case and went ahead with the craniotomy failed to appreciate the fact that the patient's prognosis was grim. The patient's wife acted out of desperation. The reality was that no potentially successful alternative existed. The operation performed was probably not indicated. In today's cost-conscious world, should this have been done to meet the wife's belief that something must be done?

B. H., an 86-year-old black man, was referred to the hospital in June 1978. A diagnosis of adenocarcinoma of the colon was established and he underwent partial colectomy uneventfully. He was seen again in November 1978 for treatment of abdominal pain, nausea, and vomiting. This problem resolved in response to symptomatic therapy. He was lost to followup until February 1981, at which time he denied any weight loss, emesis, or recent changes in bowel habits. The physical examination was unremarkable. Evaluation revealed an adenocarcinoma of the stomach. He was not obstructed, but was anemic. After consultation with an abdominal surgeon I (H.B.H.) advised gastrectomy because he was anemic, was not eating, and was losing weight, because he appeared physiologically younger than his chronologic age, and because he had recovered uneventfully from his partial colectomy. He did indeed undergo bilateral vagotomy, partial gastrectomy, and gastrojejunostomy. Postoperatively his clinical course was progressively downhill. His stomach did not function properly and despite reoperation, he continued to deteriorate. He died on the 76th hospital day.

B. H. illustrates the need to maintain a perspective on a disease with a grim prognosis when the patient is of advanced years. Undoubtedly he would have survived much longer if aggressive therapy had not been implemented. Adequate clinical indications were present, but any procedure was probably too much for a very old man with this much disease.

To do nothing but supportive care is sometimes hard to accept. There is a line of reasoning that says with no good options, take your chances even if the odds are low. Answers are not clear and there are bases for honest differences of opinion.

XI. Medical Catastrophe

D. T. was a 62-year-old white woman admitted to intensive care via the emergency room in November 1984. The patient lived alone in a boarding house and apparently had been able to care for herself. During the evening, another boarder heard a thump in her room and when he investigated found her on the floor and unresponsive to stimuli. She was immediately taken to a hospital where a presumptive diagnosis of respiratory and cardiac arrest was made. She was intubated and given artificial ventilation but started having seizures. Because that institution was unable to care for her, she was transferred and admitted to the intensive care unit on APR's service. Physical examination revealed a blood pressure of 110/60, an apical rate of 84, and a temperature of 98.4. The fundi could not be visualized. Her pupils were round, regular, equal, and reactive to light. Her fingers were deeply stained with nicotine. She was unresponsive to painful stimuli, all four extremities were flaccid, and a Babinski was positive on the right. Arterial and central venous catheters were inserted. An EKG showed changes interpreted as right ventricular hypertrophy, left anterior hemiblock, and abnormal repolarization consistent with ischemic, drug, and/or electrolyte effect. A neurologist made the presumptive diagnosis of massive left intercerebral hemorrhage. A CT scan was essentially within normal limits. A lumbar puncture was done. Culture of the spinal fluid did not reveal any growth. Hyperalimentation was initiated.

During hospitalization, the patient's condition slowly improved. She was weaned from the ventilator on the fifth hospital day. On the sixth day she was able to move all four extremities and did not have any focal central nervous system deficits. Her mental status also improved. She had several episodes of paroxysmal atrial fibrillation with rapid ventricular response and experienced a gastrointestinal hemorrhage. Evaluation after extubation showed changes consistent with chronic obstructive pulmonary disease. During this time she gave a history of ingesting two fifths of whiskey per day. She was subsequently stabilized and was transferred to a nursing home.

This patient's course was a series of potentially fatal catastrophes. Working diagnoses included cardio-respiratory arrest, stroke, cachexia, cardiac arrhythmias, gastrointestinal hemorrhage. At admission, the patient was at risk of death from any one of these clinical problems. Persistent, modern, concentrated care got her out of the hospital. With the multiple problems her prognosis is grim, but the situation is changed from that of an acute catastrophe to that of chronic survival.

XII. Relief of Suffering and Burdensome Discomforts:

Physical pain is one kind of suffering. Mental anguish, fear, depression, loss of function, and loss of future may cause as much suffering as pain, and pain is itself greatly affected by any of these other factors. Many patients speak freely of pain but are reticent about reporting other suffering. The doctor must ask.

In the care of dying patients, the relief of symptoms and the enhancement of the quality of living are the physician's primary goals. There are many actual discomforts, physical and nonphysical, that the physician can in some measure relieve. Pain is the most prominent and, for many patients, the most feared. There are many approaches to pain that give significant relief, but frequently at some cost. The starting principle must be to try to determine the cause of the pain. When a patient has an overpowering fatal illness, errors can be made by attributing pain and other symptoms to the primary disease and not recognizing that they may be caused by another disease, related or non-related, or by a treatable complication of the primary disease. So the most important first step in the management of symptoms is accurate diagnosis. Once the diagnosis is made, appropriate direct therapies are indicated. Here we are discussing the situations in which pain is due to the primary disease and is not subject to direct relief of symptoms.

A. PAIN AND THE USE OF NARCOTIC ANALGESICS

1. *Uses of narcotic drugs and their selection:* These drugs vary in chemical composition, pharmacology, mode of action, method of administration, duration of effects, side effects, and potential for addiction. Because this is about patient care rather than narcotic pharmacology, we will talk primarily in terms of morphine equivalents, recognizing that other drugs may very well be used in many circumstances and may be referred to as we go along.

2. *Importance of proper dose:* How many milligrams can be expected to give adequate relief for a given patient? Age, obesity, mental status, severity of the illness, renal function, and nutritional state must all be considered in setting a dose.

3. *Timing of intervals between doses:* This is a major problem at the present time. Most of us in medicine have grown up with a standard dose, a standard time interval, and as-needed (prn) orders for pain. Experience and thought show that this thinking does not meet the needs of many people. Many terminal patients do better on regular scheduled administration of narcotics than on a prn basis. One reason for this is, as experience now shows, is that if a patient is given narcotics before significant pain has recurred, a lower dosage will be needed to treat the pain. Additionally, in current crowded, understaffed hospital situations, patients on prn medications often do not get them in a timely manner and undergo useless and unnecessary suffering.

4. *Route of administration:* Oral administration of narcotics is becoming a preferred approach, even though subcutaneous or intramuscular administration has been standard for a long time.

Currently many active efforts are being made to give adequate relief without injections and the small number of complications that can follow them. High-potency liquid medications that can be taken in a small volume are giving sufficient relief for patients with whom oral medication is possible. Generally, the dose is about three times as high, but in many patients it is as effective—frequently with a longer duration of action. Rectal suppositories containing morphine are now being marketed for similar purposes. Rectal clysis of drug-containing liquids is another possibility for patients who cannot take oral medications. Sublingual use of narcotics has had less use but is undergoing trial at the present time. Other techniques being tried include intrathecal morphine and techniques such as the Ommaya reservoir.

5. *Significant side-effects of narcotics:* A patient with severe, intractable pain requiring rather high doses of narcotics is apt to be mentally obtunded. Anorexia is common. There may also be nausea. A combination of these may cut down food intake in such patients. The narcotized patient tends to be less mobile, allowing for more development of thrombosis, pulmonary infection, decubiti, and other ill effects of immobilization. Thirst, blurred vision, and sensations of weakness occur with high doses of medications. These, though real, are secondary to the need for pain relief.

B. UNDERTREATMENT OF PAIN:

Doctors may be responsible for undertreatment, a common complaint made by patients. The choice of the wrong drug, too small a dose, and too long intervals between doses can be major factors to a patient. The patient with severe pain must be followed closely and the time and route of drug administration must be fitted to individual problems. Observation of many critical settings leads to the inevitable conclusion that many caregivers do not recognize the amount of suffering patients may be undergoing and are afraid or are not sufficiently motivated to relieve that suffering.

Many caregivers have a strong, inherent tendency to give the lowest dose at the longest time interval possible. One reason is the fear of addiction. A flat statement can be made: *addiction will not occur in a dying patient who has severe pain.* When pain is relieved, the need for drugs stops. This is also basically true in patients with long-term, chronic pain that is difficult to treat. If pain is relieved, drugs are not needed. We have seen patients whose need for narcotics gradually increases over time. There is a clinical feeling that this is less true when medications are administered on a regular schedule rather than prn. The fear of delay and the fear of inadequate medication lead the patient to expect drug failure and to want higher doses. If enough drug to give relief is given early enough, there is less pressure for more. In many cases the declining effects of drugs are a result of the progression of the disease.

Many patients complain of lack of pain care by nurses. It is not hard to find instances in which nurses give smaller doses of medication than are ordered and at longer intervals. This appears to be a result of true concern over a number of factors, including the possibility of addiction, the side effects of the drugs, and their overall effect on the patient.

The concern that the narcotized patient eats less and is more immobilized is legitimate, but the physician and the patient have the responsibility of weighing the balance between pain relief and whether or not anorexia or other side effects are as important as the relief of pain.

C. OVERTREATMENT OF PAIN

Unnecessary medication certainly should not be used. The induction of more side effects than absolutely necessary will shorten the patient's life and lower the quality of living. There is the threat of the possible approach of euthanasia by using large doses of medication. If large doses suppress appetite, respiration, and other functions, the patient's life may be shortened. Overtreatment appears to be rare in the clinical environments we have seen.

D. NON-NARCOTIC MEDICATIONS

Either alone or in combination with the narcotics, they may permit use of lower doses of narcotics. Again, the precise diagnosis of the cause of pain is important in wise use of combination analgesia. Aspirin and acetaminophen are valuable drugs in combination with codeine or other narcotics. A combination such as Percodan or Tylox is an important level between nonnarcotics and heavy narcotics. These can be administered orally and give major relief to many patients for a long time. The nonsteroidal antiinflammatory drugs such as ibuprofen, piroxicam, and others may also give significant pain relief and either make narcotics unnecessary or usable in lower doses.

E. NON-DRUG APPROACHES TO PAIN RELIEF

Many physicians have had limited experience with these. This is an area for consultation with appropriate people, who may be neurologists, neurosurgeons, oncologists, or nonphysicians such as psychologists with experience in pain relief. One can begin with having anesthesiologists as consultants, particularly when there is the possible use of nerve blocks or other local approaches to pain relief.

Neurosurgical procedures are indicated for some patients, particularly when life expectancy is long enough for them to be of value. The use of transcutaneous electrical nerve stimulation (TENS) is worth trying. Physical medicine physicians, psychologists who work with pain, and anesthesiologists may be familiar with this approach. The use of this technique probably helps one-third to one-half of the patients and can add to mobility, freedom from pain, and improved quality of living.

Psychological approaches, such as biofeedback and self-hypnosis, can play an important role for some patients. To begin with, they give patients a role in their own situation. This is particularly true in managing anxiety, fear, guilt, and cultural conditions. The use of narcotics or other organic pain relief methods can be lessened for many patients by relief of their anxiety and fear.

F. DIRECT RELIEF OF NON-TERMINAL CAUSES OF PAIN

In a patient dying of heart disease, cancer, or some other

painful condition, the primary-disease symptoms certainly are the most common. Nevertheless, these patients may have other causes for pain or complications that can be relieved—e.g., draining abscesses, caring for ulcers, and so forth.

Watching and being involved with the suffering of another person is difficult for anyone. Each of us responds individually to such situations. Different responses are bound to cause conflict among patient, family, doctor, nurse, and others involved. Occasionally, formal efforts to resolve conflicts must be made, with the physician playing a primary role in their resolution.

G. DYSPNEA, ETC.

Dyspnea, immobility, bloating, itching, nausea and vomiting, or urinary frequency can be tremendous sources of suffering. Patients who have difficulty breathing may have tremendous fear of smothering or unpleasant death. When patients with chronic obstructive pulmonary disease (COPD) go into acute respiratory failure and are treated by intubation and external respiratory efforts in intensive care units, they frequently recover from that episode. It is not unusual for patients who have had a number of such episodes to refuse to go to an intensive care unit again, because the general level of suffering is worse than the illness. The fear of death from inability to breathe competes with the fear of treatment that might be worse than the death.

XIII. Pain Control

Most patients dying with intractable pain are cancer patients, although many terminal cancer patients do not have significant pain. Unfortunately, every oncology service always has patients for whom complete relief of pain is not possible. This is anxiety-inducing and frustrating for patient and caregivers. These patients need much care and support from all concerned.

A 57-year-old man was admitted on August 8, 1981 for biopsy of a 3 to 4 cm neck mass. Biopsy of the mass and the prostate both revealed well-differentiated carcinoma. Since then he has been followed regularly in oncology and urology clinics. His cancer has progressed slowly; various problems—especially pain—have developed and many approaches to management have been used.

On 8/28/81 he was discharged from the hospital on a regimen of diethylstilbesterol (DES).

On 5/23/83, because of pain, a bone scan was performed that showed increased activity in both shoulders, the left acetabulum, 12th rib and sternum. On 9/21/83 he complained of pain in his left shoulder. On 1/27/84 he complained of shoulder and lower back pain. DES was stopped temporarily. One treatment of intravenous Stilphostrol diminished the pain but caused enough nausea and vomiting that further treatment with Stilphostrol was refused. On 4/5/84, after 3 to 4 days of bone pain, some relief was achieved by increasing the DES dose to 2.0 mg three times a day.

4/10/84—given intravenous Stilphostrol.

6/1/84—Rib pain following overexertion. Patient is weak and depressed about wife from whom he has been divorced many years. Taking Indocin.

6/18/84—Cervical spine x-rays show patchy osteoblastic changes. Began x-ray therapy to cervical and left supraclavicular regions.

7/2/84—"Increasing disease but patient directs own treatment." "Patient wants more intravenous Stilphostrol today."

8/27/84—"Doing better." "Pain pills do not control pain." "Now complains of left posterior rib pain [bone scan 15 months earlier showed activity here] relieved by hot water soaks." Patient wanted "complete physical, including cholesterol and EKG." One can speculate on the meaning of a patient with advancing metastatic cancer asking for cardiovascular screening examinations.

9/14/84—"Patient is on a stretcher. States he is paining." "Patient complains that tylenol #3 is not effective."

9/19/84—Chemotherapy begun: Adriamycin, cytoxan, reglan, benadryl.

9/28/84—"Patient tolerated chemotherapy fairly well. Taking less pain medication and having sex." Receiving methadone 5 mgs. and ASA gr. 5 (0–2/day). Appetite is up, weight is down.

11/2/84—"Having a great deal of bone pain, which makes it difficult for him to sleep at night." Hospital bed requested from American

Cancer Society. Visiting Nurse Association arrangements made. Recently married. New wife thinks he has Hodgkin's disease and will have remission. Long explanations to her of his status.
11/28/84—Increased pain in back and hips. Did not tolerate methadone because of hallucinations.
11/16/84—On Tylenol #4 tablets every two hours. "He missed chemotherapy to see his parents in Philadelphia and now complains of intense bone pain."
12/13/84—Complains of severe pain and weakness in right arm and elbow—began since last chemotherapy on 11/26/84. Feet swollen. Pain also in mid-spine. "Fair pain control on Tylenol #4."
Began palliative x-ray therapy, 3000 v to spine.

This patient's course clearly shows the need for many approaches to give continuous personal care over many years as he slowly deteriorated. As his disease has progressed, pain control has become an increasing problem. One sees a pattern of evaluating the patient, choosing a therapeutic approach, continuing it as long as it is successful, and moving to something else when indicated. Side effects (nausea and vomiting, depression, hallucinations) are accepted or rejected.

This patient shows that when drugs lose their effectiveness in controlling pain, it is usually because of progression of the disease, not intolerance to the drug. Throughout the course of disease, this patient has actively shared in therapy decisions. For example, he refused Stilphostrol on occasion because of its side effects and requested it on other occasions.

Quality of life is a frequently discussed generalization. This patient's chart records specifics. Sexual interest and activity go up and down. The patient married three years after the diagnosis of advanced cancer.

This patient's care requires deep involvement from physicians in at least three specialties, as well as nurses and social workers. As needed, outside agencies help. This is a massive effort to care for a suffering, slowly dying person with most of the care being given on an out-patient basis. All of these people have interacted with family.

The patient is a 57-year-old white man with a 30-year history of heroin abuse. In February 1984 he underwent detoxification with methadone. In May 1984, a well-differentiated adenocarcinoma of the ascending colon was treated by right colectomy. Metastases were found in the nodes, omentum, and liver. Treatment was begun with 5FU. As an outpatient, he had considerable pain. The pharmacy noted his use of 30 to 40 Dilaudid (hydromorphine hydrochloride) tablets daily and raised questions of abuse. The patient was admitted for pain control. A psychiatrist specializing in drug abuse recommended stopping Dilaudid and giving 10 mg of methadone every 12 hours. The oncologists gave him 15 mg of methadone every 6 hours. "He tolerated his pain well and there were no problems."

This patient's history illustrates two points: (1) In today's society new pain control problems are seen in persons with long-standing narcotic use. (2) Such patients can be adequately treated but require different drug dosages or approaches than those indicated for other patients.

Conclusions

Care of a dying patient is very personal, requiring the doctor to be available to the patient (and often to the family) for communication and support, as well as to identify and meet the patient's needs. All of this is just good patient care—made poignant and pointed by the meanings of dying and death to the patient, the family, and the caregivers.

Summary Preamble: Thanatology encompasses the broad areas of death and dying, loss and grief, and the accompanying issues and problems. It stresses the need for comprehension of dying as part of a healthy outlook on living. It emphasizes the need for education and communication in these sensitive areas. It stresses the right of dying patients and their families to competent, considerate care that is responsive to their particular physical and psychosocial needs. It recognizes the necessity for new and better approaches to the care of the dying and the bereaved. It encourages inquiry into how attitudes and approaches to loss, grief, death, and dying can lead to fuller, happier living.

Summary Principle: Thanatology Is Both an Art and a Science. As an Art, It Emphasizes Humanistic Approaches to Death, Dying, and Bereavement. As a Science, It Stresses the Need for Education, Inquiry, Systematic Investigation, and Research in Approaching These Once Taboo Topics.

Summary Preamble: Thanatology encompasses the broad areas of death and dying, loss and grief, and the accompanying issues and problems. It stresses the need for comprehension of dying as part of a healthy outlook on living. It emphasizes the need for education and communication in these sensitive areas. It stresses the right of dying patients and their families to competent, considerate care that is responsive to their particular physical and psychosocial needs. It recognizes the necessity for new and better approaches to the care of the dying and the bereaved. It encourages inquiry into how attitudes and approaches to loss, grief, death, and dying can lead to fuller, happier living.

Summary Principle: Thanatology Is Both an Art and a Science. As an Art, It Emphasizes Humanistic Approaches to Death, Dying, and Bereavement. As a Science, It Stresses the Need for Education, Inquiry, Systematic Investigation, and Research in Approaching These Once Taboo Topics.

13

The Art and Science of Thanatology

RICHARD S. BLACHER

Death is a highly charged topic. It is a certainty for everyone and yet is dreaded. It is a natural stage of living and yet it is surrounded by mystery and taboo. It often follows illness and yet, until recently, it was considered more a subject for novelists, philosophers, and theologians than for medical people or behavioral scientists. It is common to all of us and yet always is felt as a unique experience. While it involves the dying person and all those whom he comes in contact with as well, everyone knows "you've got to walk that lonesome valley by yourself," as the old hymn so well describes.

While physicians and other medical caregivers have dealt with, and suffered with, the problems of the patient and the survivors, the forms surrounding the final period of life have usually concerned the clergyman more than the doctor, whose job it was to make the dying patient as comfortable as possible. In recent years there has been a growing interest in understanding what the patient approaching death actually experiences, and the science of thanatology has evolved. This new approach in no small measure was given impetus by Kübler-Ross's writing (1969), which attempted to organize the understanding of the dying patient's behavior. Feifel (1959) and Schoenberg et al. (1970) have also been catalysts in this new interest as well, as has Austin H. Kutscher, through his leadership in organizing symposiums on issues of dying and in establishing the Foundation of Thanatology. The study of suicide (Shneidman 1970) has also enlarged the boundaries of the field.

Thus in recent years, death as a special study, thanatology, has been recognized as a scientific area in its own right. As this volume so richly illustrates, the study of thanatology is a multidisciplinary one involving medicine, anthropology, philosophy, sociology, psychology, education, theology, and numerous others. It involves theoretical constructs, concepts about dying and death (these two are clearly not the same), as well as bereavement and other results of death. The prospect of death not only affects patients but also their families and caregivers. Death has cultural, medical, social, and economic implications and effects.

At various times in our history and in different socioeconomic groups, death has been viewed as a naturally occurring event and as one beset by mystery and taboo. In recent years, in our culture, it has been dealt with rather gingerly. People do not "die," they "pass away." Corpses become "remains," and many other elements of the whole situation are glossed over even though this may not be to the ultimate advantage of the survivors. The view of death as an altered state of consciousness has resulted in changes in burial cermonies that not only emphasize the continued spiritual life of the deceased, but also deal with the body itself as still living (Mitford 1978).

One of the major problems in studying death has been the very mystery with which it is surrounded. One sees in all cultures that death has been considered not the termination of life but rather as an altered state of consciousness. In no recorded society, whether advanced or primitive, is death conceptualized as an actual end of being; rather there is belief in an afterlife, either in heaven or hell, or an afterlife conceptualized as souls returning to earth (Blacher 1983). Death is sometimes thought of as an eternal sleep or else as a form of consciousness that at times may be pleasant (a blissful state) or at times a condition of deprivation ("cold in the grave").

Freud (1915) stated "It is indeed impossible to imagine our own death; and whenever we attempt to do so we can perceive that we are in fact still present as spectators . . . . in the unconscious everyone of us is convinced of his immortality." Freud speculated that the sense of immortality was based on the need to retain those loved persons who had been lost to death. "Man could no longer keep death at a distance, . . . but he was nevertheless unwilling to acknowledge it, for he could not conceive of himself as dead. So he devised a compromise: He conceived the fact of his own death as well but denied it the significance of annihilation. . . . It was beside the dead body of someone he loved that he invented spirits." Thus death became surrounded not only with a great sense of loss but with a great sense of mystery as well, and this is reflected in the feelings people through the ages have had about death.

Death, as this volume indicates, is a complex phenomenon that can be viewed from a multitude of positions. It can be looked on from the viewpoint of the subject, the onlookers, the caregivers. It can be examined over a span of time and can result in vast changes in those left behind. Death and dying can take many forms, and thus the field can become quite complicated. Death can occur in any age group and from a multitude of causes—from trauma, from illness, both acute and chronic, and can be self-induced. All of these forms have different connotations for society and survivors as well as for the individual himself.

Death has usually been associated with emotional pain—the pain of the person dying and the pain of those who survive. Thanatology looks at both aspects, recognizing the severe sense of loss on both sides. The grief of the dying patient is often not recognized (Aldrich 1963) but, after all, if one loses a loved one, one loses an important part of one's life; when one dies oneself one loses everyone. Often those who will survive are unable to tolerate the dying patient's talking about *his* loss in the situation. It is especially difficult for those who live to talk with the dying patient about his dying, since the act of surviving is often accompanied by a sense of what has been called "survivor guilt" (Niederland 1968; Blacher 1978).

Death as an ultimate loss and separation is a revival of the universal pain of separation that all human beings experience in childhood. Often, when we talk of "separation anxiety," what we really are referring to is the pain of being left out. Separation itself is frequently not painful when it is initiated by the person involved, but quite different when one remains behind. It is not uncommon for couples who have been separated for a short time to note that the person going out of town feels quite comfortable, while the one who stays home feels a great sense of loss and devastation. If the roles are reversed, then the sense of loss and pain is still experienced by whichever one is left behind. The origin of this pain seems clearly to lie in the helpless sense of desertion and rage all children experience when their parents leave them for even a short period. Children's sense of time makes even a brief separation seem intolerably long. For most people, attempts to ward off this pain occupy a good deal of effort. Death, as the final separation, is frequently experienced as a desertion. This accounts for the fact that in mourning there is often an awareness of anger toward the dead person. For the dying patient, a danger resulting from this sense of desertion is premature emotional withdrawal by those who will survive. It is as if their theme is, "As long as you're leaving us, we won't invest ourselves in you any longer." The result may be that when the patient most needs the closeness of loved ones, they are no longer there for him.

While the profound impact of grief has been known to poets over millennia, it has been only in recent years that scientists have focused on its effects. Engel's questioning paper, "Is Grief a Disease" (1961) and the volume by Schoenberg et al. (1970) have brought to the fore the problems facing survivors. Lindemann's earlier paper (1944) focused on the psychological needs and care of those who grieve. Parkes's statistical studies have indicated the physical dangers of the state of mourning (1964). Much work is being done currently to shed light on the mechanisms involved. (Schleifer et al. 1985). It is clear that the reactions to death are determined by the age of the survivor and by the emotional relationship to the deceased—sometimes an angry or ambivalent tie will result in a more difficult bereavement than a relationship that is close and loving. The survivor may also be affected by the cause of death, the length of the fatal illness, and other factors.

When the word "dying" is mentioned it usually conjures up a

situation in which someone is slowly going downhill, for example with a progressive malignancy. However, thanatology also recognizes "acute dying"—that is, sudden death during surgery, as a result of a heart attack, as well as by suicide—and the different ways these deaths are dealt with by the survivors. Thanatology recognizes the need to educate medical people, others involved with terminal care, and society at large so that the pain of dying and the pain of bereavement can be alleviated.

Ethical issues concerning dying and the prolongation of life by the newer technologies must be faced squarely. Increasing our store of knowledge about areas that once were surrounded by a mysterious aura can only lessen unnecessary suffering. In 1945, the novelist Ben Ames Williams, in an address to a medical audience, described the plight of the caregivers of the ill and dying. His words (Williams 1945) are just as pertinent today: "It is the hard lot of the doctor to know that in the end he is always defeated; his victories at best are temporary. Death he can never finally conquer. But death's ally is fear, and this ally the doctor can defeat. Let him help the patient to conquer fear, and he will win many a skirmish; and if he can never hope to win the last grim battle, he can at least do much to rob that ultimate defeat, for his patient and for the patient's family, of the terror that is its most grievous pain."

References

Aldrich, D.K. 1963. "The Dying Patient's Grief." *Journal of the American Medical Association,* 184:329.

Blacher, R.S. 1978. "Paradoxical Depression After Heart Surgery: A Form of Survivor Syndrome." *Psychoanalytic Quarterly* 47:267–283.

Blacher, R.S. 1983. "Death, Resurrection and Rebirth: Observations in Cardiac Surgery." *Psychoanalytic Quarterly* 52:56–72.

Engel, G. 1961. "Is Grief a Disease?" A Challenge for Medical Research." *Psychosomatic Medicine* 23:18–22.

Feifel, H. 1959. *The Meaning of Death.* New York: McGraw-Hill.

Freud, S. 1915. "Thoughts for the Times on War and Death." Standard Edition 14:273–302. London: Hogarth Press, 1957.

Kübler-Ross. 1969. *On Death and Dying*. New York: Macmillan.

Lindemann, E. 1944. "Symptomatology and Management of Acute Grief." *American Journal of Psychiatry* 101:141.

Mitford, J. 1978. *The American Way of Death*. New York: Fawcett Crest.

Niederland, W.G. 1968. "Clinical Observations on the 'Survivor Syndrome.'" *International Journal of Psychoanalysis* 49:313–315.

Parkes, C.M. 1964. "Effects of Bereavement on Physical and Mental Health—A Study of the Medical Records of Widows." *British Medical Journal* 2:274.

Schleifer, S.G., S.E. Keller, S.G. Siris, K.L. Davis, and M. Stein. 1985. "Depression and Immunity Lymphocyte Function in Ambulatory Depressed Patients, Hospitalized Schizophrenic Patients, and Patients Hospitalized for Herniorrhaphy." *Archives of General Psychiatry* 42:129–133.

Schoenberg, B., A.C. Carr, D. Peretz, and A.H. Kutscher, eds. 1970. *Loss and Grief.* New York: Columbia University Press.

Shneidman, E. et al. *Psychology of Suicide*. New York: Science House.

Williams, B.A. 1945. "The Greeks Had a Word for It." *New England Journal of Medicine,* 233:427–432.

Index

List of Contributors

Richard S. Blacher, Professor of Psychiatry and Lecturer in Surgery, Tufts-New England Medical Center, Boston.

John G. Bruhn, Dean, School of Allied Health Sciences, The University of Texas Medical Branch, Galveston, Texas.

Arthur C. Carr, Professor of Clinical Psychology in Psychiatry, Cornell University Medical College, New York.

Elizabeth J. Clark, Assistant Professor, Department of Health Professions, Montclair State College, Upper Montclair, N.J.

Carol Farkas, Nurse Clinician, Home Care Program, Psychiatry Service, Memorial Sloan-Kettering Cancer Center, New York.

Raymond G. Fuentes, Private Practice, Psychiatric and Behavioral Medical Associates, San Antonio.

Gary J. Grad, Clinical Assistant Professor, Cornell University Medical School; Lecturer in Psychiatry, College of Physicians and Surgeons, Columbia University, New York.

Sir Stephen Viton Gullo, President, Institute for Health and Weight Sciences' Center for Healthful Living, New York.

Mahlon S. Hale, Director of Psychiatric Consultation Services, University of Connecticut Health Sciences; Associate Professor of Psychiatry, University of Connecticut School of Medicine, Farmington, Connecticut.

Harold B. Haley, Associate Chief of Staff for Education, Houston Veterans Administration Hospital; Clinical Professor of Surgery, Baylor College of Medicine, Houston.

Austin H. Kutscher, President, The Foundation of Thanatology; Professor of Dentistry (in Psychiatry), College of Physicians and Surgeons, Columbia University, New York.

Lillian G. Kutscher, Late Publications Editor, The Foundation of Thanatology, New York.

Matthew J. Loscalzo, Assistant Director of Social Work; Social Work Behavioral Coordinator and Director of Social Work Behavioral Team, Pain Service, Departments of Neurology and Social Work, Memorial Sloan-Kettering Cancer Center, New York.

Vanderlyn R. Pine, Professor of Sociology, State University of New York at New Paltz, New Paltz, N.Y.

Therese R. Rando, Clinical Psychologist, North Scituate Medical Center, North Scituate, R.I.

Alexander B. Remenchik, Private Practice, Internal Medicine, Houston.

Bernard Rollin, Professor of Philosophy, Colorado State University, Fort Collins, Colorado.

Robert G. Stevenson, Co-Chairman, Columbia University Seminar on Death; Instructor of Death Education Programs at River Dell High School, Bergen Community College, and Fairleigh Dickinson University, New Jersey.

Margot Tallmer, Professor, Brookdale Center on Aging, Hunter College of the City University of New York, New York.

Vamik Volkan, Professor of Psychiatry, University of Virginia School of Medicine, Charlottesville, Virginia.

Columbia University Press Foundation of Thanatology Series

Teaching Psychosocial Aspects of Patient Care
Bernard Schoenberg, Helen F. Pettit, and Arthur C. Carr, editors

Loss and Grief: Psychological Management in Medical Practice
Bernard Schoenberg, Arthur C. Carr, David Peretz, and Austin H. Kutscher, editors

Psychosocial Aspects of Terminal Care
Bernard Schoenberg, Arthur C. Carr, David Peretz, and Austin H. Kutscher, editors

Psychosocial Aspects of Cystic Fibrosis: A Model for Chronic Lung Disease
Paul R. Patterson, Carolyn R. Denning, and Austin H. Kutscher, editors

The Terminal Patient: Oral Care
Austin H. Kutscher, Bernard Schoenberg, and Arthur C. Carr, editors

Psychopharmacologic Agents for the Terminally Ill and Bereaved
Ivan K. Goldberg, Sidney Malitz, and Austin H. Kutscher, editors

Anticipatory Grief
Bernard Schoenberg, Arthur C. Carr, Austin H. Kutscher, David Peretz, and Ivan K. Goldberg, editors

Bereavement: Its Psychosocial Aspects
Bernard Schoenberg, Irwin Gerber, Alfred Wiener, Austin H. Kutscher, David Peretz, and Arthur C. Carr, editors

The Nurse as Caregiver for the Terminal Patient and His Family
Ann M. Earle, Nina T. Argondizzo, and Austin H. Kutscher, editors

Social Work with the Dying Patient and the Family
Elizabeth R. Prichard, Jean Collard, Ben A. Orcutt, Austin H. Kutscher, Irene B. Seeland, and Nathan Lefkowitz, editors

Home Care: Living with Dying
Elizabeth R. Prichard, Jean Collard, Janet Starr, Josephine A.

Lockwood, Austin H. Kutscher, and Irene B. Seeland, editors

Psychosocial Aspects of Cardiovascular Disease: The Life Threatened Patient, the Family, and the Staff
James Reiffel, Robert DeBellis, Lester C. Mark, Austin H. Kutscher, Paul R. Patterson, and Bernard Schoenberg, editors

Acute Grief: Counseling the Bereaved
Otto S. Margolis, Howard C. Raether, Austin H. Kutscher, J. Bruce Powers, Irene B. Seeland, Robert DeBellis, and Daniel J. Cherico, editors

The Human Side of Homicide
Bruce L. Danto, John Bruhns, and Austin H. Kutscher, editors

Hospice U.S.A.
Austin H. Kutscher, Samuel C. Klagsbrun, Richard J. Torpie, Robert DeBellis, Mahlon S. Hale, and Margot Tallmer, editors

The Child and Death
John E. Schowalter, Paul R. Patterson, Margot Tallmer, Austin H. Kutscher, Stephen V. Gullo, and David Peretz, editors

The Life-Threatened Elderly
Margot Tallmer, Elizabeth R. Prichard, Austin H. Kutscher, Robert DeBellis, Mahlon S. Hale, and Ivan K. Goldberg, editors

Pain, Anxiety, and Grief: Pharmacotherapeutic Care of the Dying Patient and the Bereaved
Ivan K. Goldberg, Austin H. Kutscher, and Sidney Malitz, editors

Principles of Thanatology
Austin H. Kutscher, Arthur C. Carr, and Lillian G. Kutscher, editors